MW00617566

GENERAL

James G. Blunt

GENERAL
James G. Blunt

TARNISHED GLORY

ROBERT COLLINS

PELICAN PUBLISHING COMPANY
Gretna 2005

*The word "Pelican" and the depiction of a pelican are trademarks
of Pelican Publishing Company, Inc., and are registered in the
U.S. Patent and Trademark Office.*

Library of Congress Cataloging-in-Publication Data

Collins, Robert, 1965-
  General James G. Blunt : tarnished glory / by Robert Collins.
      p. cm.
  Includes bibliographical references and index.
  ISBN 978-1-58980-253-7 (alk. paper)
  1. Blunt, James G. (James Gilpatrick), 1826-1881. 2. Blunt, James G.
(James Gilpatrick), 1826-1881—Psychology. 3. Generals—United
States—Biography. 4. United States. Army—Biography. 5. Kansas—
History—Civil War, 1861-1865—Campaigns. 6. United States—History—
Civil War, 1861-1865—Campaigns. 7. Kansas—History—1854-1861. I.
Title.
    E467.1.B656C65 2005
    973.7'41'092—dc22

2004022428

Printed in the United States of America
Published by Pelican Publishing Company, Inc.
1000 Burmaster Street, Gretna, Louisiana 70053

Contents

Acknowledgments

I wish to acknowledge Roy Bird for his encouragement while I worked on the manuscript and the Augusta and Andover libraries for help with interlibrary loans and microfilm. I would also like to acknowledge Steve Cottrell for his historical review of the manuscript.

GENERAL

James G. Blunt

CHAPTER 1

A Controversial General

"He was a brave and efficient man and officer, whom Kansas should be proud to honor."—William G. Cutler, in his 1883 book, *A History of the State of Kansas.*

"[He was] unfit in any respect for the command of a division of troops against a disciplined enemy."—John Schofield, in his 1897 autobiography.

Both quotes are about the same person, Maj. Gen. James G. Blunt. General Blunt was a controversial figure in his time and has continued to be one long after his death. There's little debate about the deeds that marked Blunt's career as an abolitionist, a general, and a veteran. The debate arises when historians and authors have to explain his actions.

The active and controversial parts of Blunt's life span less than a decade. According to his daughter, Blunt moved to Kansas in the fall of 1856, but he may not have arrived until the spring of 1857. Blunt moved to Kansas to take part in the struggle over whether Kansas Territory would become a free state or a slave state. When the Civil War broke out, Blunt became an officer, first a lieutenant colonel, then a brigadier general, and finally Kansas's only major general. He served through the end of the war in 1865. But except for a few minor events in the late 1860s and a scandal in the early 1870s, Blunt disappeared from the main stage and fell into obscurity.

The decline is remarkable, considering how important Blunt was to the Union war effort in the trans-Mississippi west. The expedition he sent into the Indian Territory in the summer of 1862, although it eventually came to grief, liberated much of the Cherokee Nation and recovered Fort Gibson. His fall 1862 campaign put an end to organized Confederate resistance in northwestern Arkansas. He cleared much of the rest of the Indian

Territory of rebel forces in a series of battles in the summer of 1863. He played a key role as division commander in crushing the Price campaign in the fall of 1864. When the war ended he was preparing for one final march, a push south into Texas to end the rebellion.

As impressive as these achievements are, they can be overshadowed by Blunt's spectacular failures as a military administrator. He carried on a yearlong feud with one of his superiors. His relations with the first two governors of Kansas were notoriously poor. He did nothing to stem the rampant corruption in the military supply system. Indeed, Blunt took part in some of that corruption. And in the one incident when he was in actual danger of being killed by Confederate guerrillas at Baxter Springs, he bears some of the blame for allowing the massacre to occur.

Considering both the controversial aspects of Blunt's career as well as his importance to the region, why did he fall into obscurity after the war?

To that question I believe there are several good answers. Frankly the trans-Mississippi theater was not terribly important to the outcome of the Civil War. The western campaigns of Grant and Sherman all but determined which side would win. The eastern theater, while not quite as important, was still more important than the far west. And that theater was much closer to America's largest cities, guaranteeing that it would get the lion's share of attention then and for years afterward.

Little has been written in the intervening decades about this theater of the Civil War. Not that there aren't interesting stories and compelling people to write about. But because of the theater's relative lack of importance and profile, it's had a low priority among historians. This low profile in turn has thrown many of the region's key players into an abyss, including General Blunt.

Another reason for Blunt's "disappearance" is that he did little or nothing of importance in Kansas once the war was over. Several of the men who served under him were able to rise to prominence. Samuel Crawford became the state's first two-term governor. Preston Plumb served as an influential U.S. senator. Others were elected or appointed to high offices in the state and federal governments. A lowly sergeant, Wiley Britton, became perhaps the first author to write histories of the Civil War in the far west. In contrast, Blunt moved to Washington, D.C., four years after the war ended, where he eventually died.

Blunt himself did nothing after the war to ensure that he would be remembered. He wrote only one narrative of his experiences, an official report that was lost for almost three decades. He wrote no memoir and had no articles printed in state or national publications. Many of his official letters survived but, except for two or three letters, his personal correspondence seems to have been destroyed.

All these reasons have led to a great deal of confusion about Blunt's actions and character. There is no greater example of this than his supposed nickname during the war: "Fat Boy." The moniker has persisted in connection with Blunt despite there being only one printed instance of it being used. Blunt used it once, in a letter published in *The Rebellion Record,* a multi-volume collection of Civil War material. The words never appear again in connection with Blunt. There seems no way to know who first gave him the nickname, whether it was used in good humor or ill, or if Blunt liked it or hated it.

Reconstructing the deeds and personality of James G. Blunt isn't easy. But such reconstruction must be done to explain how a Maine boy became a significant general during the Civil War on the far frontier.

CHAPTER 2

Early Years

James G. Blunt was born in or around Trenton (now Lamoine) in Hancock County, Maine, on July 21, 1826. His family farmed in the area, and Blunt stayed on the farm until about the age of fourteen. William Cutler's *A History of the State of Kansas,* one of the few sources that has any information on Blunt's early years, says that he had "a good common school education."

Little has survived on Blunt's family. Blunt never mentioned his parents in any published source, but Maine genealogical records indicate they were John Blunt and Sally Gilpatrick Blunt. Sources are confusing as to how many siblings Blunt had or in what order they were born. Blunt mentioned having at least two brothers who moved to Kansas with him in the 1850s, and a younger sister was living with Blunt in Ohio in 1850. In the area the Blunt family was well known, with a local pond named for the Blunts. Also prominent was the Gilpatrick family, and it would be James Blunt's uncle Rufus Gilpatrick who would play an important role in his prewar career.

At fourteen Blunt left the family farm. Cutler wrote, "With a naturally energetic and restless disposition, he soon tired of the restraints and routine of his every-day life, and while still young, ran away and went to sea, shipping at first before the mast and remaining as a sailor, serving in various capacities, for four years." What this description reveals about Blunt's early career isn't clear, but as there was no fishing industry in Maine at the time, Blunt probably joined the crew of a merchant ship.

The words "serving in various capacities" might be important in understanding Blunt's next move. Blunt's later life strongly suggests that he was an intelligent person. This intelligence might have been recognized by his captain during Blunt's late teens. If so, Cutler's words suggest that Blunt did more on board than would a young man of lesser wits. Perhaps he displayed some skill in medicine, or some other ability that indicated to him that being a sailor was not the best use of his talents.

Evidence has now come to light that suggests James Blunt might not have spent as much time at sea as later biographies stated. The newspaper in Ellsworth, the county seat of Hancock County, provides a clue as to how Blunt likely spent his teenage years. In 1917 the Ellsworth newspaper ran an article about early schools in the area. One of these was a military school, which the story claimed was attended by Joshua Lawrence Chamberlain, probably Maine's most famous Civil War hero, and James G. Blunt, among others. The Ellsworth Military Academy appears to have been something of a high school for boys. The superintendent of the school from 1839 to 1845 was Charles Jarvis Whiting. Whiting was a West Point graduate who mainly served as an army engineer.

This information sheds interesting light on Blunt's record during the Civil War and could account for his battlefield success. He could well have been one of the few Kansans who had any military education when the war broke out. At the very least Blunt would know the basics of drill, military formations, and disciplined marching. If he could have passed along this information to soldiers under his command, it would have given them some advantages, such as being able to march quickly, to stay in formation under fire, and to fire volleys at a rapid rate.

So why are there so few references to Blunt's education? Blunt must have kept this part of his past a secret. The reason for this secrecy could be that Whiting was a West Pointer. Early in the Civil War, Union graduates of the United States Military Academy were not successful in the field. Blunt might have feared that such an association would hurt his chances for promotion and prime assignments. Blunt also had a running feud with another West Pointer, John Schofield, and this too might have figured into Blunt's silence.

Another reason, although it's questionable, is that Whiting or his family might have had political views that could have disgraced Blunt. James Blunt was a dedicated abolitionist and Republican when the war started. His opposition to slavery was the reason he came to Kansas in the first place. If Whiting or his family were Democrats, Blunt's education with them would have made his views suspect in the radical circles he traveled in. It would have been even worse for Blunt if they were proslavery Democrats. In either case, Blunt seemed to be ashamed of his time at the academy. We may never know if he split time between there and the sea, or if he invented his seagoing life out of whole cloth.

No matter how he spent those four years, Blunt apparently did graduate from the academy. In late 1845 he emigrated to Ohio and enrolled in the Starling Medical College in Columbus. One of his teachers was his uncle, Dr. Rufus Gilpatrick. Blunt graduated from Starling in February 1849. In January 1850 he moved to New Madison, Ohio, in the western part of the state. On January 15, 1850, he married the young Nancy G. Putman. He remained in New Madison for the next several years as a practicing doctor.

Census records for Ohio in 1850 show that Blunt was living with Rufus Gilpatrick's family with his wife and his sister Cynthia, aged eighteen. When they married, Nancy Putman was fourteen years old. A local history document, the *Biographical History of Darke County, Ohio,* states that Nancy's sister Elizabeth was married to Dr. Gilpatrick. Both girls were from an important local family. Their father Erastus Putman was a former gunsmith from Washington, D.C., who had moved to Ohio in 1819. He had laid out the town of New Madison and served as the town's first postmaster.

This history also states that while in New Madison, Blunt was active in county politics. He joined the Republican Party early and supported the presidential candidacy of John C. Fremont, the first Republican Party candidate for president; it's interesting to note this in light of Blunt's dim view of Fremont during the war.

Blunt remained in Ohio until 1856, when he moved to northern Anderson County in Kansas Territory. Blunt came to perhaps the most contested territory in American history. That contest was over whether Kansas would be admitted to the Union as a slave state or as a free state. From the moment the territory had been opened to white settlement, the two sides in the slavery issue had descended on Kansas to determine the outcome of the contest.

Up through the 1850s Kansas was part of a "permanent Indian frontier." This frontier was supposed to isolate both the "civilized" tribes moved from the East and the nomadic native tribes from white America. In the 1840s Texas was admitted to the Union; the Southwest was won from Mexico after the Mexican War; settlers began traveling across the frontier to Oregon; and gold was discovered in California, which led to a gold rush. These factors put pressure on the country to roll back the "permanent frontier" and open the central plains to white settlers.

However, the balance between the slave South and the free North in American politics was endangered. Antislavery abolitionists were more vociferous and more active, resulting in an equally active and noisy proslavery movement. Compromise between the factions was growing difficult. So when Kansas Territory was organized in the Kansas-Nebraksa Bill of 1854, it contained a provision in which the settlers of Kansas would themselves decide if the state would be admitted as a slave or a free state.

The natural result of this idea of popular sovereignty was that settlers on both sides of the slavery issue rushed into the state to determine its destiny. It seems clear from Blunt's own writing and from material written about him that he was among the many abolitionists who came to Kansas Territory to make it a free state. Blunt was different than the first settlers of this group, in that they were largely from New England while Blunt had emigrated from Ohio. But since Blunt's home state was Maine, it may be that he wasn't so different from them after all.

The county that Blunt moved into was one of the flash points in the conflict between proslavery and abolitionist forces. The massacre of five proslavery settlers on Pottawatomie Creek by a party led by John Brown had taken place earlier in the year just across the county line. County officials allied to the proslavery territorial legislature fought abolitionist settlers during the summer. Eventually the abolitionists drove out the sheriff and two county commissioners. Border Ruffians from Missouri also raided settlements in Anderson County.

Events in the county came to a head in August 1856 when an abolitionist militia partly commanded by John Brown attacked the camp of some proslavery raiders. The free-state forces carried the day, and for awhile the county calmed down. When Blunt arrived by the end of that year, he came into a county firmly under abolitionist control.

In September 1857 Blunt joined a group of men in founding the town of Mount Gilead, across the Pottawatomie Creek from the recently created Greeley. The original name of the town had been Pottawatomie, but was ultimately changed. Mount Gilead prospered and most of Greeley moved across the creek, including its post office. The town suffered when it was later discovered to have an inadequate water supply.

Blunt had arrived in Anderson County a few years after his uncle Rufus Gilpatrick. Town history suggests that Gilpatrick moved here as early as 1854, and by 1855 he had become prominent in the county's free-state circle. It seems likely, therefore, that Blunt came to Kansas Territory because of his uncle, either on his own or at Gilpatrick's urging.

Soon Blunt began to take an active part in the struggle over Kansas Territory. In 1857 Blunt joined Gilpatrick in an effort to entice locals to boycott an election. The election was over a state constitution, but the abolitionist constitution drafted in Topeka was not on the ballot. Blunt and Gilpatrick were not successful in this effort, but the next year Blunt became a senator in the territorial legislature.

Blunt also played a role in another conflict outside his new hometown. Southwest of Anderson County is Bourbon County and the town of Fort Scott. In late 1857 conflict arose between abolitionist "squatters' courts" and the proslavery county authorities in Fort Scott. On December 15 the squatters' court at "Fort Bain" along Little Osage Creek near the Fort Scott-Fort Leavenworth road was ordered by county authorities to disband. If the court refused, its members would be arrested and charged with treason. Messengers were sent to nearby counties for assistance.

The next day Blunt led fifteen men from Anderson County into Bourbon County to aid the squatters' court. Blunt arrived at the behest of Rufus Gilpatrick, who had been active in maintaining the court. According to a letter Blunt wrote in 1877, he had not been at Fort Bain more than half an hour when a posse of two hundred men arrived to make the arrests.

At first Gilpatrick and another man went out to parley with the leaders of the posse, a U.S. marshal, most likely Deputy Marshal Little, and the Bourbon County sheriff, J. Cummings. The parley went nowhere, and both sides prepared for a confrontation. The posse split into three columns and moved on the abolitionist position. Some of the abolitionists were armed with Sharps rifles and when the posse advanced they used those rifles to great effect. The firing put a fear into the posse, forcing them to retreat to Fort Scott.

While the marshal sent word to Washington via Leavenworth, the squatters' court sent out more calls for help. The abolitionary forces also withdrew north to a church along Little Sugar Creek near Mound City. Soon there were perhaps 175 men gathered in the abolitionist "army," among them John Brown and "General" Jim Lane.

James Henry Lane was born into politics in Indiana. His father was a politician, and Lane had served in the Mexican War, been Indiana's lieutenant governor, and held a seat in the U.S. House. He had voted for the Kansas-Nebraska bill in 1854 and it cost him his House seat. That vote seems to have been at the behest of Illinois senator Stephen Douglas for, upon losing his House seat, Lane went to Kansas to start a Democratic Party to support Douglas's higher ambitions.

But Kansas Territory in 1855 was already too polarized to support a Democratic Party that was mild in its opposition to slavery. The Missouri Border Ruffians who controlled the early "Bogus Legislature" wanted a proslavery party, while abolitionist settlers were creating a Republican Party that reflected their views. It was no surprise, then, that Lane's attempt failed miserably.

Jim Lane was not so easily defeated. His Indiana district was anti-slavery, so it was no real conflict for him to move from the Democratic to the Republican Party. With his colorful appearance, electric speaking style, political savvy, and ability to straddle the fence while sounding sincerely partisan, Lane quickly became one of the most powerful men in the territory.

It was Lane who led the effort to draft the first abolitionist state constitution, the Topeka Constitution. Lane skillfully led the free-state forces in the bloodless "Wakarusa War," and gained some credit for making it bloodless. When violence broke out in 1856 and the free-state forces were on the brink of collapse, Lane very publicly organized a relief "army" in the East, marched it back to the territory, outmaneuvered the proslavery men, and then nego-tiated a settlement.

By the time of the squatters' court situation in Fort Scott the proslavery partisans were losing the struggle over Kansas. Strong territorial governors rolled back some of the excesses of the Bogus

Legislature. Gov. Robert Walker held an election for the legislature in October 1857. When fraud threatened to return control to the proslavery politicians, Walker threw out the results and allowed the free-state men to gain control.

That free-state territorial legislature gave Lane the title of major general and put him in charge of the free-state militia. With his new title in hand, Lane quickly headed to Bourbon County to take command of the so-called army forming near Mound City. He chose a few men to act as his staff of military aides. Among those men were William A. Phillips, Preston B. Plumb, and Dr. James G. Blunt. But before much more could happen, regular U.S. Army troops soon arrived at Fort Scott. After some back-and-forth negotiating between the sides, peace was restored to the county.

This incident may have been the most important in Blunt's life, for in all likelihood it was the point at which he met the man who would guide much of his destiny, James Lane. The two had things in common that would have attracted each to the other. Both had lived in the Midwest, although Lane was a native. Both were raised in abolitionist areas of the United States and, by the time they met in 1857, both were active in both the free-state movement and in the Republican Party.

But there were two primary differences between the men. Lane was well known for putting on great shows of radicalism while acting moderately or attempting moderation of others' actions. Blunt was a real radical when it came to the issue of slavery, and stayed so until long after the Civil War. The other main difference was age: Lane was twelve years older than Blunt.

Before Lane could have an impact on Blunt, the young doctor would have two encounters with the most famous (and infamous) radical abolitionist, John Brown. Brown lived not far from Blunt, so it's likely Blunt had met "Old Brown" well before the crisis in Bourbon County. Once the situation had been defused, Blunt and Brown stayed in the area as guests of a local man. The two then rode back to Anderson County together, where Brown took a rest at Blunt's home before continuing on to Lawrence.

Blunt's impression of Brown was that he was a serious man who believed he was "the instrument of Divine Providence" to bring down slavery. Brown never smiled or laughed but, according to Blunt, was always polite and kind to "all classes of people." At the

Free-state fighter John Brown as he would have looked during the late 1850s. Blunt, a neighbor of Brown's, served with him in the fight in Bourbon County and helped Brown hide slaves he had liberated from Missouri. *Photograph courtesy the Kansas State Historical Society, Topeka, Kansas.*

time Blunt would have been about half the age of Brown, and he revealed in an 1877 letter that Brown made a lasting impression on him.

According to that same letter, the last time the two men met was in the winter of 1858-59. On a cold night Brown came to Blunt's house and asked him to hide a group of slaves he had apparently "liberated." Blunt quickly agreed, enlisting the aid of his two brothers, Rufus Gilpatrick, and two other men. They cared for the freed slaves for about four weeks while Brown was in Lawrence. In all likelihood, Brown spent the time trying to secure additional aid to get the former slaves out of the territory. Brown later returned for his charges and took them north where, according to Blunt, "Old Brown" had a run-in with a U.S. marshal before escaping to Canada.

The days of John Brown and violent conflict between the proslavery and abolitionist forces were just about over as Brown left the territory. The year 1859 would see the end of the control of Kansas by the "slave power" once and for all. A new constitution would be drafted calling for Kansas to be admitted to the Union as a free state. This would also be the year that Blunt would cease to be an obscure doctor in a rural county on the fringe of the frontier. He would not have known it as he met Brown for the last time, but James Blunt was beginning his own path to fame and infamy.

CHAPTER 3

The Wyandotte Convention

In March 1859 Anderson County voted in favor of the new constitutional convention 185 to 7. In June, Blunt ran against W. F. M. Arny for the post of county delegate to the convention. Blunt won and in July traveled to Wyandotte where the delegates would assemble and draft a free-state constitution for Kansas.

Rather than playing the minor role that most have since assumed, Blunt was actually one of the dozen or so major participants in the Wyandotte Convention. He took part in the important debates that framed the constitution drafted at Wyandotte. He made a handful of substantial speeches. It may well be that because he became one of the key delegates to the convention that he was able to rise so far so quickly during the Civil War.

An interesting fact later noted by Gov. John Martin was that many of the free-state and proslavery leaders did not attend the Wyandotte convention. This absence, Martin said, turned out to be a positive factor in the swift drafting of a proper constitution. There was no feud between Lane and his rival Charles Robinson at Wyandotte; ideology took a back seat to practical work; and the convention was largely free from power grabbing or maneuvering.

Aside from being a gathering of relative unknowns, Wyandotte was also a youth convention. Of the fifty-two delegates, only fifteen were older than forty. A third were under thirty, with the youngest, Benjamin F. Simpson, at twenty-three. The party makeup was thirty-five Republicans and seventeen Democrats, reflecting the change in territorial politics since 1854. Only eighteen of the men were lawyers; Blunt was one of three doctors attending the convention.

The Wyandotte convention began on the morning of July 5, 1859. Elected president of the convention was James M. Winchell, a former reporter for the *New York Times*. Solon O. Thatcher of Lawrence was chosen president pro tem. John A. Martin of

Atchison was chosen secretary. Blunt's nominee for sergeant at arms, G. F. Warren, was elected to that post. Blunt himself was put in charge of the committee on militia, even though he had no military experience. This choice, however, may have been a result of his attendance at the Ellsworth academy in Maine. Other than Blunt, there doesn't appear to have been anyone else at Wyandotte with a military education, much less formal military experience.

Blunt first spoke on an issue on July 7 when he submitted a resolution on state bonds and banking laws. This action brought about the question of whether resolutions should be considered in "the committee of the whole,"or with all the delegates, or in their respective drafting committees. The decision was made to send resolutions to the committees and allow them to decide what came before the whole convention.

A short time later Blunt proposed a resolution that would allow the convention to choose an existing state constitution as a guide. Blunt's resolution, however, left blank what state's constitution would be used. In the end Ohio was chosen, which no doubt pleased former resident Dr. Blunt. Blunt then proposed that G. F. Warren provide four extra copies of the local newspaper, the *Wyandotte Commercial Gazette*, for the delegates' use. Blunt did this to help keep the paper going. This resolution was adopted.

Blunt's first speech to the convention also came on July 7. The law forming the convention had specified fifty-two delegates and had set out how those delegates were to be elected. However, several western counties were assembled as a single district. One man each from Chase and Morris Counties tried to get in after apparently losing the election, while the Wyandotte County delegates either refused to attend or sent more than they were allowed. These questions were the subject of Blunt's speech.

His main point on the matter was that the law said fifty-two, and the convention had to follow the law if the constitution drafted was to be accepted by the people and the federal government. He expressed concern that if additional delegates were allowed, soon new delegates might come down from Nebraska Territory or up from the Cherokee Nation. This situation could then diminish the work of the convention. Later in the day the matter was disposed of, with the western men denied and the Wyandotte delegation refusing to attend the convention.

The committees were organized on July 11, with Blunt being put in charge of the militia committee. John Martin would later hail President Winchell's choices for committee chairmen, though he wondered what propelled Winchell to choose Blunt, "an obscure, dull-looking, shock-headed country doctor." Winchell selected Samuel A. Kingman to lead the judicial committee; Kingman would later serve as chief justice of the Kansas Supreme Court. John J. Ingalls was tapped to lead phraseology and arrangement; he would later be a U.S. senator. Winchell's choice to lead the education committee, W. R. Griffith, would rise to state superintendent of schools.

That day saw another Blunt speech, this time on the work of the banking and corporations committee. He was a member of that committee, and wanted to see Kansas allow the establishment of banks. "If we propose to be a mercantile and commercial people," he said, "we must have a circulating medium other than gold and silver." He assured the delegates that the committee had drafted provisions to prevent fraud, abuse, depreciation of bank stock, and charter corruption. Blunt would continue to speak out on the issue over that day and the next. It's not clear why Blunt would be interested in this topic. His speech contains no personal anecdotes on the subject, and there seems nothing in his personal life to point to an interest in banks. The most likely explanation seems to be that this was simply a civic matter that Blunt had opinions on and a willingness to express those opinions.

Over the rest of that day and the next Blunt entered the debates on the size of the new state legislature; whether or not the legislature should meet in biennial sessions; and how many votes the legislature needed to overturn a gubernatorial veto. In the latter two, as well as in other debates, Blunt would refer to Ohio as reasons for or against the matter at hand.

Blunt revealed a progressive view when the convention debated the question of women's roles in local school boards. Blunt was in favor of women taking an active role in schools. He went further than that, saying, "As far as it respects the placing of the sexes in the common schools on an equality . . . I am not opposed to that." He added that if, in the future, women "shall ask to be put upon an equality with men," he wouldn't have an objection. He didn't think that time was 1859, but clearly he could see it coming.

It's important to note that Blunt was not necessarily on the leading edge in this respect. Women had been playing a substantial role in the abolitionist movement for some time. The most powerful literary attack on slavery, *Uncle Tom's Cabin*, was written by Harriet Beecher Stowe. The Seneca Falls Declaration on women's rights had been drafted eleven years earlier. Finally, and most significantly, Blunt was not alone in his support of this position in the convention.

At the end of the July 13 session Blunt made his one committee report to the convention on militia laws for the new constitution. An attempt was made to consider the report the following day but was defeated. The three sections Blunt's committee drafted were approved. A fourth was added naming the governor commander in chief of the militia, which gave him the power to call upon the militia any time. The first section said the militia was to be composed of able-bodied white men; an attempt to strike the word "white" failed. The report was adopted and passed on to the phraseology committee.

There are two aspects of Blunt's work on this committee that, in light of his career during the Civil War, are very interesting. The first and most obvious is that, despite his lack of any military background other than the militia committee chairmanship, Blunt would go on to become the only major general from Kansas during the war. Less obvious but more intriguing is the fact that Blunt would feud with two governors over control of militia regiments and the promotion of militia officers. It's almost as if Blunt gained the prestige to rise in the ranks, but learned nothing from his work in Wyandotte.

During both the morning and afternoon session of the next day, July 14, the question of compensation for judges came before the convention. Blunt spoke out twice on the issue, supporting what he felt was a reasonably high compensation base. Both times he expressed the view that a high enough base salary would attract good talent and keep that talent on the bench for more than a year. Both times he also invoked experience from Ohio, and he once spoke of what an Ohio judge told him about the problem with that state's low salary. Since he was a doctor, and not a lawyer, his interest in the question seems to have been merely civic, but it does seem to show the wisdom of the people in Anderson County in choosing him as their delegate.

The question of "black law" dogged the drafting of the Wyandotte Constitution. Proslavery Democrats continually tried to prevent the entry of free blacks into every Kansas institution. On July 14 this debate centered around education, and Blunt spoke out against the Democrats. He was opposed to the constitution forbidding the education of blacks and expressed some anger at the "proslavery party" in constantly bringing up such provisions. He was not the only Republican to feel this way, and time and again these attempts were beaten down by the majority.

Two days later Blunt let some of his wit show when the convention debated the proposed state boundaries. There was some discussion that part of Nebraska Territory south of the Platte River be included in the new state of Kansas. There was also discussion of what the western boundary of Kansas should be; at the time the territory extended all the way to the Rocky Mountains.

Blunt spoke at considerable length about this topic. He believed that the territory already embraced enough area to make up two states. He said that drawing the western line at the twenty-third meridian, the closest of the three meridians considered, would create a state larger than New York, Ohio, or Iowa. He expressed the common view that the western high plains were uninhabitable and therefore of little value.

He observed that the chief proponent of boundary extension, the delegate from Riley County, had claimed that not pushing the state line far to the west would cut off any railroad building along the Kansas River valley and would hinder communication. In reply, Blunt wryly stated that when an imaginary boundary line could cut communication, alter commerce, bar commercial trade, or "change the channel of the Missouri River" he would believe in the delegate's assertions. He then wondered if that delegate's desire to put the state capital in Manhattan, a city along the proposed railroad route, had anything to do with his claims.

Blunt then shifted to the heart of his speech, the question of northward extension to the Platte. He was opposed to such an expansion, and his reasoning was couched in terms of the possible conflict between rural agriculture and urban commerce. He pointed out that southern Kansas was dependent upon farming, while the towns along the Kansas River and to the north were becoming densely populated and of a "commercial character."

At that point in time, he stated, the area of the Platte valley had more in common with the Kansas valley than with southern Kansas. Joining these two valleys would skew the political power in the new state toward urban commerce and upset the present balance. The agricultural interests in southern Kansas would be "like the tail of a kite," subject to the will of the urban north.

Looking at the rural economy of present-day southern Nebraska, one can see that Blunt's concern was misplaced. But in the rise of the heavily urbanized northeast and south-central Kansas, Blunt was right to be worried. These areas have since gained most of the state's population, and thus have gained or jockeyed for political control of state government. What Blunt and his contemporaries could not have known was that this imbalance would arise no matter what the borders of the state actually were.

Blunt finished his speech by stating his view that the northern extension was driven by Democrats. They were, he said, trying to maintain control of Kansas and subvert the effort to draft a free-state constitution. Blunt's arguments reflected those of his fellow Republicans and the extension efforts would fail. But Governor Martin, addressing the topic almost twenty-five years later, would call that failure the one blunder the Republicans committed at the Wyandotte convention.

The issue of slavery materialized at the convention on July 18, and Blunt once again spoke up. The question of the federal fugitive slave law had arisen during debate on the bill of rights. The law required citizens to comply with efforts to return slaves to their masters, and meted out harsh punishment for those who aided escaped slaves. The law was a red flag to abolitionists. The territory was rife with those who refused to obey it; Blunt likely knew some of them personally.

Blunt accused his Democratic opponents of trying to "come to the rescue" of slavery by protecting the law in the state's bill of rights. He wanted the bill to protect Kansans from "the aggressions of this infamous law." He was anxious that Kansas would not "be prostituted as the hunting ground for human prey." He spent a considerable amount of time denouncing the law and its supporters, and praising those who fought against the law.

Blunt could not be considered as swimming against the tide on this issue, at least not in Kansas. The Republican party was in the

ascendancy in the territory. In the convention there were two of
them for every Democrat. Actions such as the one on the fugitive
slave law were delays to the inevitable. The constitution drafted at
Wyandotte would be a free-state one. Slavery in Kansas was on its
last legs.

On July 20 a hint emerged to anyone that might have paid attention about the character of the future General Blunt. During the
debate over boundaries a reporter with the newspaper in
Wyandotte erroneously reported that Blunt had said something
that he in fact had not said. He went to the reporter and pointed
out the error. He was dismayed to see that, instead of a correction,
the reporter wrote that Blunt was retreating from his statement.
Blunt confronted the reporter again and was directed to the newspaper office, where he finally found satisfaction.

Blunt rose up on that day and recounted the situation in detail.
When he was done the president asked if Blunt had any motion to
make. He replied that he wasn't making any motion—he was
"merely" calling attention to "an abuse of privilege" on the
reporter's part. It seems a trivial thing, but similar trivialities would
trip up General Blunt time and again in the coming war.

A bit of Blunt wit also popped up that same day. The discussion
had moved to the nuts and bolts of who could hold what seat
under what circumstances, who would have what formal duties,
and so on. One of these sections had attached to it the words "and
naval." Blunt voiced skepticism that the Kansas River would ever
host a navy or naval officers, and moved to strike the words.
Another delegate then rose to strike the whole section as redun-
dant, and it was done.

Three days later Blunt was able to address a matter slightly more
in his realm as a doctor. On July 11 a resolution was put forward
granting the state legislature the power to prohibit the sale or
manufacture of alcohol in Kansas. On July 23 a similar resolution
was presented, but this one granted the legislature the power to
only regulate or prohibit alcohol, "except for mechanical or
medicinal purposes."

Blunt spoke up on the matter, saying that although he supported temperance he felt that "no good" had ever resulted from temperance laws. With several decades of hindsight one can see that
Blunt was right. But because of later rumors of his own drinking,

there is a question as to how honest his opposition actually was. In the end the motion had no real support, and prohibition was left for future legislatures to grapple with.

During the convention a delegate from Doniphan County accused a delegate from Douglas County of offering him a town lot in exchange for voting in favor of placing the state capital in Lawrence. A committee was appointed to investigate the matter. The controversy arose again on July 27. When Blunt spoke about the matter he expressed the view shared by many that he couldn't decide if the offer had been made seriously or not. He then moved to table the mess, and by an eighteen-to-fourteen vote it was dropped.

Two days later the constitution was adopted by the convention. On October 4, 1859, the people of Kansas Territory voted on the document. It passed by a two-to-one margin. Two months later state and county officers were elected and the constitution was submitted to the U.S. Congress. On April 11, 1860, the House approved admitting Kansas as a state under the Wyandotte Constitution. Kansas admission came up twice in the Senate that year and both times it was defeated. When it came up for the third time in January 1861, the nation would be on the brink of war.

In the meantime Blunt played a small but significant part in a sensational crime in Anderson County. The story of his role begins late in 1859 when an attractive woman with a poor reputation, Sarah Potter, moved in with a husband and wife named Alderman. The Aldermans arranged for Sarah to meet a local young man, Leon Phillips. In time, Potter and Phillips were married, and for a while they seemed happy.

Six weeks after the marriage, Mr. Phillips fell ill and died. Neighbors became suspicious of Mrs. Phillips when word leaked out of her buying arsenic from a local druggist. Further suspicions were aroused over will inquiries sent by one of the Aldermans. A local justice of the peace was able to empower a coroner's jury and have the body exhumed.

Blunt and another doctor were called in to examine the body and determine the cause of death. Both agreed that arsenic poisoning was the cause. On the strength of their testimony the Aldermans and Mrs. Phillips were arrested and charged with murdering Leon

Phillips. Participating in the defense of the three was a new emigrant to Kansas, a lawyer named Samuel J. Crawford.

Charges against the Aldermans were eventually dropped. But before Mrs. Phillips could go to trial, she escaped and fled the territory. When she returned to Kansas in 1862 she was arrested again and put on trial, this time in Douglas County. However, because several of the witnesses against her were in the army or otherwise unavailable, the jury was unable to convict her.

Such a case could not entirely distract from the national crisis that loomed large in 1860. The Republican nominee for president in that year's election, Abraham Lincoln, was elected. The election of an antislavery president led to a secession movement throughout the Southern states. South Carolina first voted to leave the Union on December 20. It was followed by Mississippi, Florida, Alabama, Georgia, Louisiana, and Texas, which together formed the Confederate States of America. In the spring they would be joined by Virginia, Arkansas, North Carolina, and Tennessee.

Kansas had been admitted to the Union on January 29, 1861. The nation's attention soon became riveted to the new Confederacy and the threat of a confrontation between North and South at Fort Sumter in the harbor of Charleston, South Carolina. However, in Kansas the jockeying began for leadership of the new state and, by extension, the all-powerful Republican party. This in turn led to the division of state and party between the supporters of two men, the former Midwesterner and colorful speaker James Henry Lane, and the former New Englander and upright citizen Charles Robinson.

Lane, although he came to Kansas a conservative, had by 1861 become the "Grim Chieftain" of the radical faction of the Republicans. Charles Robinson was leader of the more conservative supporters of abolition. The two had clashed during the territorial period, but now that Kansas was a state the rivalry intensified further.

Passage of the Wyandotte Constitution put Robinson in the post of governor. Lane worked the state legislature enough to persuade them to elect him as one of the state's U. S. senators. Joining him was Samuel Pomeroy, who had made a deal with Lane so that both were chosen as senators. Lane made another agreement with

Martin Conway, who had been elected the state's lone congress-man in 1859, to obtain control of federal patronage. As spring came to Kansas, James Lane had become the state's most powerful politician.

But with the coming of spring the crisis at Fort Sumter exploded. The president of the Confederacy, Jefferson Davis, ordered the bombardment of the fort to prevent it from being resupplied. The firing began on April 12 and the fort surrendered two days later. America was now to be torn apart by a civil war.

On April 15 President Lincoln called for seventy-five thousand militiamen to put down the rebellion. The North was swept by rallies that eventually came to Kansas. James Blunt quickly became one of the thousands of Kansas men who joined in order to crush the South's treason.

Blunt may have expected to be no more than an ordinary soldier or minor officer in the service of his country. But within months Blunt would begin an extraordinary career of amazing highs and discouraging lows. He would no longer be a country doctor from Anderson County. His first chance for military achievement came quickly because Kansas's neighbor to the east was racing to the brink of secession.

CHAPTER 4

1861

In 1860 Missouri elected pro-Southern Democrat Claiborne Jackson governor. Early in 1861 Governor Jackson tried to organize a pro-secession convention but was foiled by pro-Union politicians. When President Lincoln issued a call for volunteers after firing at Fort Sumter, Jackson called up the Missouri militia to resist Federal authority.

Jackson was foiled again when word of an attempt to seize arms at the Federal arsenal in St. Louis was leaked to the arsenal's commander, Capt. Nathaniel Lyon. Lyon managed to remove the weapons without Southern sympathizers knowing. In May, Lyon managed to capture a camp where Missouri militia were being trained. Lyon then took over most of the Union forces in the state.

When Sen. James Lane arrived in Washington, D. C., he found a number of Kansans already there looking for Federal jobs. Uncertain of his power, and probably looking for some publicity, Lane assembled these men into the Frontier Guard. The guard first protected the White House before moving on to more military duty. In forming the Frontier Guard, Lane was able to gain influence with and confidence from President Lincoln.

Responding to Jackson's call in April, Governor Robinson began calling up the Kansas militia. Robinson also began the process of forming regiments to enter into Federal service. By controlling which men became officers of these regiments, Robinson hoped to create a political base that could rival Lane's.

At first Robinson foiled Lane's efforts to get his hands into the formation of regiments. But by employing his new friendship with Lincoln, Lane was able to raise three regiments. Robinson was stuck for the time being. This was contentious because, in the selection of officers of a state regiment, a politician could reward his friends or allies with military commissions. These officers would not only be in positions of leadership that could yield battle-field glory, but they could also act as political bases in getting out the vote or in getting elected themselves. Usually this power rested solely with the state's governor. Senator Lane, by obtaining permission to recruit, was able to circumvent Robinson's authority.

Blunt may have already cast his lot with Lane before the war started, but he became a definite Lane man during this time. Early in May Blunt had joined a company being formed by Samuel Crawford that would be composed of men from Franklin and Anderson Counties. Blunt followed the company to Lawrence where it was supposed to be incorporated into the Second Kansas Regiment. Robinson slowed this process to gain control of the commissions. Unhappy with this delay and hearing that Lane was to raise three regiments, Blunt left the Second to aid in recruiting another at Mound City.

Previously the assumption about this period in Blunt's life was that he had enlisted as a private before rising in rank to an officer. But the major role he played at the Wyandotte convention may turn that assumption on its head. The active part he played in those debates could have made him the most important man in Anderson County. Certainly it would have made him the most famous.

Anderson County was a frontier county when Kansas became a state. This would make it hard for any well-known county figure to expect a commission to the rank of captain or higher. Certainly the county would not be expected to provide a full company this early in the war. But it does seem likely that a man with Blunt's high local profile might have expected to be commissioned a lieutenant.

If Blunt had already tied himself to James Lane, or was perceived to be a Lane man, it's hard to see why Governor Robinson would have granted Blunt any commission. Robinson's goal, stated or not, was to build his own political base. If Robinson thought Blunt was a "Lane man" he wouldn't have given him a commission. In this light it's logical to see Blunt, not getting what he thought he deserved from Robinson, going to Lane's camp in search of that commission to an officer's rank.

While Lane and Robinson wrangled over military commissions,

Jim Lane in 1861 in New York, just after he became a U.S. Senator. Blunt served under Lane in the "Lane Brigade," and as general became Lane's proxy in Kansas military affairs. *Photograph courtesy the Kansas State Historical Society, Topeka, Kansas.*

Governor Jackson appointed Sterling Price commander of all Missouri state militia units. Price was a former governor who had been a general during the Mexican War. The Missouri militia was not close to being ready to fight, so Price and Jackson were forced to retreat from Jefferson City. Price ended up having to flee all the way back to southwestern Missouri. But there he was able to drill his men in peace and prepare for a campaign to drive out the Federals and link Missouri to the Confederacy.

In early July, Price's men defeated a Union force at Carthage. At the same time his force was joined by units from Arkansas and Louisiana. By the end of the month this Confederate army had pushed Lyon's Federals back to Springfield. Among those marching with Lyon were the first Kansans who had signed up to fight.

Although outnumbered, Lyon, now a general, knew his men were better trained and supplied than the Confederates. He may have hoped that a single large battle would deplete rebel ammunition and compel them to leave Missouri. Whatever the reason, early on the morning of August 10, 1861, General Lyon launched a two-pronged attack on the Confederate camp along Wilson's Creek.

The Union assault succeeded early in holding off rebels on the north side of the battlefield. The flanking column under Col. Franz Sigel was able to push forward. But then a Louisiana regiment marched on Sigel, supposedly wearing uniforms similar to those of an Iowa Union regiment. Sigel held his fire too long, letting the Louisiana troops close in, and their counterattack drove Sigel's column back. The rebels concentrated their force on Lyon's main body. At around 10:30 A.M. Lyon was killed, and soon after the main body pulled back to Springfield.

Back in Kansas, Lane assembled three regiments, the Third, Fourth, and Fifth, into a single brigade at Fort Scott. One source claimed that Blunt enlisted in the Third Regiment as a private, but again this seems unlikely. In any case, soon after the organization of the Third he was promoted to lieutenant colonel of the regiment, putting him second in command. Leading the Third was Col. James Montgomery, a former Ohioan who had once ridden with John Brown. There were accusations at the time that the selection of officers in the Third, including Blunt's, occurred because of "corrupt combinations."

It is therefore entirely possible that Lane promised Blunt a commission before the Third Regiment was even organized. Lieutenant colonel does seem to be more fitting a rank for one of the active debaters at Wyandotte. Remember also that Blunt was head of the militia committee at the convention, and that his high school years were spent in a military academy. Indeed it's not too much to state that Senator Lane may have calculated that the presence of men like Blunt would have given his enterprise a touch more respectability. Why not, then, put Blunt in a prominent position in one of these regiments?

After the battle of Wilson's Creek, Price's Missouri rebels moved northward. Lane decided on his own to chase after them, despite Robinson's concern that any move across the border might bring retaliation. On September 2 part of the Lane Brigade fought Price's advance force at Drywood Creek. The Kansans retreated in haste from the engagement, Lane returned his brigade to Fort Scott, and Price continued north.

Lane put Lieutenant Colonel Blunt in charge of Fort Scott around this time. Blunt stayed behind while Lane took his brigade back into Missouri on September 10. He did not participate in the sack of Osceola on September 23 or in the plunder Lane's jayhawkers engaged in on their way to Kansas City to join other Union forces.

Again, Blunt's role at Wyandotte could be a reason for this appointment. If Lane thought Blunt was a more respectable member of the brigade's officers, his putting Blunt in command at Fort Scott could be an effort to groom the colonel for bigger and better things. Lane had to know there was a good chance southeastern Kansas would be raided by Confederates or their sympathizers. He also had to know that any officer who successfully fended off a raid or punished the raiders would gain instant fame across the state. Such fame would put that officer in line for promotion. It seems that if this was Lane's thinking then Blunt was the officer he was grooming for advancement.

For Lane the choice of Blunt was very shrewd. Of course Blunt would have been known from his participation at the Wyandotte Convention. Blunt would also have been known in the area for his part in the squatters' court crisis back in 1857. Blunt had knowledge of the area and the people he would deal with. And if Blunt succeeded in this assignment, he would owe some of the credit to Jim Lane.

If Lane gave Blunt the opportunity, Blunt repaid that gift in short order. On September 8, 1861, a band of 125 rebel raiders, pro-Confederate Cherokees, and half-breed Osages led by a Capt. John Mathews raided the town of Humbolt in Allen County. Most of the men in town had joined regiments Lane had raised. The raiders carried off everything of value (including plundering stores of dry goods and groceries) to the tune of about three thousand dollars, without meeting any resistance from the townsfolk. According to the *Leavenworth Daily Times* they also took "[e]ight negroes." The story does not clarify this statement, so it isn't known if these people were free blacks or recently "liberated" slaves.

The *Times* also reminded its readers that Mathews and his gang had recently committed "outrages" on settlers in the Cherokee Neutral Lands in southeast Kansas. Another account reported that Mathews had been driving settlers from Cherokee Neutral Lands. The *Emporia News* alleged that Mathews had great influence among the Osages living in a reservation along Kansas's southern border. "It is high time that this miscreant and his followers should be attended to," the *Times* opined.

To that effect a rough company of "Home Guards" and a company of cavalry were raised in the Humbolt area to go after the guerillas. Colonel Blunt was sent to take command of both companies and pursue the perpetrators. On September 18 Blunt's force found the outlaws, attacked their camp along the Neosho River, and killed Mathews along with two others during the skirmish. One period newspaper stated that Mathews fell with forty bullet holes in him. Supposedly Blunt's men found orders in Mathews' pocket allowing for the enrollment of the Quapaw Indians, who had a reservation next to the southeastern corner of the state. Blunt gave the rebels' seized property, mainly buffalo robes and horses, to his men as payment.

In 1951 the son of a founding resident of southeast Kansas gave his father's account of his Civil War experiences to a local author, who in turn wrote an article from it for the Baxter Springs newspaper. The account stated that after Mathews was killed several citizens were arrested for aiding the rebel raiders, and a court-martial was held in the settlement of Little Town. Blunt took charge of the court-martial, while one Preston Plumb of Emporia prosecuted. In the course of the trial it was learned that the charges were made by one man who was not reliable. As a result, his testimony was thrown out and the defendants were acquitted. Afterward, Union troops looted and burned Little Town; later the settlement was rebuilt as Oswego, and it became the seat of Labette County.

After the skirmish at Drywood Creek, Price continued marching north and on September 21 he took Lexington. But now Gen. John C. Fremont, placed in command of all Union forces in the West, began to concentrate his armies against Price.

Fremont had spent over a decade in the West making maps and promoting the region. Hailed as the "Pathfinder," he had run as the Republican candidate for president in 1856. Lincoln had put Fremont in command of the Western Department hoping that the Pathfinder would seek out victory for the Union.

But Fremont blew an opportunity to attack Price when the rebels had to cross the Osage River on October 8. When Fremont reached Springfield he made plans to attack Price but never did. Fremont had already put himself on shaky ground, having given orders to execute captured Confederate guerrillas and to free slaves belonging to Southern sympathizers.

After the battle of Lexington, Blunt requested permission to leave Fort Scott and rejoin his regiment. Permission was granted and, once in Kansas City, Blunt asked to take four hundred men to discover if Price remained in the area. Blunt found that Price had retreated all the way to the Osage River. He promptly reported this fact to Lane and Gen. Samuel Sturgis, the other Union commander in Kansas City.

Within twelve hours an order arrived from Fremont telling Lane and Sturgis to retreat to Fort Leavenworth because Price was approaching them. Lane and Sturgis wisely decided to ignore the order until they had passed their information on Price to Fremont's command. Fremont revoked the order and sent the Union forces at Kansas City toward Springfield.

Fremont's army was tied up for seven days while trying to cross the swollen Osage River. As it moved south Blunt famously remarked that the army's trail was littered with "the feathers of

Confederate general Sterling Price. Price took command of Missouri's Confederate forces in 1861, but Blunt did not face him on the battlefield until 1864. Price remained in charge of the Confederate forces in Missouri until the end of the disastrous 1864 campaign. *Illustration courtesy the Kansas State Historical Society, Topeka, Kansas.*

'seccesh' poultry." The army arrived in Springfield on November 1 to join Fremont who had already arrived. At that point Blunt believed the Union had forty-five thousand men and almost one hundred cannons against Price's twenty-five thousand men and twenty cannons.

Writing after the war Blunt expressed well-founded doubts that Fremont didn't understand his department or make proper use of the Union soldiers at his command. These doubts are borne out by the orders to retreat to Leavenworth, and also by Fremont's elaborate preparations to attack Price, though Fremont never took any firm action against him. Fremont's lack of movement allowed Price's men to escape to Arkansas. With controversy, failure, and stories of corruption dogging the general, Lincoln removed Fremont from command and transferred him east.

It must have troubled Blunt to some degree to see how Fremont had failed in his position. Blunt had backed the "Pathfinder" when he ran for president in 1856. Blunt was, of course, not the only one to be disappointed in Fremont's performance (or lack thereof). Fremont never really recovered from the loss in reputation that he suffered from his inability to deal effectively with the war in Missouri. While his star was on the decline, the star of one unhappy colonel was on the rise.

In a speech in Leavenworth, published in the *White Cloud Kansas Chief* on October 17, Lane claimed that he ordered Lieutenant Colonel Blunt to go after Mathews. When Blunt returned from his march through Missouri, Lane, to the cheers of a crowd, said that he was told Blunt had come back "with more slaves than white men."

James G. Blunt was now on his way up the ladder. He'd had a notorious raider killed; he was helping to "liberate" Missouri slaves; and he was a favorite of James Lane. The future appeared bright for the former doctor turned military commander.

CHAPTER 5

General James Blunt

On November 2 David Hunter replaced Fremont; about two weeks later Henry Halleck replaced Hunter. Gen. Samuel Curtis was put in command of the Southwestern Missouri District on December 26, 1861. Curtis was a West Point graduate, served in Mexico, been elected to the U.S. Congress, and had careers as a lawyer and a civil engineer. He organized his forces into the "Army of the Southwest" and decided to push Sterling Price's Confederate army out of the state for good. He began marching an army of twelve thousand toward Price's camp at Springfield.

Price chose not to stand where he was, but moved south and linked up with General McCulloch's forces at Fayetteville, Arkansas. Price and McCulloch were unable to get along, so Confederate authorities dispatched the aggressive, womanizing Maj. Gen. Earl Van Dorn to take command. Van Dorn made elaborate plans in early 1862 to drive Union forces out of Missouri, starting by marching his new army north to face Curtis early in March.

The two armies closed to within four miles on March 6, 1862. Van Dorn decided to take the offensive, sending Price forward and McCulloch toward the Federal flank and rear. But when the battle began on March 7, Price was late and McCulloch was still moving into position.

The battle of Pea Ridge saw Price's men make gains against Curtis's force near Elkhorn Tavern. McCulloch's flanking attack also gained ground. Part of his command was a brigade of Indians, notably Cherokees. Unfortunately some men of this brigade, after capturing a Union battery, scalped some of the dead. Union troops quickly recaptured the battery. The furor over this incident became a public relations nightmare for the Confederate government.

The tide of the battle began to turn when McCulloch was killed by a Union sniper while reconnoitering the field. His replacement, Texas brigadier general James McIntosh, was killed minutes later. A Louisana regiment took heavy losses and its colonel was captured. On the morning of the second day Union artillery wreaked havoc on Confederate positions. Lack of ammunition due to a wrong turn by his supply train caused General Van Dorn to order a retreat.

The main result of Pea Ridge was the end of an organized Confederate presence in Missouri. Price's men were integrated into the main rebel armies and sent east of the Mississippi. The partisan raiding continued through the spring and summer. But Federal control of Missouri was secure; the nearest rebel force was in central Arkansas.

Van Dorn had been ordered to march east to reinforce Albert Sidney Johnston's army that was about to attack Gen. Ulysses Grant's Union troops at Pittsburg Landing in Tennessee. Van Dorn wasn't able to take part in the battle of Shiloh, and, even worse for the Confederacy, his move allowed Curtis to continue south. Curtis did so and halted within ninety miles of Little Rock. He decided to continue to the Arkansas capital, but paused at Batesville to wait for a new line of supply and communication to be opened.

In the meantime, in Kansas, Governor Robinson was able in early 1862 to break up the Third and Fourth Kansas, combining them into the newly formed Tenth Kansas. Robinson then forced out the old officers in favor of ones he had commissioned. Some probably had to scramble to find new assignments, but not Blunt.

In April 1862 he was commissioned a brigadier general and placed in command of the Department of Kansas. On April 10 Brig. Gen. John M. Schofield, an aide to the late Gen. Nathaniel Lyon and organizer of the pro-Union Missouri State Militia, was put in command of Union forces in Missouri. Both would be serving under General Halleck in the Department of Missouri.

Reaction in Kansas to Blunt's promotion was fairly unfavorable. The *Emporia News* called Blunt's appointment over George Dietzler a "gross injustice." Its editor wondered who aside from Lane and his friends wanted Blunt promoted. Similar views were expressed by the *Kansas State Journal* in Lawrence, while the *Leavenworth Daily Times* wrote, "The [Lincoln] Administration has done a great many unjust and foolish things in the matter of appointments, but this last is more unjust than any before it."

One of the colonels in Lane's brigade, Charles Jennison, resigned in part due to Blunt's promotion. Jennison had been an acting brigadier general, and may have believed he deserved the promotion. The *Leavenworth Daily Conservative,* at that time allied with Jennison, expressed its dissatisfaction at Blunt's promotion and also pointed a finger at Senator Lane.

One of the few papers to support Blunt's promotion was the *Lawrence Republican,* edited by Lane's good friend John Speer. Speer quoted a colonel who had been in Lane's brigade as saying that Blunt was "one of the very best men in the service." The colonel praised Blunt's actions after Humbolt, his opposition to jayhawking (pro-Union raids on Missouri), and added, "I like his style." Speer claimed that this endorsement alone had brought Blunt his promotion.

Early in May, Brigadier General Blunt took command of the Department of Kansas from Samuel Sturgis. Blunt took over a wide area that included Kansas, the Indian Territory, and the unorganized territories of Nebraska, Colorado, and Dakota. Few newspapers knew Blunt's modest record like the *Fort Scott Bulletin.* But all editor E. A. Smith had to say about Blunt's advancement was to hail the promotion of Capt. Thomas Moonlight to assistant adjutant general. "If Gen. Blunt does not run the 'machine' in good style," said the *Bulletin,* "it will not be for lack of good assistants."

Other Kansas newspapers and editors were not so shy in making their sentiments clear about Blunt's new duties. Although no friend of Lane or Lane's allies, Sol Miller of the *Kansas Chief* wrote the following headline on May 8, "THANK THE LORD!" In the story Miller wrote, "we hope the like of Sturgis will never be seen again." The report ended with the following: "Let us hope for the best from the new commander; and . . . to traitors he may always be—Blunt."

The Leavenworth Conservative, which just one month earlier criticized Blunt's promotion, hailed his appointment to department command. It was confident Blunt would restore the "loyal Indians" to the territory, praised his selection of staff officers, and wrote this: "The Department of Kansas is restored and a man is placed in command who knows his rights and knowing dare maintain."

The Leavenworth Times also did something of a turnaround in its earlier views. Less than a month earlier it had called Blunt's promotion "unjust." Now it was willing to wait and see. The newspaper reported that it had heard Blunt was opposed to pro-Union raids, or jayhawking, and because of this it would "score a point in his favor, and will concede him the game as soon as he shows himself capable of playing it out."

Confederate officials believed that Blunt had replaced Sturgis because Sturgis had failed to invade the Indian Territory. This belief was echoed by an editorial in the *Freedom's Champion* in Atchison. On May 20, editor John Martin claimed that Sturgis's ouster would be "received with the utmost satisfaction by the patriotic people" of Kansas. He implied that Sturgis had done little, and the change would improve the situation. As to Blunt's promotion to department command, the editorial expressed a preference for state militia commander Col. George Dietzler. But the Atchison paper promised to support Blunt if "we deem him worthy of it."

The only discouraging words appear to have come from the *Emporia News*. Its editor wrote that Blunt's posting was "the severest military joke that had been perpetrated on the Department of Kansas."

It wasn't until May 31 that the *Fort Scott Bulletin*, the Kansas newspaper that "knew" Blunt the best, finally weighed in on Blunt's promotion and abilities. The occasion was apparently Blunt's preparations for a Union move toward the Indian Territory, and the more favorable newspaper reaction to this. Noting this change in tone the *Bulletin* observed, "The reviled of yesterday is the hero of today." It continued by saying that Blunt was now revealed to be "the greatest military man" of Kansas after Senator Lane. If the *Bulletin* had had any objections to Blunt's advancement, it was because he was promoted over George Dietzler. However, it said, "Blunt was smart enough to win the stars; and this is a sufficient guaranty that he will not dishonor them."

The *Bulletin's* observations are telling. It may be that most of the state's major papers were able to accept Blunt's promotion. It might also be true that, with the bad experiences of out-of-state commanders, the Kansas editors had decided that any Kansan in charge of the department was better than no Kansan in command. With much of the press now on his side, Blunt could focus his attention on running his new command.

With this command partly due to Lane's influence, Blunt quickly came into conflict with the Kansas governor and his allies. The first bone of contention was Robinson's attempt to break up the "Lane Brigade." Robinson had broken up the Fourth Regiment and removed its commander, Col. William Weer. Parts of the Third and Fourth had been combined into a new Tenth Regiment. On April 12, 1862, the War Department issued Special Order 80 revoking the breakup of the Fourth and Weer's removal.

Despite this order nothing appears to have been done, for on April 28 Weer wrote to Secretary of War Edwin Stanton protesting the breakup. He asked to be placed in command of a new Fourth Regiment made up of the old Third and some of the old Fourth. He also pointed out various vacancies in other regiments that the officers of the new Tenth could be assigned to. General Sturgis, at that point still in charge of the Kansas district, endorsed Weer's letter. Apparently days later the revocation of the breakup was reissued.

On May 23 Governor Robinson wrote to Secretary Stanton on the Weer matter. Robinson complained about Lane's part in raising the Fourth and appointing officers, including Weer. He then claimed that in early 1862 when the regiment was remustered it only had five companies. Because of this, General Hunter had mustered out Weer as colonel. Robinson claimed that General Halleck supported his consolidation of the regiments.

Blunt entered the fray on May 27 when he told Secretary Stanton that he was not getting any cooperation from Robinson in the Weer matter. With that message was Blunt's order to his subordinate to tell Robinson that no other officers would be mustered in until displaced officers (like Weer) were given assignments. The message to Stanton also included Robinson's refusal to carry out Special Order 80. Around May 30 the adjutant general told Blunt that the secretary of war had sent a request to Robinson to put Weer in command of the new Third Regiment. Since it appeared that both Robinson and the lieutenant governor were out of the state at that time, Blunt was ordered to put the request into practice.

Weer's placement didn't entirely resolve the matter and it was handed over to the U.S. attorney general for a decision. On June 16 he decided that Robinson was wrong in breaking up the Fourth and deposing Weer. As evidence, the attorney general cited the fact that the regiment was mustered into United States service, not

Charles Robinson, Kansas's first state governor. Robinson had been Jim
Lane's political rival during the territorial period, and their rivalry contin-
ued when Robinson became governor of Kansas in 1861. Blunt believed
Robinson slighted him in the forming of Kansas's first two regiments at
the start of the Civil War. *Photograph courtesy the Kansas State Historical
Society, Topeka, Kansas.*

into the Kansas state militia. Therefore the regiment was under the control of the president, not the governor, and thus not subject to Robinson's orders or his interference.

A short time later Robinson and some of his supporters at Fort Leavenworth supposedly held a meeting in the town of Leavenworth. According to Blunt, the topic was the mustering of officers. Blunt issued orders forbidding this mustering without his permission. He also made it clear that he would treat harshly those who tampered with Federal troops by creating "dissension and discord." This allowed Blunt to win the round, but these hardball tactics probably didn't win him any friends or sympathizers among the Robinson crowd.

But they were not particularly adept at getting back at Blunt, at least in the summer of 1862. The July 3 issue of the *State Journal* in Lawrence, a pro-Robinson paper, presented the claim that Weer hadn't been deposed by Robinson, but by the department commander. A week later the paper criticized an expedition Blunt sent into the Indian Territory, despite the fact that within a few weeks Union forces were able to take control of the territory.

This was not the only troubled relationship Blunt had after becoming department commander. Blunt had additional run-ins with his superior, Gen. Henry Halleck. Halleck was a renowned officer who had written extensively on strategic military theory. Upon taking command of his department, Halleck gave Brig. Gen. R. B. Mitchell the task of raising five thousand troops for an expedition to New Mexico Territory to secure that region and perhaps invade Texas from the west.

Halleck also ordered Blunt to send him all available troops for his operations in Tennessee. Blunt sent Mitchell's men east only to learn afterward that Halleck had not attacked the Confederates, and Blunt's dislike of Halleck increased. What Blunt didn't acknowledge, either because he had kept out of it or because he chose to forget, was that the New Mexico expedition was another scheme of Senator Lane's to allow him to be both senator and general. The scheme threatened the authority of generals Hunter and Denver. Denver was able to undermine Lane's intrigue in the end.

Another source of friction between Blunt and Halleck was that Halleck was not a committed abolitionist. As department commander he ordered that escaped slaves, or "contrabands," be prevented from crossing the Union line. To a radical abolition-ist like Blunt this order was unforgivable. In his mind the war was about destroying slavery as much as about crushing the rebellion. When Halleck was appointed general in chief in July he allowed the taking of rebel property including slaves, but in Blunt's eyes the damage to his superior's respect was done.

Blunt rather brazenly sent a letter to Edwin Stanton stating his perceived grievances with Halleck. In this letter Blunt vowed not to communicate with Halleck and only with Stanton. Perhaps under pressure from Lane, and perhaps not wanting to open up this can of worms, Stanton supported Blunt's position on this matter.

Trouble for Blunt's administration also came from nearby his headquarters in Leavenworth. At least three newspapers were being published in that city at the time: the *Times,* the *Conservative,* and the *Inquirer.* The first two were Republican, albeit on differing sides of the Lane-Robinson feud. *The Inquirer,* though, was a Democratic paper and had only been in operation since March. In an increasingly radical Kansas, its leaning marked it as a traitorous pro-Confederacy rag. By June of 1862 the criticism of the *Inquirer* was coming from around the state. On June 12 the *Conservative* published denunciations of its rival coming from Doniphan County and Oskaloosa to reinforce its own attacks. Three days later it printed a letter from "One Interested" decrying *Inquirer* "insults" directed at General Blunt's staff.

That must have been the last straw for Blunt for on that day, June 15, he sent men of the Third Wisconsin to arrest Burrell Taylor, the *Inquirer's* editor. Supposedly the first thing the Union soldiers found when they entered the newspaper's offices were loaded muskets. The *Conservative,* in reporting about the seizure and Taylor's arrest two days later, did so with much gleeful humor and wry illustrations.

The *Times* was just as opposed to the slant of the *Inquirer* as its rival the *Conservative* was. Two days after Taylor's arrest the *Times* printed several *Inquirer* excerpts that seemed to demonstrate Taylor's "factious opposition" to the Union. Most damning was the last excerpt, in which Taylor concluded with, "Abolition success and American national degradation are synonymous in meaning." This would be bad enough in any Northern state; in Kansas this was treason, pure and simple.

The *Conservative,* editorializing in its both daily and weekly editions of June 19, roundly praised Blunt's suppression of the *Inquirer.* This was "no blow . . . [to] freedom of the press," but a strike against treason similar to killing a rattlesnake. It offered support for its position from a speech by a congressman and an editorial from a pro-Union Democratic paper in St. Joseph, Missouri.

The *Times* was just as supportive of Blunt's move, but far less gleeful and mocking. It viewed Taylor as a tragic figure, a dignified and successful man who had "ignored" the Democratic views of Stephen Douglas in favor of the "Democracy of Jeff Davis." But the *Times* did not sympathize with Taylor, nor with another editor who took over the *Inquirer* and was forced out a month later for writing "libelous articles on Kansas affairs" and sending them to Wisconsin newspapers for reprinting. It had no qualms about the closing of any newspaper that expressed sympathy for the Confederate cause or attempted to undermine the war effort.

The *Inquirer* was not the only paper in the north to be shut down by Union authorities. Nor was Blunt the only general to have problems with Kansas newspapers. In shutting down the *Inquirer,* Blunt wasn't doing anything unusual for the time. Modern sensibilities may object to such actions in a democracy even during wartime. But Blunt was a man of his time, not the present, and if others were closing "seditious" newspapers, it's no surprise that he would also do so. And on the topic of sensibilities, Blunt was not a man who reacted well to criticism. If the *Inquirer* had insulted him or his staff, much less opposed the war or sympathized with the "slave power," Blunt would not have suffered its existence for long. Add to this his radical patron Senator Lane, and it's no wonder that Blunt put an end to the *Leavenworth Inquirer.*

General Blunt had a more pressing problem as head of the Department of Kansas than newspapers and politicians. The guerilla war between abolitionists and proslavery Missourians was now carrying on into the formal Civil War. Part of the mandate of his office was to protect Kansas from incursions from Confederate raiders.

To that end, Blunt took seriously the standing order that guerillas were not to be treated as soldiers but as criminals and executed upon capture. Indeed on June 26 Blunt issued his own orders regarding the Confederate bushwhackers. General Orders No. 13

gave field commanders permission to treat any captured guerrilla not as a prisoner of war. Instead of undergoing a formal trial, they would be "summarily tried by drum-head court-martial, and if proved guilty be executed [by hanging or shooting on the spot]."

This policy was carried out on July 28, 1862, when a Jeremiah (also known as "Perry" or "Solomon") Hoy was executed at Fort Leavenworth. Hoy rode with the already infamous guerrilla William C. Quantrill. Hoy was captured and put on trial on July 23 for his part in the March murders of a civilian and a Union soldier just across the border. He eventually admitted his part in the killings but pleaded for his life by saying that he was pressed into Quantrill's band. These pleas went unheard, Hoy was found guilty, and he was sentenced to be executed by firing squad. The sentence was carried out on July 28. Five others were reported captured along with Hoy but had been freed by Blunt's predecessor, General Sturgis.

General Blunt wasn't satisfied to wait for guerillas to be captured. He also sent units under his command to smoke out the raiders. One such mission was carried out by a company of the Sixth Kansas Cavalry. Based at Paola, Kansas, the Sixth had some responsibility for protecting the state border from raids. A company of this regiment was able to get into the Snibar Hills of Missouri, a popular summer hiding place for the guerillas. In the raid that appeared to have occurred in June, the Sixth found and destroyed eight guerilla camps and killed three dozen raiders.

Blunt continued to deal with the situation through the summer. Late in July, when it was ordered that the Missouri state militia be enrolled, there was what the *Atchison Freedom's Champion* described as a "stampede" among the guerrillas toward Kansas. In response, Blunt ordered them expelled or arrested as "rebels or vagrants."

While Blunt treated bushwhackers harshly, he refused to apply such treatment to people he viewed as "honest" civilians. Later in the year when elements of the Ninth Kansas Cavalry reached Bower's Mills in southern Missouri, one of their corporals took sick. The Ninth was part of Blunt's command, and the general approached the mistress of a local house to request care for the soldier. When the woman said her husband was in the Confederate army and expressed a willingness to aid the ill soldier, Blunt promised to repay her for her help. Of course he added to this promise that he would "burn your house over your head" if the man was mistreated. The soldier did die of his illness, but Blunt seems to have kept his promise to the wife and did not burn her home.

By the end of July the *Emporia News,* which had called Blunt's move to department commander a joke, conceded that Blunt was doing a good job. He was, it reported, "a man of good hard sense and sound judgment." No doubt this turnaround was in large part because of the swift and unexpected success of the expedition Blunt had sent into the Indian Territory to drive out the Confederates.

CHAPTER 6

Blunt Returns to the Field

The trouble in the Indian Territory dated back to fall 1861, when Col. Douglas Cooper had ousted pro-Union Creeks from the territory and drove them to Kansas. Gen. Albert Pike organized three regiments of Cherokees, Creeks, Choctaws, Chickasaws, and Seminoles to fight for Confederacy. The Cherokees took part in the Battle of Pea Ridge. Members of some of these tribes held slaves, which aided Confederate recruiters. Also helping push these tribes into the Confederate camp was that, before war broke out, many Indian agents in the territory were Southern sympathizers.

Some Kansans were aware of Pike's activities as early as September 1861. On Saturday, September 21, 1861, the *Leavenworth Times* told its readers, "The red men of the forest are gathering to the standard of the South." The *Times* went on to report that Pike was contacting all the tribes he could. He was even said to be trying to enlist "the wild Comanches, heretofore untamable. . . ." In fact, Pike did not gain support from them, but he did meet with success with other tribes. This success did not go unnoticed in Kansas or in Washington. The only problem was figuring out how to counter Pike's efforts.

At first the Lincoln administration opposed organizing friendly Indians to fight in the Civil War. Eventually this policy changed, but Blunt's predecessor Samuel Sturgis refused to carry it out. In his postwar report of his experiences, Blunt blasted Sturgis for not allowing the raising of these regiments, despite orders from the secretary of war. Senator Lane persisted in asking for Indian regiments, and his lobbying was supported by the commissioner for Indian affairs. The effort was further helped by the fact that Confederates were doing so and that Pike's Indian units had fought at Pea Ridge.

On April 6, 1862, General Halleck ordered General Sturgis to send a force under General Denver into the Indian Territory. Sturgis either refused or dallied, which led to the criticism of his leadership in Kansas. The next month when Blunt took over the Kansas department he pressed the issue far more vigorously. This had the effect of turning around some of the opposition to his appointment. Soon two "home guard" Indian regiments were assembled from the ranks of the Union Indians who had fled to Kansas.

These regiments were to be part of an expedition organized in the spring of 1862 to defeat Cooper's and Pike's commands. Plans also called for the expedition to speed the return of Indian refugees in Kansas to their homes. The commander of this "Indian Expedition" was Col. Charles Doubleday of the Second Ohio Cavalry. His plan was to march into the territory and either defeat or chase out the Confederates and Confederate Indians, but he would not chase them through Arkansas if they fled there. Doubleday's goal was mainly to occupy the territory, and perhaps later to move south into Texas.

Doubleday started his forces south in early June, but he marched without the two Indian regiments being organized and equipped for action. Col. William Weer, whose Tenth Kansas Infantry had also been left behind, sent word to Blunt's headquarters of Doubleday's decision on June 5. The next day Weer also wrote to Doubleday and asked him to wait. He wrote again to Leavenworth on June 7, still concerned about consolidating Union forces aiming for the territory.

At the same time, the commander of Union forces in Missouri, Brig. Gen. John Schofield, informed Blunt that rebel forces were massing in northwestern Arkansas. Schofield asked Blunt for his cooperation in dealing with this threat. Blunt replied to Schofield by informing him of a successful skirmish by the expedition. He also gave his estimate of Confederate strength, and pledged to assist Schofield's forces in Missouri in dealing with the enemy in front of them. This pledge would cause the expedition much grief toward the end of the summer.

While these letters were going back and forth, the state's leading newspaper, the *Leavenworth Conservative,* which expressed displeasure at Blunt's promotion just two months earlier, now expressed confidence in Blunt's expedition south. On June 19 it

General Blunt shown in a regular Union uniform. Blunt's signature appears below the undated portrait, so this picture might have been a personal photograph of him held by a friend or an acquaintance. *Photograph courtesy the Baxter Springs Heritage Center and Museum, Baxter Springs, Kansas.*

stated that soldiers and officers would be satisfied with Blunt taking command of the force. These men knew Blunt and had "the fullest confidence" in him, the paper said. "The only discontent will come from us who are left behind," it continued. At the end of its brief report the *Conservative* predicted, "After its departure we shall hear no more of secession in Western Arkansas, Texas and the Indian country."

Unfortunately the expedition still hadn't departed for the territory by the end of June. But on June 26 a message was sent to John Ross, principal chief of the Cherokees and a leader of the pro-Confederate faction of the tribe. The message, from the expedition's commander, Colonel Doubleday, promised that Union forces were coming to restore loyal Indians to their homes. Word had leaked north that Ross was wavering in his support of the Southern cause, and, therefore, the message told Ross that the approaching forces would give him the opportunity to show his true loyalty.

Despite this message to Ross, Doubleday's lackluster leadership of the expedition and its failure to move fast enough led Blunt to remove him. Blunt decided to put Colonel Weer of the Tenth in command of the force. Weer was a lawyer, a one-time jayhawker, and a notorious drinker. Blunt hoped that Weer would do well, and in July he advised the new commander to be careful marching into the territory. He informed Weer that there was a chance that the new rebel commander, Gen. Thomas Hindman, might try to get behind Weer's column and either wipe it out or invade Kansas.

Not everyone in the expedition was pleased with the change in Union commanders. A solider in the Second Ohio Cavalry wrote in his diary that the officers he knew were "astonished" by the change. Doubleday was "enraged" by what the diarist called the "intrigue and rascality of Kansas officers and politicians" and considered resigning. Of course it seems that the Kansas officers were unhappy with Doubleday for at first not moving, then trying to move without the Indian regiments. These disputes were not entirely resolved and later would lead to additional problems.

On the expedition, Colonel Weer took with him the Tenth Kansas; three Kansas cavalry regiments, the Second, Sixth, and Ninth; the Ninth Wisconsin Infantry; the Second Ohio; the First Kansas and the Second Indiana batteries; and two Indian regiments. Weer hoped to crush rebel Indians in the territory, restore Union Indians to their homes, and position a force to attack Confederates in western Arkansas. A correspondent for the *Leavenworth Times,* writing from the expedition's camp on the Neosho River, said that the rebels only numbered three thousand or less and therefore "no danger [is] to be apprehended."

In response to Weer's moves, John Ross tried to call on Albert Pike for help in fending off the Union invasion. Pike refused to leave "Fort Ben McCulloch" near the Red River. Stand Watie, commander of the Confederate Cherokee units, appealed to the new commander in Arkansas, Gen. Thomas Hindman. Hindman was a driven man who had eloped with his wife when her father placed her in a convent, and he had built a brick home despite not being able to pay for it. Despite this drive Hindman had no troops he could spare because he had his own plans.

Hindman did order Albert Pike to send the Cherokees reinforcements. Pike hesitated before sending Col. Douglas Cooper with a force of Chickasaws and Choctaws. But then Pike failed to tell Hindman that he had made this deployment. Hindman therefore sent a battalion of Missourians to help Watie. This confusion in the Confederate leadership was further damaged by persistent rumors that suggested Colonel Cooper was a heavy drinker.

On July 3 Weer took three hundred men and attacked the Missourians' camp at Locust Grove in the territory about thirty miles north of Tahlequah, the capital of the Cherokee Nation. The sudden attack routed the Confederate Cherokees, resulting in the capture of one hundred men and the camp baggage, including ammunition. Among the other items taken were orders to the Confederate commander from General Van Dorn to march into Kansas. Also captured was one Colonel Clarkson, former Leavenworth postmaster.

On that same day, the Sixth Kansas Cavalry defeated a force under Stand Watie. Weer reported accurately that the enemy was in confusion and that some Cherokees were starting to surrender. In that same message, dated July 6, Weer stated that he felt the Cherokee Nation had been conquered, but that he wasn't sure what he should do next.

The Union assault continued on July 14 when a detachment under Capt. Harris Greeno of the Sixth Kansas marched into

Summer Campaign, 1862

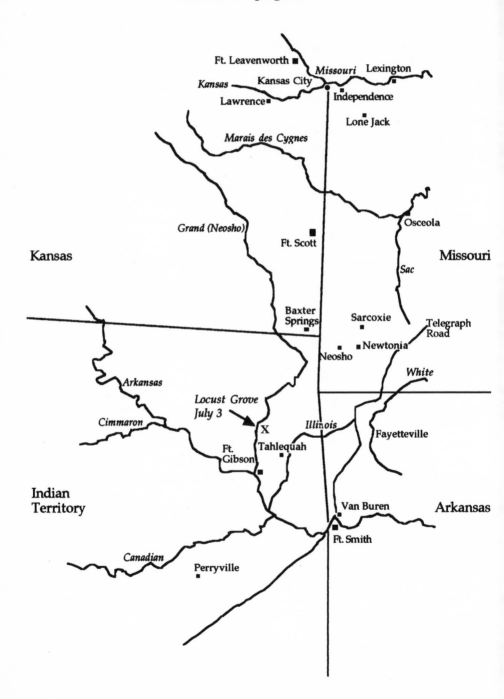

Tahlequah without opposition and captured two hundred men. The men of the Sixth then took Fort Gibson on July 19. A few days before, on July 15, Greeno met with John Ross, the wavering Cherokee chief. Col. Douglas Cooper, Ross reported, was asking for all Cherokee males between eighteen and thirty-five to be drafted into the Confederate army. Instead Ross's men switched sides and joined the Union, with the new Cherokees formed into the Third Indian Regiment under Col. William Phillips, a former reporter for Horace Greeley's *New York Tribune*. Also taken in these engagements were over fifteen hundred head of cattle, five hundred stand of arms, and thirty-six loaded mule teams.

On July 20 Blunt informed Secretary of War Stanton of the successes of the "Indian Expedition." Blunt proclaimed that the areas the expedition had secured were more prosperous than they had been since the war had started. But countering this good news were rumors Blunt passed along that the Confederates had between thirty and forty thousand men under arms in Arkansas, southern Missouri, and the Indian Territory, vastly outnumbering the Union forces.

Blunt also told Stanton that his department was lacking enough small arms and ammunition for the expedition and for repelling guerrilla raids. The only force close by was the Missouri militia, and he pointed out that they were not in his department. He called for reinforcements and weapons, and warned of having to call up the Kansas militia. Significantly, he did not ask for his department to be enlarged to obtain the Missouri militia. Blunt didn't think they'd leave Missouri, and he expressed to Stanton his lack of trust in them.

Whether Blunt sent this message reflecting only his views, or whether he sent it at Jim Lane's request, it got results. On August 4, 1862, Senator Lane opened a recruiting office in Leavenworth. Naturally, Lane's power to raise these regiments came into conflict with Governor Robinson's power to commission officers in regiments raised in his state. Lane had the backing of Stanton and the War Department, and was able to raise the Eleventh, Twelfth, and Thirteenth Kansas Volunteer Infantry Regiments. Robinson refused to back down, and when Lane presented his formal request for commissions in early October, Robinson refused to accept them. Robinson sent the matter to Gen. Samuel Curtis when he took over the department, who allowed the commissions to go through.

Whatever Blunt's motivation was in writing to Stanton, the result was the subversion of the powers of Governor Robinson. Lane was able to reward his friends and supporters with commissions. He became the most important politician in Kansas, and he used that status to get his candidates elected governor and U.S. representative in the fall elections. Thus it was General Blunt who, possibly unwittingly (but probably wittingly), put Senator Lane "in command" of Kansas.

Well before Blunt could give Kansas to Lane, he had to deal with a crisis in the Indian Expedition. On July 18 a dispatch was written by Col. Frederick Salomon, commander of the Ninth Wisconsin, to the officers of the expedition saying that he had arrested and relieved Colonel Weer. The reasons were not given openly, but references were made to the fact that the force was well into the Indian Territory, they had gotten there through forced marches, and the Union camp did not have drinkable water. In addition, on July 17 Weer had supposedly disregarded the advice of his subordinates to fall back. In the dispatch Salomon also seemed to worry that no communications had reached them for two weeks, and that no one knew if any supply trains were en route. Salomon claimed that he had reliable information that "large bodies of the enemy were moving on our rear."

The next day two Indian agents sent a message to Blunt on the deposing of Weer. They said that the white forces were already retreating, leaving three Indian regiments in the field. They reported fears among the Union Cherokees that they would now be attacked or even murdered. The agents termed the arrest a "mutiny" and added, "These honest people, who believe in the United States Government and flag, care more at present for life and virtue than the making of brigadiers."

The main source of the mutiny appears to have been the lack of provisions for the men, especially a lack of water. Luman Tenney, a solider in the Second Ohio, wrote to his family on July 11 that the troops were already suffering from a lack of water. One sergeant who went to a spring just outside the line of march was reduced in rank, he reported. Tenney also wrote of rumors that on the other side of the river that the men were following there was plenty of water. There had been "no rain of consequence for about two months," Tenney said, and the temperature had been recorded as high as "one hundred and twelve in the shade."

A soldier who served in the First Kansas Battery also wrote about the men's dire situation. He said that for water the men had to rely on "stagnant pools" in dry creek beds. The water was "so impregnated with foreign matter" that the men had to boil it, skim it, then blacken it with coffee just to drink it. As to food, the soldier reported that the men were down to three days of rations left when Salomon took control.

Yet another solider, Isaac Gause of the Second Ohio, wrote later that the men had plenty of beef, but nothing to season it with to prevent those who ate it from getting dysentery. Gause added that "our old clothes were fast giving out," and the only shade came from lying blankets on top of stacked arms. Disease and exhaustion were rampant, and the men were lashing out at each other. Gause and Tenney seemed to confirm the claim that Weer was drinking. "I do not know what he had to eat," Gause wrote at one point in his narrative, describing Weer, "but I know he had a ten-gallon keg strapped to a mule." For his part, Tenney claimed that during the battle of Locust Grove Weer was so drunk that "he could neither receive the report of the battle or give any orders." After enduring all this, Tenney wrote, Salomon had had enough and ordered his regimental camp guards to arrest Weer.

On July 20 Salomon wrote Blunt saying that he "had the honor to report" Weer's arrest. In this message he claimed Weer was "abusive" in talking to his fellow officers, "intemperate in habits," and "rash in speech, act, and orders." Weer had not kept up communications with the Union rear. The expedition had camped in a poor spot from July 9 to July 19 and had not taken any action one way or the other. Salomon's letter also claimed that Weer had agreed in a council of war to retreat but then ordered the men onto half rations and prepared to advance. At that point Salomon and the others relieved Weer and pulled back. By the time this message was written, Salomon's command had withdrawn to Wolf Creek, some thirty to forty miles north of Tahlequah.

But Salomon may not have been the best man to take over from Weer, for on July 25 Col. R. W. Furnas, commander of the "Indian Brigade" that was left behind, reported that the commanders of the three Indian regiments had not been told of Weer's arrest until July 22. Salomon had left "indefinite orders" to Furnas and the other commanders. Furnas also reported desertions in two of the regiments. Furnas did have one bit of good news: a detachment of one of the remaining regiments had marched into Fort Gibson to secure that important post. He added that he held the Indian Territory north and east of the Arkansas River. Furnas said he had asked Salomon for some reinforcements to maintain control, but as of that day he hadn't heard from Salomon.

Four days later Salomon again reported to Blunt. This time he told of all the positions the Union held, including Fort Gibson, Tahlequah, and the upper crossing of the Arkansas River. He also said that a "vigilant system of scouting" was operating to keep watch over Confederates in the area.

On August 3 Blunt wrote to Salomon saying that he was happy about all the points held. From the message it seems that he hadn't yet heard that Salomon had retreated. Blunt ordered Salomon to send the Sixth and Tenth Kansas to support the Indian regiments. Importantly, he stated clearly that he opposed a complete withdrawal of the white regiments from the territory.

Though Blunt had not heard about Salomon's retreat, a message written on August 3 to General Schofield in command in Missouri reported that force's movements. The reference to Salomon was supposedly caused by the news that Gen. Thomas Hindman, having raised a Confederate army in Arkansas, was heading toward the territory. The author of that letter, Brig. Gen. E. B. Brown, stated that from what he had gathered, Hindman was marching toward General Curtis in northern Arkansas.

As soon as Blunt heard about Weer's arrest and Salomon's movements, he sent orders for the column to halt. Blunt believed that Salomon was retreating because of rumors that a Confederate force was on the column's right flank. Blunt left Fort Leavenworth on August 8 to take personal command of the Union force. When he got to Fort Scott he found Salomon there, even though Salomon admitted he'd received Blunt's order at Baxter Springs. Blunt allowed the captured Cherokees from Tahlequah to formally organize into the Third (Union) Indian Regiment.

When he arrived, Blunt said, he found the soldiers "disorganized and demoralized" due to the dispute among the officers. Blunt convened a general court-martial to investigate the mess. But he discovered too many officers had taken part, and there wasn't enough time to fully investigate the situation. The newspaper in Atchison expressed a disgust with Salomon similar to that of Blunt's, for on August 2 it described Salomon's "strategical policy" as one of "masterly inactivity." It voiced a hope that when Blunt took command the expedition would start advancing again.

The men might not have been quite as angry with Salomon as Blunt was, however, and that may have played a part in Blunt not pressing the matter. Luman Tenney wrote in his diary that when Blunt and Senator Lane arrived on August 11 to speak to the men, they "didn't cheer much" when Blunt criticized the officers who arrested Weer. They did cheer when Salomon's name came up during their remarks, though.

The *Bulletin* in Fort Scott, reporting the situation on August 2, summarized the problem Blunt faced in dealing with the Weer-Salomon mess. It was able to present clear rationales for the actions of both men. Weer could be seen to have endangered his men, while Salomon could be seen as a coward and a mutineer. The only opinion the *Bulletin* could manage to express was the hope that Blunt would "bring things into better shape" and take personal command of the expedition. Blunt wasn't able to take command, but the day after he spoke to the men he seemed to put aside the whole mess.

While Blunt was trying to reorganize the expedition he sent John Ross to Washington to meet with President Lincoln and other Federal officials. Blunt believed that most of the members of the "Civilized Tribes" were loyal to the Union. Cut off from the government and with only Confederates speaking to them, the tribes had cast their lot with the South. Blunt seemed certain that if a Union army could hold the territory, the tribes would remain loyal and aid the Northern cause. It's a fairly straightforward argument that probably made sense. There would be little chance to test Blunt's belief, for rebel activity was again on the rise in Missouri.

Before traveling to Fort Scott to deal with the expedition's failures, Blunt attended a war meeting in Leavenworth on August 4. Senator Lane was the featured speaker, but Blunt also spoke as he was in charge of all troops in Kansas. Some two thousand people listened as he addressed the regional situation. Blunt began by expressing his reluctance to speak on military matters, but felt justified because he was speaking "on matters pertaining to your own welfare." He asked why the rebellion had not yet been crushed, then answered that it was because while the nation fought the rebels the nation also sought to "conciliate" the Confederacy. The lesson of the last fourteen months, Blunt said, was that "we must make war in earnest."

To him and other radical abolitionists, that meant one thing: "The man must be demented who believes that this rebellion can be put down and the institution of slavery be preserved." In commenting on this remark a few days later, the *Leavenworth Times* put Blunt's position this way: "Sympathizers must keep quiet, hereafter, or they will be summarily gagged." No doubt this was directed at those who still supported the editorial policies of the defunct *Inquirer.*

After expanding on his statement to the cheers of the audience, Blunt told the crowd that when the campaign in the Indian Territory was about to be reversed, he authorized his men "to arm everything, black and white, rather than give up one foot of territory." He called for the enlistment of black troops, even going so far as to state that if blacks "won't go in voluntarily I intend they shall go in anyhow."

Although Kansas might seem to have been a hotbed of radicalism during the Civil War, this was not the case. Few ordinary citizens, perhaps reflecting the sentiments of their mostly Midwestern states of origin, did not support the enlistment of black soldiers. As the war dragged on, however, this view started to change. Blunt was almost certainly trying to do his part to change that view by making these remarks.

Of course, enlisting black soldiers would mean regiments, and that would mean commissions for officers of those regiments. This too had to have been a motive for Blunt's remarks. But given Blunt's long association with the abolitionist cause and his apparent lack of interest in a political career, this probably wasn't as strong a motive as his determination to destroy slavery. After all, once he took command of the department, Blunt gave orders forbidding any blacks to be removed from Kansas to nearby departments. This sort of order, which effectively prevented slaves who fled into Kansas from being returned to their masters, could only have come from a dedicated abolitionist.

Blunt encouraged the men in his Leavenworth audience to enlist, to get others to enlist, and to oppose those who discouraged enlistments. He then engaged in a little Robinson bashing, saying that the governor's "re-organizations" of Kansas regiments had left them demoralized. He said he had done "justice" to those officers wronged by Robinson and that he had the support of nearly every officer under his command.

He concluded by telling his listeners that he would be back in the field soon. He pledged to protect the state with his "small force." His army would be a "bulwark of fire" between them and the enemy, and that "if your homes are invaded it shall only be over a field drenched in blood."

Senator Lane followed Blunt with a rabble-rousing speech echoing and expounding upon what the general had said. After Lane came Marcus Parrott, who when he said, "The institutions of Missouri are not [to] be interfered with," the crowd went into an uproar. It took some minutes for the audience to calm down, and when they did they gave Parrott none of the cheers they gave Blunt and Lane.

The soldiers defending those "institutions of Missouri" were on the move again as Blunt and Lane spoke in Leavenworth. In mid-August, General Schofield received reports that the rebels were on the move in southern Missouri. He asked General in Chief Henry Halleck in Washington if he could get Blunt to assist him in fending off this threat. Halleck assented, and on August 15 Schofield wrote to Blunt to send all the men he could spare to stop the Confederates.

Springfield, Missouri, was once again under threat from a Confederate army. The commander of Union forces there, Brig. Gen. E. B. Brown, apparently called on Blunt for help. Blunt, perhaps because he was still busy with the problems of the expedition, didn't send any help to Brown at first. On August 10 Brown wrote to Schofield that Blunt wasn't aiding him and that he might have to abandon Springfield.

But the next day Blunt wrote to Brown that he did want to cooperate. He reported that he was trying to get reliable information on rebel movements. Blunt asked Brown to prevent the rebels from heading north. Blunt promised to prevent them from moving south, and expressed his desire to catch them in a vise and destroy them. Of course what Brown might not have known was the mess Blunt had to grapple with at Fort Scott. Until Blunt took a few days to get a handle on things he would be unable to send out any of his units.

That same day, August 11, Blunt ordered Col. William Cloud of the Second Kansas to both secure Fort Scott and prepare to resist the rebel column. Blunt had a message sent from department headquarters calling up the militia in Leavenworth County. Perhaps a day or so later the commander of the Sixth Kansas reported that Independence, Missouri, had fallen to the rebels.

As he was restoring order and planning to continue the campaign, Blunt was informed that Confederate cavalry under Shelby and Coffey had just penetrated into Missouri. He turned his force east at Fort Scott and gave chase. He found the rebels' trail at Pappinsville and after marching for a hundred miles "with but little rest," he found the rebels at Lone Jack.

On August 16 the Confederates overwhelmed a force of eight hundred Federals there, killing their commander. Blunt arrived two days later, the Confederates pulled back, and Blunt resumed the pursuit. His advance guard was able to attack the rebel rear at the Osage River; the main body was able to escape to Arkansas.

While all this was going on Blunt changed his headquarters from Fort Leavenworth to "the field." This move, along with Blunt's role at Lone Jack, were hailed by the *Leavenworth Conservative*. Despite the fact that Blunt and his men played only a modest role in fending off the rebel raid, the *Conservative* devoted much space to the Kansas general and his troops. Their march from Fort Scott to Lone Jack was "not paralleled in the history of the present war." Blunt had "anticipated every movement [the Confederates] designed" and "saved [Kansas and western Missouri] from the ravages of a reckless and unprincipled enemy."

This epic article was in all likelihood an attempt by the *Conservative* to bolster morale in Kansas. The early gains of the Indian Territory expedition had ended in mutiny. The Confederates had raided all the way to Independence. War news from the rest of the country was bad or unclear. So when Blunt's men were able to win a skirmish with the rebels, the *Conservative* hyped the minor action as a major victory.

This is probably even more true considering that the raiding rebels were able to elude Blunt at Lone Jack. Luman Tenney, writing in his diary, claimed that Blunt made a mistake in allowing their escape. He said that all the officers were "enraged and disgusted" by Blunt's error.

Despite the rebel withdrawal, the situation in Missouri was still fluid, and turning bad in the territory. By then many of the Union Indian regiments had left the territory. In their absence the Confederate Indians fell upon their opponents once again and sent another stream of refugees back to Kansas. Blunt took his troops back to Fort Scott, organized them into three brigades, and prepared for another foray into the territory to deal with the enemy there.

On August 23 Brown informed Blunt of yet another rebel strike into Missouri. He suggested that his command and Blunt's combine to drive this new force south. That same day Schofield told Blunt to stay close to Springfield to aid Brown. Schofield wanted Blunt to stay on the defensive until he could assemble enough reinforcements to allow for an offensive drive south.

Three days later, in reporting on a skirmish his men had with rebels near Lamar, Missouri, Blunt told Schofield that he had information that the organized Confederate forces had retreated to Arkansas. Blunt suggested to Schofield that all Federal troops in the state, except for those necessary to garrison certain strong points, be assembled for a massive offensive to push the rebels out. Blunt wanted this campaign to cooperate with Curtis's drive along the Mississippi. He didn't want this push stopped at the Arkansas border but carried on all the way to Texas. Blunt's idea was to compel the Confederates to fight or "jump into the Gulf of Mexico."

Blunt's suggestion was no doubt ambitious, but perhaps borne out of frustration and desperation. Certainly the rebels could not continue to raid into Missouri. No doubt the Union needed an offensive to boost morale and increase support for the war. And perhaps Blunt was looking after his own prospects for if such a campaign succeeded, its commanders would earn glory and promotion.

Blunt seemed to believe that both Arkansas and Texas had

enough supplies to maintain an army. Such a move would take the war to the enemy, a strategy that Gen. Ulysses Grant was beginning to undertake farther east. Blunt might well have been onto something.

Schofield, either thinking along the same lines or inspired by Blunt, wrote to General Halleck on August 28 about a push toward Fort Smith, Arkansas. Schofield asked for reinforcements that could be combined with Blunt's and Gen. James Totten's men. He wanted to move into western Arkansas before the Confederates could organize. He hoped that this drive would end the hopes of Southern sympathizers in Missouri about a return of Sterling Price.

That same day, General Totten informed Schofield that the rebel governors of Missouri, Texas, Louisiana, and Arkansas had met some days before and called for an invasion of Missouri so that they could regain control of the Union-occupied state. Totten called for more troops to deal with this threat and promised to watch for any invasion. But at the end of his message he reported that Blunt was not cooperating and suggested that he be put under the command of the general in charge of Union forces in Missouri.

On September 1 Totten informed Blunt that the rebels were once again moving north. He estimated their strength at fifteen thousand and growing, and Totten urged Blunt to move east to assist him. On September 5 Colonel Phillips wrote to Blunt that rebel forces were southeast, southwest, and south of his position at Neosho. He wasn't as certain at Totten of what their intentions were, however. Three days later Schofield ordered Blunt to move as many men as he could east to support Totten. This was to either resist another rebel raid or to initiate a push south into Arkansas.

Weer presented more definite information to Blunt on September 12. He was able to report changes in Confederate high command in Little Rock. He said that there were two large rebel forces: one at Maysville, Arkansas, the other southeast of Neosho, Missouri. Weer recommended that Blunt's division at Fort Scott be moved to deal with the situation.

Schofield wrote to Halleck on September 14 that he was getting "no valuable assistance" from Blunt. He decided to leave his headquarters in St. Louis and personally go to Springfield. That same day Schofield asked Blunt to go to Springfield to assist Totten and asked Blunt to reply to him. Totten also wrote to Blunt on that day repeating his request for help. Totten told Blunt that together "we can thrash the whole damned rabble," but separated their task was much more difficult.

Blunt may not have been as uncooperative as Totten and Schofield thought, but instead was keeping quiet while waiting for his own intelligence from Weer and the newly promoted General Salomon. Two days later he wrote to his patron, Sen. James Lane, asking for all the troops that could be spared. He reported Totten's intelligence and said he was to get moving soon, perhaps within a day or so.

Blunt wrote to Totten on September 17 that he had heard from Weer and Salomon at Carthage, Missouri. He told Totten that he was ordering them to harass the Confederate flank and to be ready to assist Totten in defending Springfield. He said he couldn't move immediately because four of his six infantry regiments, all new, were waiting for their small arms to arrive. Once they came he promised to move to support Totten, and asked him to keep in contact with him, Weer, and Salomon.

On September 22 Samuel Curtis's leave of absence was revoked and he was put in charge of the Department of Missouri. Curtis's department embraced Missouri, Arkansas, and the Indian Territory, but Kansas was still separate. On September 27 Curtis told Blunt that he should combine his forces with Schofield, that he was to obey Schofield's orders, and that he was to keep in touch with Curtis until he joined Schofield. It seems that any planned major campaign south was put on hold until the present situation became more clear to the Union leadership.

Part of this lack of clarity stemmed from the fact that no one seemed to be in overall command in the field. Three days before Curtis's message to Blunt, Weer wrote to him saying that he was struggling to make sense of orders from four separate brigadier generals. Weer warned Blunt that if someone didn't "take command of all these scattered forces we will be cut up in detail."

Weer was ostensibly part of a brigade Blunt had sent under General Salomon toward Carthage to deal with the rebels nearby. Salomon moved his forces to Sarcoxie, and on September 29 he decided to see if there were in fact Confederate units in the area.

He sent a small force toward Newtonia to make contact and determine the strength of any Confederate army nearby.

While the Union forces were reacting to one rebel raid after the other, Maj. Gen. Thomas C. Hindman was able to raise a new Confederate army in Arkansas seemingly without the Federals noticing. To that end Hindman declared martial law, rigorously conscripted men, arrested deserters, and even shot some of them. By doing these things, he was able to raise an army of twenty thousand men by early July. At the time General Curtis began to worry that he wouldn't be able to hold Batesville, so he decided to pull back to Helena. Hindman sent a Confederate force to prevent Curtis from reaching Helena. The effort failed and Curtis marched into Helena on July 13.

After some confusion among Confederate leadership, Hindman was allowed to organize an expedition to retake Missouri as autumn approached. When there was a buildup of Confederate strength in southwest Missouri in September, concern spread throughout the region. General Curtis ordered the district commander, General Schofield, to assemble all Union units and stop Hindman's invasion. Curtis gave Blunt the choice of heading back to Fort Leavenworth to run the new District of Kansas from there, or to join General Schofield and for the time being run the district from the field. Blunt chose the latter, left Fort Scott on October 1, and reached Sarcoxie the next day. Before he left, Blunt was again told by Curtis to cooperate with Schofield and obey his orders.

In the meantime around four thousand rebels reached Newtonia, Missouri, on September 28. Twelve miles to the north was a brigade of Blunt's men under the command of Frederick Salomon. Taking command of the Confederate column was Douglas Cooper, who replaced Albert Pike as commander of the Indian Brigade. Despite orders not to bring on an engagement, Salomon sent a reconnaissance force toward Newtonia.

They struck the Confederates early on the morning of September 30. The Union troops were quickly overwhelmed as Confederate reinforcements swarmed them. A charge by Cooper's Choctaws and Chickasaws sent the Federals into a full retreat. Salomon's main force moved forward and met the retreat about six miles from Newtonia.

Confederate general Thomas Hindman. Hindman faced Blunt in Arkansas in the last few months of 1862. Hindman's retreat under a flag of truce after the battle of Prairie Grove was in Blunt's eyes an act of cowardice. After the Van Buren raid, he never again faced Blunt in the field. *From the collection of Dr. Tom and Karen Sweeney, General Sweeny's Museum, Republic, Missouri.*

Salomon was then able to rally his men and make a stand. He counterattacked the pursuing Confederates and held his ground. Cooper threw the whole of his command at the Union line. The Union troops gave way again, but this time their retreat didn't stop until they reached Sarcoxie, where Salomon's men had started.

Union leaders believed Cooper's force to be from five thousand to ten thousand men. For his part, Cooper believed he was outnumbered, six to seven thousand to his four thousand. He described some Kansas units as "jayhawkers," expressing his contempt for them. In Fort Scott, however, the Kansas units were hailed for their "gallantry," except the Ninth Kansas which had been the first to flee.

The battle at Newtonia now alerted the rest of the Union army in the region. The Confederates were assembled, had fought well, and were planning to move north. If they were to drive back the rebel threat, Blunt and Schofield would have to work together to stem the reverse their forces had suffered.

CHAPTER 7

Into the Ozarks

After Newtonia, Blunt was given formal command of a division in General Schofield's new Army of the Frontier. Blunt's division consisted of the Second, Sixth, and Ninth Kansas Cavalries; the Tenth, Eleventh, Twelfth, and Thirteenth Kansas Infantries; the Third Wisconsin Cavalry; the Ninth Wisconsin Infantry; the Eighteenth Iowa Infantry; and the First Kansas and Second Indiana Batteries. Blunt's force numbered around six thousand men.

He and Schofield immediately began to plan how they would take back the offensive from the Confederates. They decided that a frontal assault would be too obvious. They agreed that Blunt would move his division right while Schofield would take the rest of his force left. The idea was to hit both flanks, get into the rebel rear, and by routing them drive the Confederates back into Arkansas.

Blunt ran into two delaying actions around Granby, and he worried that he would be too late to support Schofield. When he arrived at the rebel camp Schofield wasn't there. Blunt decided to attack anyway, certain the enemy didn't want to fight, and after a brief engagement the rebels retreated. After they fled, Schofield's column arrived on the scene. Blunt later claimed that Schofield had five fewer miles to march than he, and that on the march Schofield hadn't run into so much as a picket.

This may have been the crucial point at which the relationship between Blunt and Schofield began to deteriorate. Back on September 30, when he had been informed of Curtis's taking command, Blunt had seemed unhappy that he had to hear of this from Schofield and not from Curtis. But he did pledge his full cooperation to Schofield and even expressed a desire to see Schofield in person to plan the next Union move. This message, combined with Blunt's postwar comments, suggests that it was in the days after the battle of Newtonia that things started to go bad between Blunt and Schofield.

On October 4 Blunt's command returned to Newtonia, this time to stay. They engaged troops under Confederate commanders Marmaduke and Shelby and after marching in rain and with the help of Union batteries, drove the Confederates back. When Union troops entered town rumor among locals was that Confederate general Cooper had been "drunk as a lord." His reputation was sinking as fast as Blunt's was rising.

Schofield wrote to General Curtis on October 13 that he planned to "clear out Northwestern Arkansas." Once that was done he would send Blunt's division into the Indian Territory to finish that campaign and restore the refugee Indians to their homes. He promised Curtis that he would not advance farther than was possible, but he also stated that he would not advance and then retreat until loyal men in the area could be mustered to hold any ground that was gained.

By October 16 Blunt's men reached the old Pea Ridge battlefield. During this time various cavalry units skirmished with partisans and scouted the terrain for Cooper's army. After an engagement by the Second Kansas Cavalry on October 18, Blunt resumed his march. On October 21 his men reached Maysville near the border of Arkansas and the Indian Territory.

Supposedly Schofield paused for a week there to survey the ground and map the roads. Blunt was incensed by this waiting and later claimed that Schofield didn't say anything to him until October 20, when he asked if Blunt had any suggestions about future movement. Blunt proposed to head toward Maysville and attack Confederates under Cooper and Stand Watie. Schofield agreed and Blunt set out with thirty-five hundred men. Blunt said Schofield promised to attack other rebels at Huntsville.

If Blunt and Schofield weren't on the best of terms, they could comfort themselves that at least they weren't on the opposing side. A letter from the Eleventh Kansas appeared in the *Leavenworth Conservative* on October 29, well before Blunt's men marched. The author of the letter described the rebel army as "in rags . . ., on short rations of beef and corn dodgers only, half armed, half starved, and good only at a foot race." Such talk might be seen as

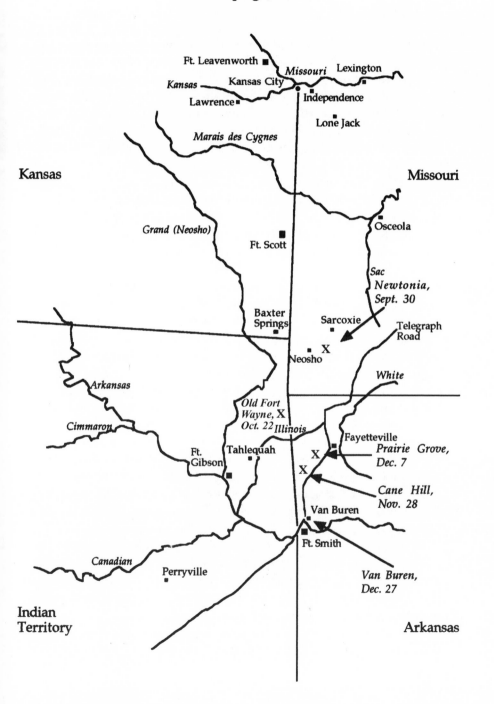

Fall Campaign, 1862

Ft. Leavenworth ■

Missouri   Lexington ■

Kansas   Kansas City ●

Lawrence ■   Independence ■

Lone Jack ■

Marais des Cygnes

Kansas

Missouri

Osceola ■

Grand (Neosho)

Ft. Scott ■

Sac
Newtonia,
Sept. 30

Baxter
Springs ■

Sarcoxie ■

Telegraph
Road

X

Neosho ■

White

Arkansas

Old Fort
Wayne, X
Oct. 22 *Illinois*

Cimmaron

Ft.   Tahlequah ■
Gibson ■

Fayetteville ■   *Prairie Grove,*
Dec. 7

X

X

Cane Hill,
Nov. 28

Van Buren ■

Canadian

Perryville ■

Ft. Smith ■

Van Buren,
Dec. 27

Indian
Territory

Arkansas

Union bravado, but would find some proof when Blunt's men made contact with Cooper's force.

On October 15 Gen. James S. Rains had ordered Cooper to invade Kansas. Cooper ordered all Confederate Indian regiments to meet his white units at Old Fort Wayne in Indian Territory just across the border from Maysville, Arkansas. He arrived on October 17, found that not all the units had assembled, and decided to wait for them to come in. He had heard on October 21 that Federal troops were marching toward him from Bentonville, but he assumed they were scouts. He could not have been more wrong.

Early on the morning of October 22 Blunt found Cooper's camp with his entire command behind him. He decided to call up the Second Kansas to hold the rebels until the rest of his army arrived. The first pickets those men struck were driven back. Blunt rode forward while he waited for the Second to arrive on the scene. He came upon the black slave of a rebel officer. Assured of his freedom, the freed man told Blunt where Cooper's men were camped and the overall lay of the land. The man climbed onto a captured officer's horse and rode with Blunt.

Blunt was joined by Capt. Samuel Crawford, a sergeant, and three men of his bodyguard. They rode toward a small group of Confederate cavalry past the town of Maysville. The small group chased the rebels down a road until they ran into eighty enemy horsemen. The sergeant wasn't able to stop his horse in time, and was captured

The two groups looked at each other for a moment. A rebel officer fired a shot that went over the heads of Blunt and his men. Captain Crawford fired two shots back. The Confederates were suddenly put off balance and hesitated. While the officer was trying to urge his men forward, the soldiers of the Second Kansas came onto the scene.

Blunt had ordered his whole column forward, but only the Second Kansas Cavalry received the order to march. He saw that the Confederates had pulled back to their camp, which was eight miles east of Maysville. Blunt ordered Crawford to take five companies of the Second and two cannons, and move through a wooded spot to the enemy camp. Blunt took direct command of the rest of the regiment and two other cannons and followed the retreating rebel cavalrymen. He attacked the rebels in the front while sending Crawford to assault the flank.

The following battle, known as Old Fort Wayne for a former post nearby, only lasted about half an hour. The Second did most of the fighting, but during the attack was joined by the Sixth Kansas Cavalry. The short and sharp fight sent the Confederates into full retreat before the rest of Blunt's force arrived on the battlefield, with many of Cooper's men throwing down their rifles as they fled.

The turning point in the battle came as Crawford's battalion arrived through the woods, dismounted, and began firing their carbines in support of Blunt's attack. At first the rebel artillery fired over his men's heads, but eventually they found their target. Confederate musket fire also increased, forcing Crawford to choose between charging or retreating. Crawford decided to charge, and his attack swept back the Confederates and captured one of their batteries.

Part of Blunt's success at Old Fort Wayne was due in part to the scouting he did personally. Aside from the help he gained from the freedman, Blunt also had disguised himself as a Southern soldier and went to a large house near the prairie where the rebels were camped. Blunt was able to get the woman of the house, whose husband was a soldier in the camp, to tell him of the Confederacy's strength and the location of their pickets.

Before Crawford's charge the Confederates tried to use their superiority in numbers to drive back Blunt's frontal attack. But as they pushed forward, the Sixth Kansas and the Third Indian regiments came up. Following this was Crawford's capture of the rebel battery. After that, the Second Indiana Battery arrived in time to fire a few shells at the fleeing rebels. Cooper's men fled all the way back to Fort Gibson.

To explain his defeat Cooper claimed that of the Indians he had sent for before the battle, only Stand Watie's force had arrived on the field. He also claimed to be ill during the battle. He insisted that he was outnumbered fifteen hundred to five thousand and that he had inflicted more casualties than he had taken. Cooper shifted the blame to General Rains, who had taken four Texas regiments from his command; to the disobedience of one of his colonels who did not arrive with his men; and to his illness, in that he had to delegate command. He believed the Indians were not used to taking orders from other whites. This is why, he reported later, they retreated so quickly.

Stand Watie, in his report, didn't blame anyone. Instead he wrote that during the battle he personally rode out to learn how many Union soldiers were approaching. He observed a force of three thousand infantry and cavalry, and decided it would be best to withdraw. While doing so he learned of the capture of the Confederate cannons. He also admitted that during the retreat continued Union attacks and cavalry charges threw his command into some confusion.

Cooper may not have been "ill" at Old Fort Wayne as he later claimed. At least one Union soldier, Vincent Osborne, wrote in his diary about how Cooper was "intoxicated" and "managed the battle unskillfully." He also wrote that the rebel cannons consistently missed the Union batteries and that when more Union batteries arrived the rebels ran. Another solider writing to the *Atchison Freedom's Champion* said many rebels were without shoes and "almost destitute of provisions."

The one black spot on the victory came from Blunt's bodyguard early in the fight. In temporary command of the guard was one Sergeant Cooper of the Third Wisconsin, because the lieutenant usually in command was sick. In the days before the battle Cooper claimed to be a nephew of Gen. Douglas Cooper, but apparently no one took him seriously.

When Blunt's bodyguard neared the Confederate pickets, Cooper promptly rode up to the enemy and surrendered. The sergeant supposedly had a reunion with his uncle, and during the battle pointed out Blunt so that the rebels could pick him off. There's no verification for this story, and Blunt never made mention of it in his report. Since it came from a writer in the Eleventh Kansas, and was directed at the Third Wisconsin, if it wasn't true then it was probably a bit of chest thumping by a Kansas soldier for consumption in a Kansas newspaper.

When Blunt rejoined the Army of the Frontier he was unhappy to learn that Schofield had not attacked at Huntsville. He asked Schofield to continue forward but was instead told to move back to Pea Ridge. Schofield, for his part, told Curtis on October 24 that he had moved toward Huntsville and, having found the rebels gone, took off after another rebel force. In this letter Schofield seemed pleased with Blunt's victory. He expressed a desire to let Blunt go into the Indian Territory.

Schofield wasn't the only one happy with Blunt's performance at Old Fort Wayne. The general was also praised by the *Conservative's* correspondent from the Eleventh Kansas. The author said Blunt had the "dash of Lee, with his cavalry at Palo Alto; nay, that of Napoleon himself for that matter, at the Bridge of Arcola." Clearly Blunt's stock in his home state was on the rise with his victory at Old Fort Wayne.

The same day, October 24, that Schofield had written to Curtis, Blunt informed Schofield that he was sending scouts as far as Fort Gibson. He expressed his desire to attack Fort Smith, and felt confident that he could do so. He ended his message to his superior by telling Schofield that he hoped his plan would meet with his and Curtis's approval so he could start as soon as possible.

Back in late September when he had taken over the Department of the Missouri, Curtis told Blunt that he didn't want to merge the Department of Kansas with any other. However, on November 2, Curtis put Blunt in command of the District of Kansas and placed it in his department. These actions were probably because of the ongoing campaign. Schofield was put in command of the District of Southwest Missouri. That order meant that Blunt had a larger district than Schofield. This almost certainly added to the growing problems between the two generals.

In the field Union soldiers found plenty to forage on the march south. These men also found pro-Confederate businesses to destroy, including a large tannery. The loss of that tannery may have cost the rebels fifteen thousand dollars. The men were unable to find other diversions, for a lieutenant in the Eleventh Kansas wrote the *Conservative,* "We are all sober—good reason—no whiskey."

On November 9 the Second Kansas dispersed a party of Confederates under Col. Emmett McDonald, provost marshal of Missouri and Arkansas, at the village of Boonsboro. The Union troops also took the rebels' baggage and supplies. In reporting this action to Schofield, Blunt added that fourteen men who had been conscripted into a Confederate regiment had deserted, come through his lines, and asked to enlist in the Union army.

Around this time Blunt learned that Schofield had pulled back to Springfield. He probably "went ballistic" when he later heard that Schofield was in winter quarters; that the other general was sick and had gone back to St. Louis; and that Schofield was saying that the Army of the Frontier had done what Schofield had desired. What he did not know is that Curtis had approved of Schofield's move; that Schofield thought Blunt's position was safe; and that both were willing to allow Blunt to march on the Indian Territory as long as the Confederates had not crossed the Arkansas River and were not moving toward him. But neither man seems to have told Blunt these things. That omission would only cause more problems in the days and weeks to come.

For a time after Old Fort Wayne, no major engagements were fought by the Army of the Frontier. Perhaps because of this inactivity, on November 11 the *Times* reprinted a story from the correspondent to the *Cleveland Herald*. In a piece dated October 23, the reporter claimed that there was a "strange insanity" affecting the generals of both sides. These leaders were failing to follow up their "obvious" victories "to [their] legitimate fruits." The reporter also displayed some skepticism with all three Union Indian regiments, which he stated were "paid by Uncle Sam for purposes of yelling." Such a view could only have been expressed in Kansas if nothing newsworthy was happening in the war.

The *Times'* own correspondent put down his impressions of the situation and the army in a long letter dated November 15 and printed on December 2. The author began by informing the paper's readers of how the Second Kansas "jayhawked" the Confederate cannon at Old Fort Wayne. He told briefly of the disposition of the Kansas forces in Blunt's division.

The reporter went on to paint an interesting picture of the war's effect on Arkansas. Wheat was easy to come by, but finding other forage was becoming difficult. He found evidence of the "ravages of armies" in the "deserted houses, vacant fields, neglected farms," and in the ruins of fences and other local property stolen or destroyed. Men were nowhere to be found; houses were occupied by "old men, women and children." Most of the black population had been driven south, but those who remained were happy to see the Union soldiers and were supposedly "always ready to 'jine de army and go nort.'"

The correspondent went into great detail about visiting a local home. Inside were three young widows and two other young ladies, "all rather good looking and quite intelligent." He talked with them for a time about the war and the hard conditions of life. Then one of the women said that tobacco was scarce. The reporter assumed she meant smoking tobacco and replied that all he had was chewing tobacco. That's just what they wanted, she told him. "But just as I was about to fall hopelessly in love," he wrote, the attractive young woman took her chaw and spat into the hearth fire. "The women do chew tobacco," he noted sourly.

He moved from that topic to the army's activities. The reporter told in great detail of a few minor skirmishes with guerrillas to show that little of substance was occurring. He decried Hindman's order allowing bushwhackers to operate as "Provost Guards." He grumbled that in Missouri, General Schofield had given orders to pay for every bit of forage, but gave no such orders in Arkansas. "I am in favor of foraging off the enemy," he said, referring to this contradiction, "but I am opposed to nursing one set and cursing another." After this comment he told of how the various Kansas regiments fared at foraging off their enemy.

The correspondent wound down his letter by passing on a rumor that the troops were to return to Kansas for the winter. He was opposed to their return, adding that the men of the Second Kansas felt that "you [should] not see us in Kansas again until after the close of the war." They wanted "to go farther into Dixie, where there are more chances of 'fun.'"

The correspondent and the soldiers were about to get their wish. Events were accelerating in northwestern Arkansas. Blunt's army was about to move and enter into battle once again.

On November 10 Blunt decided to march south toward Cane Hill, where Gen. John Marmaduke had supposedly gathered more rebel forces. Blunt sent a reconnaissance detachment toward Van Buren and Fort Smith from his camp at Lindsey's Prairie, about fifteen miles south of Maysville. They discovered that Hindman was gathering the forces of Marmaduke, Stand Watie, and Douglas Cooper. Blunt heard estimates of Confederate strength as high as thirty thousand men, but in writing to General Curtis he expressed the belief that it was no more than fifteen thousand, and possibly as low as twelve thousand. He did ask Curtis for reinforcements on November 24, but he only wanted enough men to protect his lines of communication. Blunt was confident that as long as other Union forces could tie down the Confederates at Little Rock, he could take Fort Smith.

Curtis was already trying to send Blunt reinforcements. Back on November 15 he had ordered General Totten to move the Second and Third Divisions along the Telegraph Road to aid Blunt. The next day Schofield told Blunt that they were due to move on November 17. The divisions got about thirty miles southwest of Springfield to Crane Creek, then stopped when reports came that Marmaduke was withdrawing.

On November 24 Blunt informed Schofield that the rebels had an army in the Fort Smith area. His spies had told him that the force was as large as thirty thousand men, but, as he had written to Curtis, Blunt believed the real number to be between twelve thousand and fifteen thousand. He asked Schofield for reinforcements and again expressed confidence that he could take Fort Smith.

The next day, November 25, Blunt's scouting force was attacked by Marmaduke's men. From this attack Blunt learned that Marmaduke had seven thousand to eight thousand men. Hindman was following Marmaduke with the significant force of which Blunt was already aware. Hindman's plan called for a move north toward Missouri. On November 26 Marmaduke was at Cane Hill, some thirty miles from Blunt's camp. Blunt decided to attack Marmaduke before Hindman arrived and could drive back Blunt's force. That same day Blunt took formal control of the District of Kansas. Ostensibly his headquarters would be in Leavenworth, but it would be some time before Blunt could go there. He first had to take care of Marmaduke's men at Cane Hill.

On November 27 Blunt took five thousand men and thirty cannons toward Cane Hill, marching twenty-five miles in that one day. Blunt learned that the main road he had been marching on was well defended. On the morning of November 28 he found a trail into Cane Hill that the rebels didn't know about and hadn't protected. Blunt sent the Second Kansas with artillery support along this trail to attack Marmaduke's men.

Samuel Crawford later called Blunt's order of march and battle plan "ill conceived." But Confederate colonel J. O. Shelby admitted in his report after the battle that Blunt attacked his men sooner than Shelby had expected. Since Shelby was writing at the time,

Confederate commander J. O. Shelby. Shelby squared off against Blunt on several occasions. His men faced Blunt's at Cane Hill and Prairie Grove as well as during the Price Campaign of 1864. *Photograph courtesy the Kansas State Historical Society, Topeka, Kansas.*

Confederate commander John Marmaduke. Marmaduke was another Confederate commander whose men tangled with Blunt's. He was captured at Mine Creek during the Price Campaign of 1864. *Photograph courtesy the Kansas State Historical Society, Topeka, Kansas.*

and Crawford over fifty years after the battle, Crawford's view is somewhat suspect. Crawford would have his own problem with Blunt later in the war, which might have also colored his memories of Cane Hill.

On the field as that November day began, the two sides engaged in an artillery duel while Blunt waited for the main body of his forces. Marmaduke apparently thought Blunt's main body was already there so he didn't counterattack. The Second Indiana and three companies of Second Kansas engaged but quickly were thrown into confusion. Marmaduke continued to hesitate to attack, giving other Union forces time to reach and support the beleaguered Yankees. According to a Confederate colonel in command during the fighting, Blunt's artillery could hit his guns while Blunt's own artillery was out of the rebels' range.

Blunt then found an approach on the Confederate left that he could use to his advantage, and he sent companies of Eleventh Kansas with supporting batteries to attack. The combined assaults drove the rebels back to a second defensive position. Blunt found some high ground and allowed his artillery to open up. That dismounted one of the rebel cannons and drove the rebels farther south. Marmaduke's men took up a third position on the south side of Cane Hill. The Third Kansas Battery, with three six-pounders and a twelve-pound howitzer, was able to first break up a Confederate cavalry charge, then drive back a Confederate battery on a hill near the town.

At this battle Colonel Shelby introduced a defensive strategy that afterward he would use to great effect. To stage a fighting retreat, Shelby broke his brigade down into its constituent companies. His first biographer, newspaperman and longtime aide John Edwards, said that at Cane Hill, Shelby had thirty companies in his brigade to carry out his maneuver. Shelby formed each company into a line along either side of a road Blunt's men were using to advance. When the Union forces approached the first company, the rebels opened fire at point-blank range, mounted their horses, rode past the other companies, and formed a new line behind the last company. Each succeeding company would do the same thing, thus slowing their opponents' advance and inflicting increasing casualties on the attackers.

For three miles past Cane Hill both armies engaged in a running battle until the Confederates reached a mountain and assembled a defensive line. Again Blunt's artillery was able to drive the rebel cannons back. Blunt then sent in the Second Kansas, Third Indian, and Eleventh Kansas to drive the rebels off the mountain. The fighting was fierce, but the Federals pushed up the slope. When the rebels reached the top they fell back. About every half-mile or so for the next three miles the Confederates made a stand, and every time Blunt's men pushed them back.

Near sundown Blunt decided to try to capture six Confederate cannons at the end of a small valley. The valley was formed by Cove Creek, and on one side was the road connecting Fayetteville and Van Buren. Not only would it be important to capture the cannons, but the road itself would be vital if Blunt wanted to continue south.

At first Blunt ordered the Tenth Kansas to make the assault down the valley. He changed his mind and decided to let the Sixth Kansas Cavalry attack. Their commander was away, so in charge of the regiment was Lt. Col. Lewis R. Jewell. Jewell surveyed the valley, decided that attacking with more than three companies would tangle the Union attack, and asked for volunteers.

Blunt then ordered the Tenth to make another assault on the rebels to force them out. Jewell led his men forward, and at first their march was so fast that they reached one battery before it could fire on them. But the Tenth did not support the Sixth due to Blunt's ordering them to withdraw. Perhaps he saw that the regiments might be heading into an ambush or toward an impregnable position. The Sixth didn't get orders to pull back, most likely because they were moving so fast.

The Confederates did indeed have an ambush planned, and Jewell's men ran directly into it. Jewell was struck in the chest in the first rebel volley along with many of his soldiers. More were cut down as they staggered back to the Union lines. Jewell was found by J. O. "Jo" Shelby, who managed to return the wounded Kansan to his comrades. Two days later Jewell died of his wounds.

Meanwhile the Confederates counterattacked, and while Blunt was rallying the Sixth, four howitzers came up. The guns forced the rebels back, but this time Marmaduke put his men into a position where Blunt's troops could not attack their flanks. Blunt observed that this line would allow the rebels to retreat in good order, and he decided to attack the line to prevent such a retreat. Just as Blunt was preparing for one final assault an officer from Marmaduke rode up bearing a white flag. The officer said Marmaduke wanted a truce to recover the dead and wounded. Blunt agreed, only to find out later that Marmaduke used the truce as a cover for his retreat.

According to John Edwards, while Blunt met with Marmaduke and Shelby to arrange the truce, he told Marmaduke that Shelby's men had "fought like devils." When Shelby asked Blunt how many men he sent against the Confederates, Blunt replied, "I am ashamed to tell, but more than you had to meet me."

More than a week before the battle, Schofield had returned to St. Louis. Schofield's departure left Blunt in command of the Army of the Frontier. Blunt had yet another victory to add to his record. His troops were deep into Arkansas and within striking distance of Fort Smith. When this news reached Kansas the press was ecstatic at the home-state general who had done so well.

After Cane Hill the *Leavenworth Conservative* got over any last vestige of its support for Charles Jennison. Starting on December 2 and for three straight days it printed Blunt's official correspondence on the battle at Cane Hill. That first day the headline over the report read, "THE GREAT VICTORY IN ARKANSAS! - Utter Rout of the Enemy!" Its rival the *Times* also crowed about the victory and about Blunt's leadership. The battle had "given evidence of his capabilities as a soldier."

These headlines reflected the views of many on the Union side in the region. There was a growing confidence that the rebels in the trans-Mississippi west were whipped and Union control of the region was imminent. In a report General Herron made to General Curtis on November 29 about a successful raid of his own, he said, "This movement, with Blunt's victory at Cane Hill, effectually clears the north side of the mountains of all troops, except guerrillas." Maybe at last the war here was indeed winding down.

CHAPTER 8

Prairie Grove

The Confederates still had fire in them after the battle of Cane Hill. Earlier in the year General Hindman had boasted to his men that his horse would either drink from the Missouri River or "the rivers of Pluto's regions" by the end of 1862. He now had a plan to smash Blunt in Arkansas and then invade and "liberate" Missouri. To gird his men for the coming assault, Hindman gave an incendiary address in which he called Federal soldiers despoilers and claimed that they had "defiled the graves of your kindred." Clearly he hoped his men would dash Union confidence with their battlefield performance.

But to bolster their ranks the Confederate authorities had conscripted every able-bodied man in Arkansas they could find. Some were taken by force, with suspected Union sympathizers the first to be conscripted. Some of these men would be allowed to leave, but were "compelled" to leave their horses with the army. Many of these conscripts were poorly armed and were put in front of more experienced soldiers. This treatment drove other government supporters to dash for the Federal lines to join the Union army.

While Hindman was making plans, Earl Van Dorn had been defeated at Corinth, Mississippi. Union general Ulysses Grant was about to move on Vicksburg, Mississippi, and follow up on that victory at Corinth. Hindman, therefore, was ordered to pull back to Little Rock to help fend off Grant. Instead he disregarded his orders, carried on with his plan, and marched toward Blunt at Cane Hill.

Hindman's first thought was to attack Blunt at Cane Hill. To cover his march Hindman told Marmaduke to spread rumors that he had been recalled to Little Rock. He also told Cooper to march his men into Blunt's rear to prevent Blunt from escaping. After the war John Edwards, Colonel Shelby's biographer, claimed that Hindman had orders that, no matter the outcome of the attack on

Blunt, he was to withdraw to Van Buren and then Little Rock. Interestingly, he also said that Hindman's army of ninety-five hundred men "were in good condition, well armed, clothed, and fed." This statement seems to be contradicted by Hindman, who in an official report on his campaign claimed that his army had "barely ammunition enough for one battle, and not sufficient subsistence and forage for seven days at half rations." He went on to say his supplies were "accumulated with extreme difficulty" because of an eighty-mile supply line, limits on transportation, local rivers too shallow to navigate, and the "entirely exhausted" state of the surrounding countryside.

What Hindman didn't know was that his army's movements were already known. The *Chief* in White Cloud, after reporting on December 4 of the victory at Cane Hill, printed a dispatch from Blunt that said Hindman and Marmaduke were consolidating their forces. Of Blunt's position, editor Sol Miller presumed "there is no danger that [Blunt] will be caught napping."

He wasn't napping. Blunt had information that Hindman was on the move and planned to start his own march on December 3. He estimated Hindman's strength at twenty thousand, well above Hindman's actual ten thousand, and sent a telegram with this information to General Curtis with a request for reinforcements. To that end Blunt also asked Brig. Gen. Francis Herron to march from Springfield and join him with the rest of the Army of the Frontier.

General Curtis responded by ordering Herron to take the Second and Third Divisions south and reinforce Blunt. On December 3 Curtis also advised Blunt to fall back to meet Herron. Herron echoed Curtis's advice when he told Blunt that he would march at noon on December 3, but added that he wasn't certain that he'd reach Blunt's camp in time.

Two days later, elements of Second Kansas located Hindman's advancing force. Apparently based on the reports of the Second, Blunt decided that he could hold off Hindman until Herron arrived. Samuel Crawford, serving in the Second, later wrote that he thought Blunt should have fallen back. Crawford also claimed that he told Blunt that staying would be a risk. If Blunt did get this warning, he disregarded it and strengthened his defenses.

That same day, December 5, Curtis congratulated Herron on his progress. Herron was managing to march his men over one hundred miles in three days over the Boston Mountains of the Ozark region. In that same message he warned Herron, "Be cautious. Hindman is shrewd and active. He will try hard to deceive you by drawing you into ambush." For his part, on that day Herron told Blunt, "I hope to God we will reach you before they get too close. . . . I am afraid when they hear reinforcements coming up they will back down."

The next day advance units of both armies met some miles south of Blunt's camp. The Confederates were unable to drive the Union troops back. Blunt continued to believe that Hindman would attack him first, and he said so to Herron. On the evening of December 6 Blunt, writing to Maj. T. J. Weed, his acting assistant adjutant general at Fort Leavenworth, predicted that the following day, "You will soon hear of one of the damnedest fights or foot races that has taken place lately."

As the Confederate commanders marched north they had no idea that Blunt was about to be reinforced. Although General Marmaduke had written to Hindman on November 29 asking if there were any Federal troops that could support Blunt, no word of Herron's march arrived in Hindman's camp until the night of December 6. This vital information arrived just as Hindman was to give final instructions to his commanders about the attack on Blunt at Cane Hill. John Edwards later wrote that they were debating two plans of attack: a frontal assault or a flanking attack. The rebel leaders decided on the flanking plan, then news arrived of Herron's relief column.

Hindman immediately realized that if he went ahead with his plan, Blunt would simply pull back to join his reinforcements. To counter this reaction, Hindman proposed that the relief column be dealt with first. Once Herron was driven off, the Confederates would go after Blunt. His officers agreed with their commander's strategy, and by three o'clock the following morning the Confederates began moving around Blunt's position at Cane Hill.

It is here that the most controversial aspect of the battle of Prairie Grove, and of Blunt's military career, would take place.

Blunt seemed to be aware of the possibility that Hindman might try to get around him to either attack his flank or to attack Herron, whose forces had that night arrived in Fayetteville. To that end Blunt ordered Col. J. M. Richardson of the Fourteenth Missouri State Militia to take from 250 to 300 cavalrymen and cross the "Hog-eye"

Road running from north of Cane Hill to the Telegraph Road, the main road connecting Missouri, Arkansas, and Texas. From there Richardson was to proceed to the point at which the road connecting Cane Hill to Fayetteville intersected with the road between Fayetteville and Cove Creek. Richardson was to place his men in a strong defensive position and watch the Cove Creek road for Hindman. Blunt ordered that if Hindman reached the road, Richardson should fight "to the last extremity" and promptly inform him of the situation.

At 7 A.M. on Sunday, December 7, Blunt went out with his staff and found what he thought was a considerable force at his front. As soon as there was enough light, Confederate artillery opened up on an advance outpost. Blunt ordered the men at the outpost to fall back and form up to gauge the intent of his enemy. They did so and the Confederates marched forward.

The night before Blunt had put his army into a new line to fend off the expected rebel attack. When Blunt and his staff came out the next morning, Blunt talked with a colonel in one of the regiments in the line. One of the men in that regiment was close enough to hear the officers talk. Two decades later he would tell a Kansas author about this fateful conversation, which would later be recorded in Noble Prentis's *Kansas Miscellanies*.

The colonel suggested that Blunt advance the line to the right in order to put the sun at the men's backs. Blunt replied that it would be done once the battle started. He and the colonel told each other that they would "pound hell" out of the rebels when the battle began. Then an orderly came with a flask of alcohol from General Salomon. Blunt asked the colonel if he would take a drink with him. The colonel declined, to which Blunt said, "Yes, I think we've more important business on hand just now."

The soldier reported that as the morning wore on with no sign of the rebels, the men in the ranks became anxious. Their officers had to keep getting the soldiers back into line. Even Blunt seemed nervous, according to this soldier. No doubt this was true for he had yet to hear from Colonel Richardson. Finally the rebels pushed forward to engage Blunt's men.

Not too long after the skirmishing began, Blunt seemed to realize that something was not right. He could see that the enemy line was only half a mile long. This length would have suggested a smaller force than what he knew Hindman to have. With no other

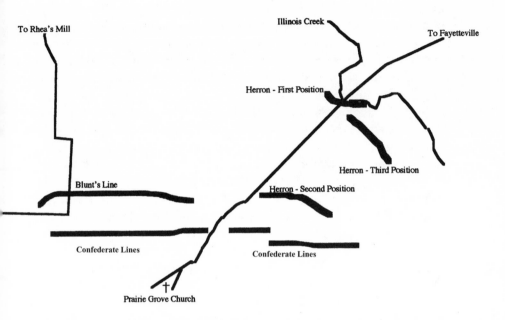

Prairie Grove
December 7, 1862

To Rhea's Mill

Illinois Creek

To Fayetteville

Herron - First Position

Herron - Third Position

Blunt's Line

Herron - Second Position

Confederate Lines

Confederate Lines

Prairie Grove Church

rebel force in sight, Blunt seemed to understand that this attack was a feint.

He immediately sent sixteen hundred cavalrymen from Herron's command that had arrived the night before to rejoin Herron. He sent messages of warning to Herron, but they did not get through. Blunt then put his whole division into motion, sending the First Brigade under General Salomon to guard his supply trains at Rhea's Mill while sending the Second and Third Brigades toward Herron on the Fayetteville road. Blunt now knew that the Confederates had marched around him without detection. His army would have to hurry if it was to reach Herron's divisions in time.

Blunt was not the only one surprised that the Confederates had gotten around him. Vincent Osborne, a soldier in the Second Kansas, wrote in his diary that men in his regiment had heard the sounds of movement. None of them had assumed it signified a flank march. Instead they had "supposed that [it meant the rebels] would attack us early in the morning."

The first formal notice of these events came from the commander of the Sixth Kansas. That colonel reported that Hindman's army was moving toward Fayetteville and advance elements were already engaging Herron's forces. Then, around 10 A.M., Blunt finally heard from Richardson, who reported the same thing. To buy time Blunt ordered Col. W. R. Judson to take the Sixth Kansas and attack the Confederate rear. En route the Sixth picked up Richardson's men. They would be the first of Blunt's command to engage the Confederates.

So how did it happen that Hindman was able to circumvent Blunt? Much of the blame has fallen on Blunt since he was the general in charge. But Richardson's own report of his actions early in the day shifts the blame onto himself.

In the report Richardson states that as he was moving east he ran into sixty men from the Ninth Kansas. They told him that the Confederates were moving in force up the Cove Creek road. He sent a messenger to Blunt to report this movement. Richardson decided that this movement was toward Blunt's position at Cane Hill, and he fell back a mile from the scene and waited for the advance. When nothing happened he sent an officer to locate the enemy. That officer discovered that the rebels were marching toward Fayetteville. Richardson sent another messenger to Blunt, then joined the Sixth when it arrived for the attack on the Confederate rear.

Richardson's account of these vital hours consists of one paragraph that is vague on details and times. He never identifies the two messengers he sent to Blunt's headquarters. He does not say when he met the Ninth Kansas, or when he sent his officer to learn the enemy position. What's more, he says his command consisted of only 100 men. In Blunt's report, the general adds 100 men to Richardson's 150-man battalion. Richardson does say he was joined by a captain from the Third Wisconsin Cavalry, but he does not say if the captain had any men with him.

Richardson's actions during this time are confusing, to say the least. He does not explain why he assumed the Confederates were moving on Cane Hill when he received news of enemy movement from the men in the Ninth. Considering how wrong he turned out to be, it is odd that he never bothered to justify himself. He could easily have faced a court-martial for this lack of judgment. He seems to be a competent officer, so this lack of an explanation is troubling.

More troubling is the matter of the first messenger. Blunt stated that the first news he heard from Richardson was at ten in the morning. Blunt states that in this message Richardson claimed the rebels had been moving north since midnight (though in reality Hindman's men didn't start moving toward Herron until 3 A.M., and their movement was slow due to the poor condition of the road). Though the messenger brought the news that the rebels were moving north, Blunt was already able to hear the sounds of battle as Hindman's forces attacked Herron's relief column. The messenger who brought this news to Blunt obviously wasn't the first messenger, who would have likely arrived around dawn, long before Hindman could reach Herron.

So what happened to that first messenger sent to bring news of the Confederate march up the Cove Creek road? The first possibility is that the messenger deserted. Desertions were not uncommon during the Civil War, especially on the eve of battle. But why would Richardson send a potential deserter on such an important mission? Why wouldn't he send a man he trusted, namely an officer? And where would this deserter go? If he was from Richardson's battalion, he'd have a long way to travel to reach Missouri. If he was part of the extra force Blunt said he gave the colonel, he'd had even farther to go to reach Wisconsin. Either way, he would need to head north. That route would not take him to immediate safety, but toward Herron's division and possible arrest. All these factors make it unlikely that the man deserted.

The second possibility is that the messenger was captured. If the messenger had been captured, why didn't Hindman, in his report on the battle, boast of this important capture? He could have claimed not only to have safely skirted Blunt, but also to have taken prisoner the one man who might have informed Blunt of the Confederate march. This possibility also raises the question of why the Confederates did not notice or react to Richardson's movements. Presumably a Union force of any strength heading toward the Confederate line of march would be regarded as a threat. This is even more true considering the danger of being attacked while forces are stretched out along a road. Therefore either the rebel generals didn't see Richardson's men, or they didn't think his command was a threat.

There is a third, and more disturbing, possibility: there was no first messenger, only the one who actually reported to Blunt at 10 A.M. Richardson made up this first messenger to cover his grievous error. Before writing his official report, perhaps on that very morning, he realized that his initial assumption about the direction of the Confederate advance was terribly wrong. He may have concocted the first messenger to avoid blame for his mistake. This explanation might also explain why he was vague in his details and timeline.

Additionally it gives a reason why Richardson wasn't concerned about the fate of the messenger. After all, whether he had one hundred or three hundred men, his force was small and moving close to the enemy. If he discovered something about the rebels' movements, not only would he want to report it, but he also would want to know if the information affected his orders. Should he move to safer ground, continue his original mission, or return to camp? He didn't have enough men to fight the whole Confederate army, and if he got into trouble rescue was some distance away.

But if Richardson realized that he had made a serious mistake, the invention of a first messenger gets him out of difficulty. His report might be vague but it doesn't contain evidence of misconduct. Without that messenger Richardson would have to explain why he had made the assumption he had. Instead he could say that he had sent someone and he was not accountable if the man never arrived. The invention allows Colonel Richardson to avoid admitting that he was responsible for Blunt's ignorance of Hindman's flanking movement and that his incorrect guess brought on the battle of Prairie Grove.

Blunt was enraged with Richardson, and remained so well past the end of the war. And he was not the only one upset with Richardson. A correspondent for the *St. Louis Democrat* expressed his displeasure with the Missouri colonel when he wrote of the battle. The reporter called Richardson's action "a piece of neglect" that, in the middle of a war, was "almost unpardonable." Theodore Gardner, a veteran of the First Kansas Battery, put it more plainly. When he later learned of what Richardson had done (or failed to do), he said that history would view the colonel as "either a d——d coward or a traitor."

However history views John Richardson, at midmorning on December 7 his error meant that Blunt's division would have to scramble. Advance elements of Hindman's army were already engaged with Herron's men. A large force of rebels were between the two parts of the Union army and close to Blunt's supply train. Blunt and his men were in a race to reach Herron before the "relief force" was driven back and they were in danger of annihilation.

Blunt's force was five miles west and five miles south of Herron's position when the battle opened. The battle to the north had begun when Shelby's men captured a Union wagon train and their escort. Herron immediately marched his men out of Fayetteville to meet the attack. Hindman had put Marmaduke's men in the advance, and just before dawn they ran into Herron's cavalry advance. Marmaduke attacked and drove the Union cavalry back.

The battle turned into a general engagement between the two armies. Hindman decided to form his men into a line on a ridge near Prairie Grove Church. Herron crossed Illinois Creek in front of Hindman's line, formed up his men, and attacked. After a bloody action on the Confederate right, Hindman prepared an attack only to learn that one of his conscripted regiments had deserted.

At one point during the morning's action, one of Herron's regiments, the Twenty-ninth Wisconsin, managed to capture a rebel battery. The Confederates sent four regiments to retake the guns, and they drove the Wisconsin men off with heavy losses. An Iowa regiment took another battery but was forced back in the same manner. Herron did not let these setbacks keep him from staying on the field as he waited for Blunt to come to his assistance.

During the fighting, confusion arose among the Confederates over the location of their forces, for Hindman later claimed he saw smoke coming from Rhea's Mill. He assumed that Blunt had burned his supplies and was retreating to join Herron. But Hindman took no more offensive actions. Perhaps this was because his men were on good ground, positioned on the side of a mountain, and on a wooded plateau. Herron continued to throw his men against Hindman, while seemingly waiting for Blunt.

The first units of Blunt's force, the Sixth Kansas, had been sent with two howitzers to hold a mountain pass twelve miles southeast of Rhea's Mill. Upon arrival they found that Hindman's army had already gone through the pass, and in front of them was the

Confederate rear guard. Union colonel Judson ordered his artillery to fire into the enemy to disorganize their forces.

Facing his small command were ten infantry regiments, two batteries, and fifteen hundred cavalrymen. Judson's gunners tossed some shells at their foes, who replied with one gun and a musket volley that went high. Judson and Richardson then decided to withdraw since they were badly outnumbered. They were amazed that the rebels did not pursue them. The reason seems to be that Hindman had assumed those men were Blunt's advance guard. He was expecting a strike on his rear instead of his left, where Blunt's main body was actually moving toward him.

Blunt in fact had moved his division north to Rhea's Mill to protect his supplies. From there they were to move east to link up with Herron's line, which would put them into Hindman's left flank. At first the movement of Blunt's troops was confused. Blunt personally brought order out of the chaos. As one veteran told it, as the men struggled forward he heard Blunt order someone to, "Tell the —— fool to turn to the right and come on." The veteran described Blunt's profanity as "sublime" and that upon hearing it, the men cheered, knowing that their commander was on the scene and taking charge.

A chaplain with the Union army paints another portrait of Blunt as his division marched to Herron's relief. The chaplain saw Blunt sitting on the ground talking to a young man whom the chaplain believed to be a scout. Blunt listened to the young man's report, occasionally asking questions and constantly cutting sticks with a pocket knife. After the man made his report Blunt scribbled a few words on a piece of paper and handed the paper to an attendant. In moments Blunt's division was in motion, racing to Herron's aid.

Hindman had left a small force to hold Blunt at Cane Hill. Not only did they fail to hold Blunt, but they also failed to report to Hindman that Blunt was on the move. Hindman was therefore unpleasantly surprised when Blunt's artillery joined Herron's to pour fire on the rebel line. The first of Blunt's regiments to arrive at Prairie Grove were the Tenth, Eleventh, and Thirteenth Kansas, followed by the First Indian Regiment and part of the Second Kansas Cavalry.

To counter Blunt, Hindman threw in his reserve. The two sides fought for three hours, but Hindman's men were unable to drive back Blunt's forces. The Second Kansas at first attacked mounted but as soon as the rest of the infantry arrived they dismounted. Their combined fire was directed at some thick underbrush that kept them from actually seeing their enemy. Though this led to some confusion over whether they were firing on their own side, they found that they weren't and kept up their attack for the rest of the afternoon.

When the Confederate counterattack came, Blunt ordered his artillery to fire canister shot. For the First Kansas Battery now joining the battle, this meant firing a tin can filled with eighty-five one-ounce lead balls. The effect would have been like firing a large shotgun, and it was devastating to massed ranks of men. The Union artillery fire was once again true to form and broke up the rebel assault. At sunset Blunt's cannons also sent a rebel attack reeling. Some Confederate soldiers tried to hide behind haystacks to avoid the Union guns. In response the artillerymen fired "hot shot" (cannon balls heated on a fire, an early type of incendiary round) at the hay and set it ablaze, causing the Confederates to flee.

Wiley Britton, a Kansas soldier who later wrote much about the war in the region, observed that Union artillery was both skillful and brave in combating the Confederates. They seriously damaged some gun carriages, and many horses and men serving the rebel batteries were killed or wounded. The rebel position, obstructed by trees, prevented rebels from both sighting their attacks and from moving to counter Union fire. The position of the enemy forces allowed the Federal artillery free reign to target their enemy and move when threatened or when needed elsewhere. John Edwards, writing from the Confederate perspective, echoed Britton. "If the Federal fire at Cane Hill had been admirable, here it was perfect and unsurpassable," he later wrote. It would seem that any rebel superiority in numbers was equalized by the skill of the Union artillery.

But it was not Union artillery that played a part in making the battle of Prairie Grove an unusual battle for the Civil War. That arose from Hindman's own conscription policy. One Union veteran later spoke of finding hundreds of bullets at the feet of dead Union men in Hindman's army. It seems that many "rebel" soldiers had fired blank rounds at Blunt's and Herron's troops. Some of those men were even driven against Union batteries but still refused to fire bullets at their "enemy." The most obvious sign of this disaffection was the fact that at least one Arkansas regiment fired off one volley, threw down their arms, and fled, with some even deserting to the Union lines!

Not all the rebels deserted, of course. Most stayed on the field to combat their opponents. One of the first of Blunt's infantry to face rebel fire was the Thirteenth Kansas. Recruited in northeast Kansas, the Thirteenth was only a few months old when it joined Blunt's command. The Thirteenth held off all Confederate attacks, despite facing "hot and heavy" fire. The Thirteenth fought all day and remained on the battlefield until well after the field had quieted down.

The older Tenth Kansas Infantry went into action at three in the afternoon. The Tenth ran into one enemy force, withdrew under heavy fire, then moved forward again. This time the men of the Tenth found a depression in the ground. They laid down to avoid being decimated by the larger force and remained in their position for an hour and a half. A major in the regiment later commented that it was "a miracle that the command was not annihilated."

Meanwhile the Eleventh Kansas Infantry ascended a ridge and ran into a Confederate charge. The Union regiment was forced back but then rallied around the Union batteries. The Confederates tried several times to take the battery, but all efforts failed, resulting in serious casualties for the rebels. At sunset, two Confederate regiments turned the Tenth's right flank. The Tenth retreated in good order and formed around a battery. Rebel cannons fired on their position but were silenced by Union cannons.

The battle of Prairie Grove was probably the most intense in the region to date. Soldiers who had participated in this and other major battles called Prairie Grove the most destructive they had seen. One called Pea Ridge "a chicken fight" compared with Prairie Grove.

Another veteran later remarked on the many prominent men who fought for the Union cause in Blunt's division. Four men who saw action that day became U.S. senators, one of whom would also become a Kansas governor. Another man would also be elected Kansas governor, and two others would be elected governors of other states. Others became state legislators, judges, prominent civic leaders, and appointed officials. One private even rose to become Kansas's assistant state auditor.

Almost every one of those men, as well as many others on the Union side, fully expected another day of hard fighting ahead.

Blunt planned for a second day of battle to force Hindman onto the open prairie and allow the Union cavalry to smash the rebels. Whether or not Herron's forces were originally part of Blunt's plan, his divisions were low on ammunition. Once the battle had ended, Herron sent word back toward Fayetteville to move his ammunition supply train closer to his lines. The wagon train was parked several miles away, waiting for guards to arrive to protect it from raiders. The train moved some distance without guards, paused, finally joined with the guards, but didn't arrive on the field until December 10!

Luckily there was no attack the morning of December 8. Instead General Marmaduke rode up to the Union camp at sunrise to ask for an armistice. Hindman had decided to ask Blunt for a truce so that both sides could retrieve their wounded and bury their dead. The request seemed reasonable, so Blunt agreed. What happened next has become yet another controversy surrounding the battle of Prairie Grove.

Hindman, by his own admission, had already sent his infantry from the battlefield in retreat. After meeting with Blunt, Hindman sent a message to him complaining that some of Herron's men were collecting arms from Confederate soldiers. In the belief that the battlefield was still contested ground, Blunt ordered Herron to stop his men's activities.

Shortly thereafter Blunt learned that Hindman's infantry had already retreated despite Hindman's claim that the field was his. Blunt sent word to Hindman that using a truce to cover a withdrawal was a violation of the rules of war. Blunt also expressed skepticism of Hindman's claim of victory by writing, "If you claim the field of Prairie Grove, . . . why did you not remain there?"

The next day Hindman sent another message to Blunt complaining of Union behavior, insisting that his men had won the field, and stating that he had only retreated because his men lacked food. Blunt repeated his charges of the abuse of the truce arrangement and added that Hindman's claim of victory was "a good joke." Then on December 12 Hindman sent an officer under another truce flag to make a plat of the battlefield. Hindman's intent may have been to record the locations where men had been buried, but it was clearly the last straw for Blunt.

Blunt replied that he would yield to such a request, but only if Hindman allowed him to send an artist to sketch Hindman's camp. After this note, communications finally broke off between the two men. Union officers were disgusted with Hindman's "trick" of using the truce to cover his retreat. Interestingly Hindman, in his report after the battle, dated December 25, only made mention of a first truce offer by Blunt and completely omitted his claims of Union abuses and a Confederate victory.

Although it had been a close battle, the Union forces were still on the field, and Blunt and Herron claimed a victory. The Union victory was proclaimed in newspapers around the state and around the nation. An account even surfaced in Kansas City that said rebel papers admitted heavy casualties. Actual casualties from the battle of Prairie Grove are hard to determine because there was such a wide variety in numbers from just as many sources.

General Blunt estimated Union killed, wounded, and captured at 1,100, and Confederate losses at 3,000. General Curtis estimated 1,000 Union casualties and 2,000 Confederate losses. General Hindman claimed his losses as only 350 men, and Union losses as 1,000. A newspaper published from the field by men under Blunt reported about 25 killed and 175 wounded in Blunt's division, and enemy losses were reported as 450 killed and 2,000 wounded. Among Blunt's regiments, the Tenth Kansas was said to have had 6 casualities and 63 wounded, while the Thirteenth Kansas had 8 casualties and 43 wounded.

There is additional confusion over the actual numbers of men involved, as both sides posted various claims in their official records. Blunt believed the Union had 10,000 men on field and 8,000 engaged, while Hindman had 28,000 men. Hindman claimed to have only 11,000 men against 11,000 to 14,000 Federals. John Edwards, writing after the war, estimated Blunt's force at 10,000 and Herron's at 6,000. And in reporting on Blunt's victory, the *Conservative* in Leavenworth gave the numbers as "8,000 Kansans Against 25,000 Butternuts."

Although uncertain of how many rebels they had fought, the

Union leaders were pleased with the outcome of the battle. Colonel Richardson called Hindman's march around Blunt a work of "military genius," but that Blunt in turn had fooled Hindman by hitting the rebel left. Herron called Blunt "a good fighting man." Even General Schofield, in his annual report on the events of 1862, complimented Blunt and Herron for their "brilliant victory."

For his part Hindman insisted that he did not lose due to Blunt's skill but due to the fact that he was outnumbered; his men had no food; and he didn't have enough ammunition for more than one day of battle. He put additional blame on the system of electing noncommissioned and low-ranking officers from within the regiment and the low pay of soldiers, although it is not clear why he thought this was a problem.

Hindman also called for every able-bodied male to be conscripted into the army with few allowable exemptions and strict martial law to enforce conscription; this he said would bring the Confederates victory. It is probably a testament to his modest ability that he made this suggestion despite the evidence from his own army that this policy only led to desertions, demoralization, and ultimately defeat.

If Hindman seems out of touch, one of Blunt's officers was very much in touch with the men. Before the battle at Cane Hill, Preston Plumb had found an abandoned printing press. Plumb decided to start a newspaper for his army, which was dubbed the *Buck and Ball*. He hoped this paper would be the start of a nice run that would give him experience in publishing before his return to Kansas. Officially published by the Eleventh Kansas, the *Buck and Ball* was supposed to be printed on December 6. The events of the next day prevented its printing, and although the final issue still had that earlier date, a small note reported the actual publication date as December 15.

The newspaper contained a history of the regiment to that day, accounts of the battles of Cane Hill and Prairie Grove, and other bits of news. Among those bits and pieces was information on the dire condition of civilians in the region. Where the two armies had been "nothing has grown"; the "sounds of war" were in every valley; and there was "[s]carce a fireside circle that does not mourn some one of its number slain in battle." This description was followed by a call to local men to abandon the Confederate cause,

join the Union, and "return in peace to your homes." One wonders that if Hindman had read that excerpt and thought about its
message, would he have changed his tune about conscription?

Naturally there was some information in the *Buck and Ball* on
General Blunt. Blunt and his officers were reportedly "reprobated"
or appalled by acts of pillaging by Union soldiers and threatened
to inflict "severest punishment" on those caught. Blunt's leadership in the two battles was hailed, and the paper claimed that his
name "gives assurance of victory." After his actions at Prairie
Grove, Blunt, the author wrote, would gain "another well-earned
star which will soon adorn his shoulder."

Before any stars could be handed out, Hindman's army, still in
the field, had to be faced. To deal with that army Blunt and
Herron decided to strike at Van Buren. The town was just north of
Fort Smith, and both believed that a successful raid on Van Buren
would further demoralize the South. They had wanted to move
soon after Prairie Grove, but bad weather held them up. Other
reasons for the strike were that Blunt was concerned that
Hindman would join Confederate troops in Little Rock and attack
him again. General Curtis was also worried about such a prospect,
for on December 23 he wrote to Blunt, Herron, and Schofield that
such a relief force was indeed moving from Little Rock to assist
Hindman.

By then Schofield had recovered from an illness that had tem-
porarily taken him away from the field and was on his way south to
resume command of the Army of the Frontier. On December 24
he wrote to Blunt telling him not to risk a battle unless he was certain to win. Herron and Blunt met Christmas night and decided
that they could take Van Buren. On December 27 they set out with
a picked force from both commands. Blunt's subordinates
opposed the plan, but he went ahead anyway. Before marching
south he allowed word to leak out that he was returning to
Springfield so that Hindman's spies would carry that false information to their complacent commander.

Late on December 26 advisory orders came from General Curtis
requesting that Blunt fall back and not take unnecessary risks.
Orders also came from General Schofield to pull back. Blunt considered Schofield a general who had "deserted his command in

the face of the enemy" and refused to obey. He sent a message to Schofield saying that he was in command of the Army of the Frontier and that until or unless a superior officer came in person to relieve him he would continue advancing on Van Buren.

On December 27 the Second and Sixth Kansas defeated a unit of Texas soldiers at Dripping Springs, capturing their baggage train. This was the last formal battle in Blunt's Arkansas campaign. However, Blunt had heard that more Texans were eight miles north of Van Buren, so he sent the Second Kansas, followed by the Sixth Kansas. They hit the rebel pickets who fled immediately, allowing the Union cavalry to attack the rebel camp. As the cavalry swept in, Blunt called up the infantry and artillery. The Confederates were in a good position, on a hill with fields between them and the Federal attackers. After a few volleys were fired, Blunt ordered a cavalry charge. The Second, Sixth, and Third Wisconsin drew sabers and charged. The Texans fled in panic, leaving their supplies behind.

Blunt then had the cavalry move at the gallop toward Van Buren, and in an hour they had traveled ten miles and entered the town. The locals, watching as the Federals chased their foes through the streets, previously had had no inkling of the Union attack. Blunt's men found that large quantities of supplies were at Van Buren and that four steamboats were bringing in more.

On December 28 Blunt began his report to General Curtis with "The Stars and Stripes now wave in triumph over Van Buren." The four steamboats on the Arkansas River had been taken promptly along with the other supplies in town. The boats had been loaded with food for hungry rebels, but Union soldiers ate them instead. Hindman later admitted to losing only three steamboats, but he also claimed that two more were burned after he removed their supplies. He again claimed to be outnumbered, this time four thousand to seven thousand. Once Blunt took Van Buren, he had the supplies taken off the steamboats and burned. The townspeople thought Kansas soldiers were savages, but Wiley Britton later wrote that he did not hear any complaints from locals on ill treatment from Kansans.

The supplies taken had included large amounts of hard bread, sugar, and molasses; forty-two wagons of provisions and military equipment; numerous horses; and twenty-five thousand bushels of burned grain. One Kansas newspaper reported that the blow at

Van Buren caused three regiments of Missourians to desert along with two Tennessee regiments and one Texas regiment.

The rebels who were to relieve Hindman were first sent toward Vicksburg. At Little Rock they were stopped and countermarched toward Hindman. Blunt told General Curtis that the relief forces had probably arrived at Van Buren, but two days later Schofield told Curtis that reports he had of that column consisting of ten thousand men were "exaggerated." In all likelihood they had probably joined those who had retreated when the Union soldiers swept into Van Buren, or they pulled back to Little Rock before Blunt and Herron attacked.

The storage of the captured supplies would lead to an interesting incident in the life of James G. Blunt. It seems that some of the whisky, brandy, and unshucked corn seized from the steamboats were placed in a brick warehouse. A fire broke out in the warehouse, and Union soldiers scrambled to douse it. They were able to form a fire line and put up a ladder. Colonel Cloud of the Second Kansas climbed the ladder, crawled onto the roof, and took control of the firefighting.

In the midst of this effort someone repeatedly ordered Cloud to come down. Cloud refused at first, then paused when he realized that it was Blunt telling him to come down. At that point Blunt lost his temper. A soldier observed that "Blunt raved and swore and dashed aimlessly," vowing to court-martial any officer that dared contradict him and "demoralize the army."

Blunt's display did not bring Cloud down. Indeed a short time later the fire subsided. Even though the materials in the warehouse were lost, the walls and the roof of the warehouse itself remained intact. When Cloud descended from the roof, the soldiers roared with approval for his bravery.

The soldier who witnessed this scene does not say how Blunt reacted when the amateur firefighters cheered Cloud. Later reporting suggests that Cloud wasn't upset with Blunt over this incident. What it does show is that the Kansas general was developing a bad temper. That temper would get Blunt into trouble time and again in the coming year.

While Blunt was marching on Van Buren he had sent twelve hundred men under Col. William A. Phillips back into Indian Territory. During the fall campaign Pike and Hindman had gotten into a dispute over how the Confederate Indian units ought to be deployed. The result of the dispute was that Pike was discredited and resigned in a flurry of controversy. This controversy as well as the defeat at Old Fort Wayne left the Confederate Indians a demoralized and unorganized force. Blunt wisely decided to exploit these problems and finish what the summer expedition had failed to accomplish.

Phillips began his campaign on December 22. He defeated one small force of Confederate Indians and burned their fort, driving some to Fort Smith, while he forced Cooper almost entirely out of the territory. Phillips's men also sacked and burned the homes of pro-Southern Indians. With these Union victories, the Confederacy finally lost control over the northeastern part of the territory.

Blunt later claimed that he had defeated and demoralized an army of thirty thousand in just thirty days with less than half the number of soldiers his enemy had. In January another Union army captured the Post of Arkansas, an important city and river port. Combined with Blunt's victories the Federals now controlled northern Arkansas, Missouri, and much of eastern Indian Territory belonging to the "Five Civilized Tribes." General Curtis commended the "Commanding Officer of the Army of the Frontier" (he likely intended to include both Blunt and Schofield) for "gloriously" wrapping up the campaign in northwestern Arkansas. In the whole of the campaign, possibly a million dollars of Confederate property was lost, not including all the lost men and equipment.

Blunt did not continue his attacks, instead deciding to go into winter quarters closer to supply bases. On December 31 Schofield resumed command of the Army of the Frontier. He broke up Blunt's and Herron's divisions, sending Blunt to Elm Springs. Schofield did allow Blunt to leave the three Indian regiments, a battalion of the Sixth Kansas, and a four-gun battery in the region. Blunt delegated command to Colonel Phillips of the Third Indian.

In early January, Blunt was reporting that the Creeks, Cherokees, and Choctaws were so beaten by Phillips's Indian regiment that they were considering surrender. He made it clear that he had advanced although he had orders to retreat to the Missouri state line. Blunt was not pleased to hear that the Union army might retreat despite their victories. He believed the rebels were demoralized and that a retreat would be the same as losing a battle. He later said that he thought the department commander (Curtis but possibly meaning Schofield) was out of touch with the reality of war in northwestern Arkansas.

Wiley Britton, possibly reflecting the views of the men in the army, would have agreed with Blunt's assessment. Britton seems to have liked Blunt as a military commander. He wrote in his *Memoirs of the Rebellion on the Border, 1863* that Blunt was "probably able to meet any movement his opponents are able to make on the military chess board." He added that if the campaign had been conducted Schofield's way, or the "West Point" way, the army would have gone on the defensive and been destroyed. If Schofield had had his way the Van Buren raid would never have taken place. Britton, writing at the time, wondered why the army should fall back if no rebel force could stop their advance. He also hinted that Schofield was jealous of Blunt's success. His view of Blunt's superiority was shared by the men, for during a review Schofield held after taking command of the Army of the Frontier, Britton overheard a soldier who looked at Schofield and his staff and said, "Too much fuss and feathers for a fighting general."

James G. Blunt was the real fighting general. His successes on the field were about to be rewarded with a promotion and acclaim throughout Kansas. As the new year got underway, Blunt was the man of the hour.

CHAPTER 9

Major General Blunt

When Blunt returned to Fort Leavenworth to take command of the District of Kansas, he met with the new governor, Thomas Carney. Carney promised to support Blunt, who hoped that this would be a change from his poor relationship with Governor Robinson. Part of the reason for his confidence was no doubt due to how Carney had gained office.

Carney had obtained the governorship through the machinations of Sen. James Lane. Governor Robinson had been caught up in a confusing and dubious scandal involving the sale of state bonds. Lane's allies in the state legislature began investigating the matter in early 1862. Their investigation led to impeachment charges against Robinson, the secretary of state, and the state auditor. In an impeachment trial in June the latter two were convicted and Robinson was acquitted, but Robinson's reputation was damaged. In the 1862 fall elections Carney, known as the richest man in the state, was chosen governor by a landslide over the anti-Lane Republican candidate.

With Carney's support of Blunt, Blunt's own record of success in Arkansas, and an expected promotion, Blunt's profile was rising in Kansas and in the nation. This made him a target of both praise and criticism. Like most people he had no problem with the former. But his reaction to the latter would create serious problems.

The *St. Louis Democrat* wrote highly of Blunt's actions in the wake of Prairie Grove and Van Buren. It lauded him and his staff for being in "the very thickest of the fight" despite Confederate volleys and sharpshooters. It called Blunt's foe Hindman "the trickster" who was beaten by the "clear-headed, . . . decided," and dedicated General Blunt. This story appeared in the January 3 issue of the *Freedom's Champion* from Atchison. At the end of the month the *Champion's* correspondent with Blunt's army lent his support to the general by saying that Blunt "displayed his usual sagacity" in allowing Colonel Cloud and the Second Kansas to lead the Van Buren raid.

More praise for Blunt came from as far away as New York. Just days after Prairie Grove, the *New York Times* said that although Blunt was a "civilian General," he was a "magnificent commander." The *Times* wanted Blunt turned loose to clear out Arkansas and march on Texas, where he might do better than Gen. Nathaniel Banks, "whose whereabouts have been for sometime unknown."

Parts of this piece appeared in the *Leavenworth Conservative* on December 16. Five days earlier the *Conservative* had published and endorsed a *Times* opinion that Blunt should be promoted to major general. The endorsement was repeated on December 13 and given further impetus by a meeting held on December 27 in Leavenworth, which passed a resolution calling for Blunt's promotion.

However, not everyone in Kansas was eager to see Blunt's advancement. Jacob Stotler at the *Emporia News* expressed the belief that while Blunt had performed nobly, General Herron had done most of the fighting at Prairie Grove. The newspapers that opposed Senator Lane were naturally the harshest critics of Blunt and his prospects. The *Journal* of Lawrence, in an issue that came out two years to the day after Kansas's admission to the Union, dismissed Blunt by claiming that he "has done well in the two or three skirmishes he has been engaged in." Its editor added that "few men have succeeded to the 'Stars' with reason so vapory."

Two weeks later came perhaps the most controversial correspondence the *Journal* ever printed. On February 13 it printed a letter in which both the author and its recipient were left unnamed. The letter accused Blunt of being asleep or "sitting up with some of the female hangers on" while Hindman marched around him at Prairie Grove. It claimed that Blunt was taking credit for the work done by one of his brigade commanders, Colonel Cloud.

Upon further examination it might be concluded that the *Journal* letter was not entirely true in its reporting and its accusations. As to the matter of Colonel Cloud, the December 28 issue of the *Conservative* printed a letter from Cloud in which he said, "I am proud of my success in whipping my part of the enemy, and losing few men." Cloud added that Blunt was "the most popular" of all the Western generals "by reason of his courage and success." Cloud even compared Blunt with "Old Rough and Ready," Andrew Jackson.

To reinforce his case, the author of the *Journal* letter expressed the view that Blunt was taking credit for what Cloud accomplished at Prairie Grove, while insulting Cloud and his men. The author stated that Blunt's official report said little about Cloud's brigade and censured its commander. And while Blunt's report does not praise Cloud, it does praise Samuel Crawford, one of Cloud's officers. The report doesn't mention the commander of Blunt's third brigade either. Blunt only censured two people in his report: Richardson, the man who failed to report the movements of the Confederate forces, and Hindman, for retreating under a truce.

The letter's author went on to say that when Cloud found out about Blunt's report, he sent a message to Blunt's immediate superior, Gen. John Schofield. Cloud supposedly called for Schofield to start an investigation of Blunt's report, yet no such letter appears in the official records or elsewhere. When Schofield asked Halleck to be transferred from the region on February 3, he stated several grievances against Blunt, Herron, and Curtis; a falsified battle report is not one of them.

Another argument against the letter's statements is the fact that Blunt's postwar narrative contains no hint of a message from Cloud to Schofield. If at any time during the war he had uncovered such an accusation from Cloud, he almost certainly would have launched a tirade against him. It is possible that Blunt was ignorant of Cloud's accusation, but since he was able to find out what Schofield was later saying about him, that possibility seems unlikely.

After making the charge about Cloud's supposed anger, the *Journal* letter concluded by sourly noting that Schofield, Blunt, and Herron were all in line to be promoted to major general. In actuality, while Blunt and Herron were indeed getting promotions, Schofield's reward failed to pass through Congress. That failure would become another point of friction between Blunt and Schofield in the coming year.

The most interesting fact about the *Journal* letter is that both the author and its recipient are anonymous. Without the identity of the writer there is no way to be certain whether or not that writer was indeed at Prairie Grove, in communication with someone who was, or was simply passing along secondhand rumors.

At one point the author asserted that Blunt had lost his popularity with the men in the army. Wiley Britton, who served in the ranks and later wrote extensively about the Civil War in the region, noted that because Blunt won battles, he was popular with the men. Britton suggested that Schofield was jealous of Blunt because Blunt was a winner and therefore popular. These are strong arguments against the letter writer's identity as an ordinary soldier or a low-ranking officer. Since the author is not aware of the growing Blunt-Schofield feud, he probably wasn't a high-ranking officer either.

It's likely, therefore, that this wasn't so much a "letter" as a disguised editorial. Considering that the *Journal* was the anti-Lane paper in the senator's hometown, it is not surprising that it would be critical of General Blunt. Since much of what discounts the author of the letter is inside information, readers would have no way of knowing the truth behind its statements. It is interesting to note that the two chief Lane organs at the time, the *Leavenworth Conservative* and the *Weekly Tribune* in Lawrence, declined to refute the *Journal* and its letter.

Indeed, the only newspaper in Kansas to comment on the *Journal* piece was the *Emporia News,* and it put an interesting spin on it. While editor Jacob Stotler expressed support for the letter and said that Blunt was lucky that Herron had arrived, he presented a different view on his front page. That view, from the *New York Times,* praised Blunt and Herron for giving a "most tremendous whipping" to Hindman at Prairie Grove. But when General Schofield arrived, the correspondent wrote that he stopped the army's progress, and added, "It has not been heard from since." That correspondent claimed that Schofield was sick with "West Point," the lack of success from which West Point generals seemed to be suffering at that point in the war; said he was happy that Blunt was free of such a sickness; and wondered why Blunt wasn't allowed to "finish his work."

The *Journal* seems to have been part of a very small minority in its sour view of General Blunt. When he and his staff arrived in Fort Scott on his way to Leavenworth, Blunt was cheered and treated to a grand ball. When he arrived at Leavenworth on January 15 a crowd gathered at his hotel just to see him. He was too tired to speak to the crowd that day, but did so the next day at a formal reception. Blunt gave a short speech thanking his men, which was met by "three long and deafening cheers from the crowd." As he left the public reception, a twenty-three-gun major general's salute was fired; Blunt still had not been officially promoted to that rank.

The *Conservative* of January 15 reported on Blunt's arrival with an almost breathless quality. After describing the reception, the paper's reporter took time to describe what General Blunt looked like. His appearance had changed since Blunt left Leavenworth back in July. "His naturally healthy complexion is now browned by exposure," readers were told, "and instead of whiskers, he now sports a heavy black moustache . . ., giving a decided military cut to his appearance."

A month later Blunt had the opportunity to express his own views at a public gathering in Leavenworth with other dignitaries. His speech was peppered with radical rhetoric, perhaps part of his attempt to gain favor with the crowd but, in light of his later writings, perhaps also reflecting his own views. Again and again in the speech he denouced traitors and Copperheads and expressed pleasure that such "treason" was not accepted in Kansas.

There are three things worthy of note that Blunt said at this gathering. The first was an odd choice of words, as he claimed that the aim of the Copperheads and Confederates was to "cripple the Government and *procrastinate* the rebellion." Considering that Blunt was a well-educated doctor and an experienced speaker, such misuse of the word "procrastinate" is unusual. It could be that Blunt was misquoted. It could also be that Blunt was invoking his patron Senator Lane, who was notorious for his linguistic eccentricities before ordinary citizens.

The next noteworthy remark of Blunt's was this statement: "Whenever I have heard any objection to rebels being killed by negroes I have always noticed that it came from some fool in shoulder-straps." The most radical abolitionists in Kansas had advocated the arming of blacks as soon as the war began. But the general population, in Kansas as well as in the nation, had no stomach for black men in army uniforms. The tide had started to turn the previous fall in the wake of the Emancipation Proclamation, but there was still opposition to the concept. Despite this opposition a black regiment had already been created in Kansas and was in training in Leavenworth when Blunt spoke.

In this light Blunt's remark seems to be part of an overall effort among the radicals to gain public support for the concept of black soldiers. Blunt had made these remarks after he told his audience that the soldiers he knew had no objections to getting help from black troops. It's also important to note that his statement might have been another attempt to lend support to Lane, who was the driving force in creating the black regiment.

The third of Blunt's important comments came toward the end of his speech and immediately after his remark on black troops. "Let me here say to the Copperheads that when this rebellion is put down," he vowed, "and when this army returns home there will be a day of fearful retribution. There will be the biggest crop of black eyes ever heard of in this country."

Needless to say, Blunt's contempt for those he termed traitors was, in this remark, clear for all to see. Clearly he did not desire accommodation and a peaceful reconstruction; he was still the radical abolitionist bent on crushing the slave power. He wanted to carry on the dream of "Old Brown" to utterly destroy the slave holders and their wicked institution. With his impending promotion to major general, Blunt would have even more ability to carry out this extreme program.

Blunt's speech not only contained his plan of action, but it also lent no small support to Blunt's patron Senator Lane. News of Blunt's victories would have come too late to help Lane and his allies in the fall election of 1862. But they almost certainly bolstered Lane and Kansans' view of him. After all, Lane could argue, it was he that had made Blunt a general and put him at the head of the Kansas department. With that power and position Blunt beat the Confederate army at a time when Union triumphs were hard to come by. If Lane's influence in Kansas increased through 1863, Blunt could rightly claim credit. Is it any surprise, then, that Lane was energetic in getting Blunt promoted to major general?

While many Kansans were pleased with the general's "blunt talk" and record of victories, his superior in the Army of the Frontier was not. General Schofield began expressing his contempt for Blunt on the first day of 1863. Within months, Blunt would begin viewing his commander as his "bitter personal enemy." Blunt thought that Schofield was the provocateur of this feud, and he may not have been all that far off the mark.

In a January 1, 1863, letter to General Curtis, Schofield reported

Gen. John Schofield shown well after the Civil War. Schofield was Blunt's immediate superior, and he became Blunt's personal nemesis inside the Union army in the far western theater of operations. *Illustration courtesy the Kansas State Historical Society, Topeka, Kansas.*

that Blunt wanted to return to Leavenworth to attend to his affairs as commander of the District of Kansas. Schofield expressed a desire for Blunt to choose between district and field command. He preferred that Blunt take the district.

Schofield then described the actions of the Army of the Frontier before he had returned as "a series of blunders, from which it narrowly escaped disaster where it should have met with complete success." He then claimed that Herron and Blunt had been beaten at Prairie Grove and that Hindman had only retreated when he heard rumors that Schofield was coming with reinforcements. Since Hindman made many excuses for retreating from Prairie Grove, it seems logical that if Schofield's claim was true, Hindman would have cited that as another reason. Hindman didn't, so where did Schofield get this idea? He would never say, which casts the Missouri general in a fairly unfavorable light.

The next day Curtis sent some sort of message rebuking Schofield, for on January 3 Schofield wrote back in response to his superior. He explained that he wanted Blunt out of the field because of those "series of blunders" that he had charged two days earlier. He repeated the "reinforcements excuse" as well as his statement that this was a "fact" he had passed along "without intending to pass censure upon any officer." One has to question why passing along such a "fact" would not have that effect.

In his letter Curtis had rebuked Schofield for trying to co-opt Blunt's and Herron's reports by inserting his own comments in advance. Schofield replied to this charge by telling Curtis "that you regard it as no business of mine that I find on my return my command cut up and demoralized." But then Schofield said that he had always spoken of Blunt and Herron positively and expressed "regret that their success [at Prairie Grove] had not been as complete" as he had wanted. Schofield concluded this letter by promising not to write about subjects that would hurt the feelings of his subordinates.

In the coming months, Blunt would say and do things that would give Schofield headaches. Blunt's behavior would become increasingly outrageous and his comments ever more vitriolic. Yet from these letters, it appears that at first Blunt was the victim of Schofield's bitter attacks. Blunt found out what his superior in the field was saying about him and replied in kind. Thus were sown the seeds of their later feud.

Schofield would later admit that at first he had liked and praised Blunt. But at some point, which he never made clear, Schofield decided that Blunt was "unfit in any respect for the command of a division of troops against a disciplined enemy." In his autobiography Schofield said that he had written to Curtis in confidence, expressing his preference for taking command of the district, and he alleged that Curtis had shown his letter to Senator Lane and other Blunt backers. Since Blunt did indeed find out what Schofield had said about him, that accusation was almost certainly true.

Schofield wrote in his autobiography that this betrayal made him seem hostile to the men who had won the battle of Prairie Grove. He claimed that it was this "perception" that killed his promotion to major general. It seems odd that Schofield would be surprised at that outcome, considering that he was simultaneously praising and damning Blunt and Herron. It is also odd why Schofield thought that Curtis would fail to keep his letters secret when promotions for all three men were in question.

Schofield's attitude toward Blunt is even more puzzling when reading his annual report on the activities of his command during 1862. He had concluded this report by stating that he and the country needed to thank Blunt and Herron "for their prompt and cordial cooperation with me in the discharge of every duty." He added that it gave him "great satisfaction" to say that "the gallant Blunt and Herron" had defeated Hindman at Prairie Grove.

In his next letter to Curtis, Schofield tried to turn Curtis against Blunt. On January 6 Schofield wrote to Curtis that he had a question as to whether Blunt's "Kansas Division" (the term Schofield gave for Phillips's command in the Indian Territory) should be supplied from Springfield or Fort Scott. In this letter Schofield told Curtis that Blunt was describing Curtis's ordering the retreat of the Second and Third Division the previous fall as part of a "disgraceful scheme."

Schofield must not have liked how Curtis responded to that statement, for a month later he was telling tales about Blunt, Herron, and Curtis to General Halleck. On a letter dated February 3 he said that it was Curtis who was foiling his accomplishments. He said Curtis had ordered him to fall back the previous year. He accused Curtis of detaining him in St. Louis for a week after Schofield had wanted to resume command of the army so that Blunt and Herron could conduct their Van Buren raid. He wanted to take Little Rock, but Curtis was holding him back. He added that Blunt and Herron were Curtis's favorites. He accused both Blunt and Herron of being incapable of command and of having blundered into success. He told Halleck that he was not dissatisfied with his command but merely wanted to "be permitted to use it."

Reviewing this letter, one has to wonder if Wiley Britton wasn't right in his judgment that Schofield was jealous of Blunt. Whatever the cause, as long as Schofield and Blunt shared the same level of authority, their views of each other were not a serious problem. Both were still brigadier generals and district commanders. One or the other could be removed from the field without much harm to the Union cause, or to each other's reputations. So long as one wasn't put in administrative command of the other, their feud was a manageable situation.

Perhaps to bring some peace between the generals, early in 1863 the Army of the Frontier was reorganized and Blunt was relieved of his divisional command. By late February, Blunt was back at Fort Leavenworth, administering the District of Kansas and maintaining his distance from Schofield. As soon as Blunt returned to Kansas he had to deal with a local crisis.

Days before Blunt's move, a mob had demolished the offices of the one Democratic newspaper in Kansas, the *Leavenworth Inquirer*, still printing despite Blunt's closure the previous June. The attack was apparently sparked the night before, when a gang fired shots at Daniel Anthony, the Leavenworth mayor and publisher of the *Conservative*. The gang either came from or fled to the *Inquirer* office, it is unclear which. In response Anthony and Charles Jennison led a group of citizens to the *Inquirer* office and destroyed its press. Blunt was not bothered by the matter; he was quoted in a Kansas City newspaper as saying that "a dirty job was taken off [my] hands." Thus the *Inquirer* crisis was solved, more or less.

There was, however, other illegal behavior occuring that Blunt could not ignore or allow to continue. The border region of his district was now overrun with criminal gangs known as the Red Legs. They were supposedly pro-Union guerrillas, but by this time they were robbing and murdering indiscriminately. Blunt cracked down on them despite his claim that he received death threats from supporters of the Red Legs.

The problem of these Red Legs, or jayhawkers, as they were also called, dated to the internecine warfare of the territorial period. With the coming of the Civil War, the "pro-Union" raiders first became known as jayhawkers. Depending on which side of the Lane-Robinson feud a newspaper stood, one either praised or denounced the jayhawkers. In a well-known piece from 1861 the *Leavenworth Conservative* had written, "Jayhawking was got up in Kansas. It is one of our things. It works well; we believe in it[;] we are going to have it." Their rival the *Times* decried the jayhawkers' actions as "a reign of terror glazed over with the specious plea of loyalty to the Union."

Throughout the next two years the raids continued. As time went on, however, the raids became less about supporting the Union and more about simple plunder. By the time the problem was placed in Blunt's lap in 1863, no one in Kansas felt safe from the Red Legs. So while Blunt might have had some sympathy for this style of guerilla war, it was clear he had to crack down on these attacks.

He began to do so on March 2, when he issued a circular ordering the suppression of this "piracy" by all officers within his command. Next he sent out orders banning "secret organizations," which "under the guide of patriotism" were committing robbery and plunder. In the meantime Blunt's promotion to major general was passed through Congress.

On April 3 Curtis told Major General Blunt that people in Missouri believed that Blunt was too easily providing the Red Legs the liberty to continue their raids. In another letter to Gen. Ben Loan in command in Jefferson City, Curtis expressed worries about allowing Blunt to take over some counties in western Missouri to deal with the Red Legs. Perhaps Curtis was concerned about Blunt's alleged ties to these gangs. But he also wanted other commanders in the adjacent areas of the border to work together to suppress the Red Legs threat.

Blunt wrote to Curtis on April 17 that he did not have to worry about his combating the Red Legs. He enclosed the orders he had sent to one of his colonels that called for strict border defense against all armed groups, including the Red Legs. Blunt promised Curtis that he would "hang a few [captured Red Legs] soon" to discourage others from outlaw actions. One Kansas newspaper, the

Oskaloosa Independent, reported that Blunt had even ordered his officers "to take as few prisoners of this class of outlaws as possible."

Blunt's policy fell firmly on the head of one John Shirley on May 6, 1863, when he was hanged at Fort Leavenworth. Shirley and two other men had been turned over to Blunt by Mayor Anthony of Leavenworth. Anthony described the three prisoners as leaders of a gang of "professional thieves" and part of a larger group that included women. In handing them over Anthony expressed the hope that the trio would be "speedily punished."

What happened to the other two men is unknown, but Shirley was convicted and sentenced to death. It was only the third time during the war that a man was executed for "thieving and other lawlessness." On the day of the hanging, the Leavenworth *Conservative* wrote:

> "GEN. BLUNT was praised by all the papers when he only talked and made orders against lawlessness. As soon, however, as he puts his orders into effect what a terrible howl is raised. Punishing criminals is one of our things, and we shall adhere to it."

The problem of dispensing justice to outlaws in Kansas largely moved beyond Blunt's control later that month in Atchison. Days after the Shirley hanging, General Blunt traveled up the Missouri River to Atchison to speak. He not only recounted Union victories, but he also encouraged his listeners to "knock down" anyone who uttered "a disloyal word" against the Union. Blunt then told the crowd that if they had proof that someone had assisted the rebellion, they should send that person to him for punishment.

But when a group of men robbed a local man and seriously wounded his son, the people of Atchison didn't send the criminals to Blunt. Instead, on Sunday, May 17, 1863, they hauled the six accused robbers into town, convened an immediate "jury trial," and at least two were hanged that afternoon, while two more of the six men were hanged later. In addition two men were hanged in a separate incident in Highland in Doniphan County.

Blunt faced some criticism for allowing these lynchings to take place. The *Conservative* accurately claimed later that two of the men in Atchison were hung before Blunt knew what had happened. Blunt, acting on the advice of the local sheriff, allowed the other two men to be handed over to "the citizens of Atchison

County" for trial and punishment. Blunt later claimed that his actions were supported by the people of Kansas while the only opposition came from Carney, rival general Thomas Ewing, and possible Copperheads.

Incredibly, the same day the *Atchison Champion* told of the May 17 lynching of the two men, it published criticism of Blunt for unjustly arresting two men apparently associated with a stage line and rivals to another line that supported Blunt. The outrage expressed by one "J. Gray" to the arrest cited the rule of law as well as the contrast between civilian and military authorities, and accused Blunt of having a "swell[ed] head." But in light of the events of the seventeenth, this rhetoric seems hypocritical, and even more so when a month later the *Champion* praised the hangings as a warning to scoundrels.

The Red Legs were not the only irregular forces Blunt had to deal with. Confederate guerrillas resumed their attacks on pro-Union towns and targets in Kansas. Blunt continued the general Union policy of treating these guerrillas not as soldiers but as criminals. This led to an extraordinary exchange of letters published in Kansas City's *Journal of Commerce* on May 16, 1863.

The first letter came from Col. B. F. Harker of the Confederate army. Harker stated that captured Union soldiers were treated as prisoners of war, while Confederate "soldiers and citizens" were arrested and executed. Harker refused to accept the rationale Union officers gave concerning these individuals and their aid to bushwhackers.

"What, sir, can you expect from a people whose rights are trampled in the dust?. . ." Harker asked. He demanded that all armed Confederates be treated as soldiers, that seizures of persons and property stop, and that people be compensated for their losses. Harker concluded his letter by threatening to kill five Union "soldiers or citizens" for every Confederate "executed without due process of law."

Blunt, of course, was neither scared nor impressed with Harker's comments. His reply was published after Harker's letter, and he was short and to the point. He told Harker that he and his "motley crew" were rebels engaged in attacks on "unarmed loyal citizens" and therefore exempt from "all rights and considerations extended to prisoners of war."

Blunt also said he had instructed his officers that every guerrilla and guerrilla sympathizer be "destroyed or expelled" from his district. He warned that women would not be excluded from suffering if they aided the rebel cause. The executions would continue, with Blunt promising that the only rights to be granted to the guerillas "will be the right to make choice of the quality of rope with which they will be hung."

If Harker thought he might scare off Blunt, he was sadly mistaken. Blunt was dedicated to ending slavery and combating those who, in his view, fought to preserve it. No doubt Harker's comments confirmed every negative notion Blunt had of the Confederate army and its officers. Nothing would get in Blunt's way; slavery would be destroyed, and there was no price too high to pay to achieve that end.

This correspondence may have stemmed in part from an attack in late March in which the Sixth Kansas killed seventeen bushwhackers and, according to the major in charge, "hung two." These men also burned twenty-one houses belonging to guerrillas who earlier attacked a steamboat carrying freed slaves. As the spring progressed the cross-border raids continued to the point that on May 16 the *Champion* called for Blunt to "clean out the country from Independence to Lexington" and leave nothing for the guerrillas "or their sympathizers."

Though the guerrilla problem showed no signs of abating, the situation with the Red Legs was under control by the summer of 1863. The *Journal of Commerce* reported to its readers on July 23 that Capt. George Hoyt was now cooperating against them. Hoyt had *"legitimate authority"* to assist in the search and arrest of suspected Red Legs. He was described as a man of "good abilities and impulses," had previously denounced their thieving, and the *Journal* wished him success in his new duties as a defender of law and order in the border region.

Blunt would, of course, take full credit for the suppression of both the Red Legs and the general lawlessness that plagued Kansas at the time. After the war he would also claim that Governor Carney had admitted to him in early in 1866 that Blunt's actions in the "Atchison incident" were correct. Blunt said Carney only opposed him because he was interested in replacing Senator Lane as the state's chief powerbroker.

Thomas Carney, the pro-Lane candidate for governor in 1862. As governor his ambitions rose, and he not only feuded with Lane but also with Blunt. Carney's actions during the Price Campaign of 1864 would lead to the fall of his popularity. *Photograph courtesy the Kansas State Historical Society, Topeka, Kansas.*

Almost as soon as Thomas Carney was sworn in as governor, he began asserting himself and lusting after Lane's Senate seat. They clashed over several matters, including the raising of a "home guard" regiment in Johnson County after more guerrilla raids. Lane believed that the raising of such a regiment would reflect poorly on Blunt, who was still dealing with the guerilla problem.

On June 5, 1863, Blunt was appointed as a special recruiting commissioner by the War Department. Blunt was to raise another white cavalry regiment in Kansas as well as a black infantry regiment. Blunt would also have some power to commission the officers of the white unit.

Carney viewed this as an attack on his power as governor, just as Robinson had with the "Lane Brigade" back in 1861. He dashed to Washington to have Blunt removed. Carney left in mid-June, stopping first in St. Louis to gain Schofield's backing for raising a regiment for border defense. In a letter to his friend James McDowell, Carney stated his desire to put Gen. Thomas Ewing in charge of the Kansas District. He hoped that placement would push Blunt out, and he told McDowell, "This I am doing in self defense."

The next day Carney told McDowell that Schofield had indeed given him the authority to raise a regiment. Once in Washington, Carney wrote to President Lincoln about the Kansas situation as he saw it. He reported the incidents in Atchison and Leavenworth and complained that Blunt had usurped civilian authorities. He told Lincoln that he felt Blunt's interference might cause anarchy and that under Blunt "no man's life will be safe." He also protested Blunt's appointments of officers for the new regiments. Carney asked Lincoln to "absolutely" suspend Blunt's administrative authority and to revoke the War Department's grant empowering Blunt to appoint officers in the new regiments.

Lane's influence over both Lincoln and Stanton was too great for Carney to overcome. The day after writing to Lincoln, Carney sourly reported to McDowell that Stanton refused to back Schofield in the creation of a "home guard" regiment. Perhaps to effect some peace among the rivals in Kansas, Blunt was ordered by the War Department to allow the men to elect company officers and to let company officers nominate field officers. Blunt was assured that the orders wold not affect "appointments which may have been duly made" before the order was sent. In the end Blunt did take a hand in those appointments, despite the wishes of the War Department.

When the regiment entered service as the Fourteenth Kansas, Blunt claimed at least part of it as his personal escort. Blunt was also able to maintain control of the selection of officers for the black regiment. Jacob Stotler in Emporia knew who was the beneficiary of Blunt's prestige, and speculated on June 20 that while his commissions might not give Blunt a Senate seat, "Perhaps somebody else is interested in that line—the man that runs the General."

The *Leavenworth Times* was even more direct. By the summer of 1863 it was distinguishing itself from the *Conservative* by opposing Lane and Lane's friends. This of course included Blunt, and the *Times* spared no ammunition. On July 2 it presented, without any substantiation, the news that Blunt had been arrested and ordered to Washington. Because this story was dropped the next day, it isn't clear why Blunt was supposedly arrested.

Most likely it was the recruitment matter, for the next day the *Times* commented on that subject. It printed the "full text" of the order allowing Blunt to organize the cavalry regiment and focused its readers' attention on a paragraph that allowed the governor to commission the officers. It asked, "Will some of Blunt's friends explain this?"

A little more than a week later, the *Times* was in a more jaunty mood. Its pleasure was due to a reading of Blunt's orders that said he had only thirty days to nominate officers for the regiment. That period had begun on June 5 and as of that day, July 11, Blunt's power had expired. "The powers at Washington are beginning to learn that there is a Governor in Kansas," the *Times* announced.

In the end, however, Blunt and Lane got their way. But in the process a new political division had been created in Kansas. The Republican Party was once again split into two factions. From this point on Lane and Carney would be vying for control of the party and, by extension, state politics. As for General Blunt, his fortunes hinged on Lane's influence now more than ever. He would need that support for his feud with Schofield had now heated to the boiling point.

Despite these political maneuvers, the situation in the region appeared hopeful to the *Leavenworth Conservative*. In its issue of

May 6, 1863, a piece called "The Kansas Military District" painted a picture of refugee Indians heading home; a pro-Union government taking control of the Cherokee Nation; Union enlistments increasing in western Arkansas; rebel forces in disarray; and Blunt ordering crackdowns on guerrillas. The one area of dissatisfaction was in the Union military leadership. On that score, if on no other, Generals Schofield and Halleck might have agreed with the *Conservative's* editors.

Schofield had wanted to send part of his command to assist Grant with the capture of Vicksburg earlier in the year. His superior, General Curtis, had disagreed and prevented the transfer. This in part led to Curtis's being relieved of department command on March 10, but his replacement died before he could arrive.

Halleck then ordered Curtis to send more troops east. Curtis replied that he had no more that he could spare. Curtis added that he was not receiving much cooperation from the pro-Union Missouri governor. Washington then reversed its decision about the two generals, and on April 1 Schofield was relieved. This apparently wasn't satisfactory because on May 11 Lincoln decided to relieve General Curtis, and two days later he put Schofield in charge of the Department of the Missouri. Kansas would be divided into two districts, with Blunt getting the southern one and General Ewing the more populous northern district.

This was bad news not only to Blunt, but also to most of Senator Lane's allies. They may have feared that the no-nonsense West Pointer would not support their hands in the military till. Corruption in the region was an open secret, and Lane's friends were believed to be the chief beneficiaries. Certainly the Lane faction viewed Schofield as less than radical when it came to the abolition of slavery.

About a month after Schofield was appointed department commander, the *Kansas Weekly Tribune,* the Lawrence newspaper edited by Lane's friend John Speer, published a long denunciation of the new general in charge. The denunciation can be boiled down to two separate attacks. The first was that Schofield was far too close to conservative Missouri politicians. This seems more "guilt by association" than a reflection of reality. Schofield may have been from Missouri, but that hardly made him a conservative on the issue of slavery.

The second attack was based on Schofield's views of Blunt, Herron, and Curtis. Whoever wrote this piece (probably Speer himself) had to have seen Schofield's letters to Curtis from earlier in the year. The editorial almost directly quotes Schofield's previous assertion that the Army of the Frontier was demoralized and that it was word of his coming that caused Hindman to retreat. Schofield was described as "egotistical," "pretentious," and a "would-be hero [of] battles he never fought." The editorial went on to say this:

> "We find in the appointment of Gen. Schofield a continuation of the policy associated with his name: —a policy which first insulted us, then took our trains and supplies, removing the base of operations to Missouri for the benefits of pet towns therein, in whose streets to-day, rebels of the 'she-adder' stripe are allowed to insult Union soldiers; which slandered our heroes and our dead after their hard fought victories, and which boasts of hating our very name because we win victories, kill rebels and sympathizers, and fight to destroy the cause of the all the 'wild woe of war' which now desolates the land—Slavery."

On June 12 the *Times* expressed its satisfaction that Ewing had been put in command of the border region. The *Conservative* replied the next day by saying that if Ewing did as good a job as Blunt had, Ewing should consider himself lucky. Blunt had been providing for the state's defense and punishing lawless elements, and in their view had done well in such difficult circumstances. It then used this opening as an opportunity to further editorialize on the situation.

Perhaps revealing its own ties to Blunt, the *Conservative* reported that Blunt was happy to be rid of "this police duty." Blunt had wanted a field command, and now he had one. Blunt was eager to fight Price and his army, and he expected that once Vicksburg fell to Grant he would have enough men to go after the general the rebels viewed as "one of their ablest leaders."

Ewing, by contrast, supposedly was not as eager as Blunt to fight the Confederates. The paper reported that he had recently gone to see Schofield in St. Louis. Upon his return, he seemed to prefer "the duties of a police officer than to meet the enemy force in the field." Ewing moved his headquarters from Leavenworth to Kansas

City, which the *Conservative* said proved that Ewing's ambitions were political rather than military.

That paper also disputed the *Times'* comments with respect to the view of the War Department. Blunt, it pointed out, had been given the authority by the War Department to raise two new regiments. Such authority, as well as the patronage in commissions, could advance a man to the U.S. Senate. But instead, wrote the *Conservative,* Blunt would give these commissions to enlisted men in old regiments so as to enable these new units to fight.

Although not part of the *Conservative's* editorial, elsewhere the paper contained praise of Blunt's new orders to stop distribution of "treasonable newspapers" from out of the state. It claimed, "The Orders . . . will be read with the greatest interest and satisfaction by all loyal men." Among Leavenworth newspapers Blunt now had a friend and a foe.

A slightly less partisan view came from Kansas City. There the *Journal of Commerce* expressed some pleasure at the change in districts, but its reasoning was that the division would make it easier to protect the area from guerrillas. That newspaper had no problems with the way Blunt had managed affairs, but it was confident of General Ewing's abilities. Of course, the *Journal* was a major supporter of the railroad that Ewing had been working to aid over the past few years, so its view of Ewing might be colored by its railroad allegiance.

A few weeks before this interchange between the newspapers, the *Tribune* had called for Blunt to be put in charge of the Missouri department. When first promoted to general, conceded the *Tribune,* "he had opposition, but his gallant conduct has entirely eradicated all opposition with loyal men." Unfortunately his conduct over the next six weeks would prove less than gallant and opposition to him would resurface.

After taking command, Schofield reorganized his department. In orders dated June 9, 1863, Blunt was placed in command of the new District of the Frontier, consisting of Kansas and the Missouri border counties south of the thirty-eighth parallel as well as the Indian Territory. North of the thirty-eighth parallel would be the District of the Border under General Ewing. E. B. Brown replaced Ben Loan as commander of the District of Central Missouri.

Schofield also assigned Maj. L. C. Easton as not only the chief quartermaster of the frontier and border districts but also the Nebraska and Colorado districts.

Within days of the reorganization Blunt attempted to give orders to Major Easton at Fort Leavenworth. This was not the first time that Blunt had a conflict with Easton. In March, Blunt had asked General Curtis to remove Easton, charging him with disloyalty and disobedience. At the time, Curtis threw his support to Blunt and decided to remove Easton. However, either Easton was not removed, or Schofield returned him to Kansas despite his earlier removal.

While records do not indicate why Blunt was trying to give orders to Easton, the most obvious reason was that Blunt wanted Easton to direct business toward a supply contractor with which Blunt was connected. With this scenario Blunt would have been part of an epidemic of Union corruption in the trans-Mississippi theater.

One account of this sort of skullduggery surfaced late in 1862 in the Atchison newspaper. The story reported of a Lawrence man who had a contract to supply the U.S. Army with beef. It claimed that the man was obtaining confiscated cattle at one and one-half cents per pound, but he was selling the beef to the army at five and three-quarter cents per pound, pocketing a substantial profit.

In late 1863 the Union post chaplain at Fort Smith saw additional evidence of chicanery. He reported that some officers would obtain Confederate or private property and sell it to the government. Some of the property was stolen from citizens who had been declared rebels. Other soldiers were using government funds to speculate in cotton, liquor, and horses.

The most common form of corruption was connected to the delivery of supplies to Union forces in camp and in the field. The army contracted out the work of delivering supplies to private shipping firms, some of which already had connections to suppliers. The army had chosen this method because it had experienced problems trying to bring supplies to units in the field during the Mexican War.

Unfortunately this system was ideal for officers, politicians, and others who wanted to get rich at the army's expense. A shipping firm could be started by men who wanted to favor suppliers that they already had investments in. This would give them profits from the shipping firm and from the supplier. A firm also could bribe officers in order to induce them to favor that firm over their competitors for deliveries to posts or field units. As in the above example on beef shipments, suppliers and shippers could (and apparently did) overcharge the army for goods and services. The corruption was never largely dealt with because this theater of the war was not a high priority to the Lincoln administration.

The one person the administration consistently relied on for information about the theater was Sen. James Lane. The following year allegations would surface as to Lane's connections to the corruption. Lane's allies and supporters would be tied to the situation, including General Blunt. Long before those stories surfaced, however, Blunt's conflict with Major Easton would dig him into a very deep hole with his superiors.

On June 18 Easton reported to his superior, department quartermaster Gen. Robert Allen in St. Louis, that Blunt had attempted to give him orders. Blunt was claiming that the order appointing him head of the Frontier District allowed him to give Easton orders. Easton disagreed, reasoning that Blunt only had authority over the quartermaster in his own district. He told Allen that according to his reading of military rules, the district commander had to make requisitions through the district quartermaster. Those quartermasters in turn could apply to him for their supplies. Easton asked Allen to obtain clarification from General Schofield.

General Allen did so, and on June 24, Schofield made a short and direct decision. "Respectfully referred to Major-General Blunt, with information that the views expressed by Major Easton are correct. He receives orders only from department headquarters and the chief quartermaster of the department."

Six days later Blunt sent a message trying to claim that because Easton was chief quartermaster for the district, Blunt could indeed give Easton orders. The only way he could not give orders to Easton, Blunt claimed, was if Easton was not the chief quartermaster. Blunt was clearly in the wrong on this issue because he was trying to bypass the chain of command. And at any rate, Major Easton was working out of Fort Leavenworth and therefore was physically outside of Blunt's new district.

On July 5 Schofield referred this question to General in Chief Halleck in Washington. He repeated his argument that Easton, by virtue of being depot quartermaster at Leavenworth, was chief quartermaster of all the districts that drew supplies from said depot. He said that Blunt "can no more command Major Easton than he can the chief quartermaster of the department." On July 23, Col. E. D. Townsend, assistant adjutant general at the War Department in Washington, sent word to Schofield that Halleck had reviewed the matter and had agreed with Schofield. Schofield was to instruct Blunt that he had "no authority" to give orders to Major Easton.

Previously on July 15 Schofield had written to Townsend that he had official and unofficial reports of "fraud, corruption, and mal-administration" in his department and in Blunt's district. He conceded that the reports were too circumstantial to make specific charges, and he called for a court of inquiry appointed by President Lincoln to investigate the situation.

Blunt found out about this request and on July 23 he wrote an incendiary letter to Secretary of War Stanton. Blunt took the opportunity to make the claim that Schofield's "abuses and irregularities" had begun with Blunt's advance the previous fall in the face of Schofield's retreat and Blunt's victories at Cane Hill, Prairie Grove, and Van Buren. The next "irregularity" Blunt mentioned was that Schofield had ignored Blunt's repeated requests for more troops to reinforce Fort Gibson and that even without these troops Blunt had again marched into Indian Territory to beat back the rebels. In his message Blunt sneered that, "Schofield has been guilty of no such 'irregularities' since he has been in the service."

Blunt charged Easton and Capt. J. P. Ray, the commissary at Leavenworth, of being "traitors" who would be in Richmond if Confederate money was worth more than American money. For good measure he also accused Governor Carney and the superintendent of Indian Affairs of having robbed the refugees from the territory. Blunt claimed that "Copperheads" in Missouri and Kansas were trying to get rid of him and sacrifice his command. He pledged to Stanton that his private grievances wouldn't interfere with his duty. This was why he had not already left the field to await the outcome of an investigation. He concluded by expressing a hope that "these base calumniators shall be called to an account."

Blunt threws plenty of verbal grenades in this letter to Stanton, but not once did he address the actual issues that were the cause of all this trouble. He never explaind why he tried to give Easton orders in the first place or why he had to go around the chain of command. Rather than directly attack the charges of fraud and corruption, Blunt trotted out his battlefield record. He failed to justify any of his administrative actions as district commander, which seemed to be the cause of Schofield's concern. He even omitted specifics when he made his vicious accusations against Easton, Carney, and the rest.

Blunt didn't seem to understand that his case would have been strengthened by making his situation as clear as possible. If these charges against him were false, he had a responsibility to provide explanations for his decisions and actions. By the same token, if the charges he made against his opponents were true, he needed to state any facts that could support them.

These omissions strongly suggest that Blunt had no such reasons or facts to support his case. Without such ammunition Blunt chose to cite his war record, irrelevant to the matters at hand, and to insult those who he believed were his political opponents. The letter suggests a man with a guilty conscience or a man so egotistical that he didn't take these charges against him seriously.

Two days later Blunt wrote to Governor Carney to tell him that he knew Carney had gone to Washington to present charges against him. He demanded that Carney "present said charges to the President with as little delay as possible, and prepare yourself to substantiate them." He closed his letter by saying that he had "for the present disposed of the open enemy in my front, and I now propose to attend to *thieves* and secret assassins in my rear."

For his part, Governor Carney would continue to protest Blunt's actions over the Fourteenth Kansas. As late as November 16 he was writing to Stanton to explain his side and fight what he perceived as an attack on his authority as governor. In the meantime Blunt had continued his letter-writing campaign by appealing directly to the top. On July 31 he wrote a long letter to Pres. Abraham Lincoln. The ostensible cause for this letter was Carney's trip to Washington. Blunt believed that Carney was accusing Blunt of being tied to the Red Legs, that Blunt was supporting their raids, and that he had even shared in some of their ill-gotten gains from defenseless citizens.

Blunt replied to these allegations by denouncing Carney as a thief and liar and assuring that he had proof of his allegations. He repeated his charge that Carney had taken part in the plunder of refugee Indians, and added that Carney was trying to make Blunt's command subservient to Carney's political goals. He also repeated his insults of Easton and Roy. He said they were aided by Schofield who, Blunt claimed, was an imbecile and a coward. In his defense to the president, Blunt again brought up his record of victories and his requests for reinforcements for Colonel Phillips's command in the territory. He even hinted that if he couldn't deal with his political enemies through legal means, he might take extralegal action once out of the service, perhaps suggesting settling the dispute by duels!

Lincoln replied to Blunt on August 18, reassuring the general that while Carney had left "some papers" with him, Lincoln hadn't felt overly impressed by them. He added that those papers may not have been as harsh as Blunt was assuming. Lincoln expressed dismay with Blunt's denouncing so many people and with the language that he was using. Lincoln also told Blunt he was dissatisfied only with Blunt's part in the Atchison incident and his submission to "Judge Lynch."

More than a month later, Blunt replied to Lincoln's letter with a much more subdued tone. He presented a new version of his charge against Schofield, adding that his denunciations merely reflected the views of many ordinary Kansans. As to the Atchison hangings, Blunt said that he believed that the hangings had a "salutary" effect and that the people agreed with him.

Lincoln did not reply to that letter, but early in his previous message he had asked Blunt, "Your position looks critical, but did anybody force you into it?" Indeed it was critical for Blunt was once again on campaign in the Indian Territory. Once again he was facing a strong Confederate army. And once again the balance of power in the trans-Mississippi theater hinged upon the outcome of battles in the region.

CHAPTER 10

Greater Glory

Back on February 23, Blunt had ordered Colonel Phillips in Fort Gibson to contact the tribes that had turned toward the Confederacy. He told Phillips to promise them pardons and protection. He also expressed the intention to retake the rest of Indian Territory. He said he was already talking to the superintendent of Indian Affairs to arrange for the delivery of seeds so that once the campaign was over the tribes could plant crops and feed themselves, refugees, and the troops in the field protecting them.

Phillips had taken a position in Fort Gibson to maintain Union control over the Indian Territory. The withdrawal of Union forces in Arkansas, combined with the renewed vigor of the Confederate resistance in the territory, placed Phillips in danger. On March 3, Phillips asked Blunt to allow him to engage nearby Confederate forces despite his admission that forage for his animals was low. In April, Blunt cautioned Phillips not to cross the Arkansas River, but not to wait to be attacked either.

The prospect of another Blunt campaign in the territory had some Confederate generals nervous. On March 31, Brig. Gen. William Steele, commanding at Fort Smith, wrote to his superior, Gen. T. H. Holmes, that he believed Blunt was planning a march south. He said, "Whether I have anything to fear from him depends upon the strength with which he moves." In anticipation of this move, on April 1 the Confederate government in Richmond gave Stand Waite the authority to raise a brigade to protect against the Union incursion.

In early April the rebel troops skirmished with Phillips's men. Blunt warned Curtis about these actions and expressed concern that instead of marching back to Missouri, this presaged an invasion of Kansas. He said he gained this intelligence by infiltrating spies in a pro-Confederate, secret organization called "Knights of the Golden Circle." The scale of the situation was brought home to Blunt personally when on May 6 he was informed that his uncle and good friend Rufus Gilpatrick was killed in a rebel attack. According to Phillips, Gilpatrick died during an engagement while he was giving aid to a wounded rebel soldier. Gilpatrick lost his life while carrying out his duty as a doctor, not as a soldier.

No one knows how Gilpatrick's death might have affected Blunt, but it had to have been a terrible blow. Aside from being his uncle, Gilpatrick was the man who had encouraged Blunt to come to Kansas. They had fought together in Bourbon County before the war. Gilpatrick was even married to a sister of Blunt's wife. Blunt certainly grieved for Gilpatrick, but the mourning period must have been short, for the war required his attention.

Colonel Phillips's situation in the territory was deteriorating. On May 9, Phillips wrote to Blunt that he was running out of supplies and that the recruiting of two more Indian regiments had suffered as a result. His men were still in good spirits, though, and he had strengthened his defenses. He also proposed to rename the fort Fort Blunt. Phillips concluded with a plea for more food saying, "a command that has behaved so well deserves better than to be half starved."

Two days prior, the commander at Fort Scott had reported that bushwhackers were increasing their raids. Among other things, they were threatening the wagon trains carrying supplies between that fort and Fort Gibson. That officer stated that he was pleased to hear that Blunt had established a post at Baxter Springs to increase protection of the supply trains.

While this trouble was transpiring in the Indian Territory, Blunt seems to have expressed concerns about the loyalty of the Osage tribe, which held a large reservation in southern Kansas. Indian refugees had been crossing back and forth over their land, and Blunt may have thought that some of those refugees could have been spies or provocateurs. But on May 17, P. P. Elder from the Neosho Indian Agency office reassured Blunt that the Osages were indeed loyal. He said that two days earlier they had intercepted a party of "robbers" and killed them. These robbers would later be revealed as a group of Confederate officers and recruiters.

With that situation under control, Blunt's attention was drawn back to Phillips and "Fort Blunt." Union supply trains were still under threat, and on June 20, Phillips sent a force to meet one such train en route to the fort. He reported to Blunt that a rebel force was only a few miles away.

Those Confederates were under Douglas Cooper and Stand Watie. They decided to intercept this supply train despite a warning from their superior that Blunt might launch a surprise attack on his camp while Cooper's men were dealing with Union wagon trains.

To bring in the train safely, Phillips dispatched Col. James Williams and the First Kansas Colored to Baxter Springs. The First had been in training for some time, and by now they felt ready to enter the war as a unit. At Baxter Springs they joined the wagon train and moved south, aided by the Second Colorado Infantry, companies from the Ninth and Fourteenth Kansas, and the Second Kansas Battery. They would be further assisted by the Third Indian Home Guards, who were coming north from the fort to meet them.

The escort left Baxter Springs on June 26 and traveled unhindered until they reached Cabin Creek at noon on July 1. There they were attacked by Cooper's and Stand Watie's forces, positioned on the opposite bank where the train had to cross the creek. For the first time during the Civil War, black and white units would fight side by side.

Williams began the battle by firing his artillery at his enemy. Since he had discovered that the creek was too high to cross, he decided to wait one day to force a crossing. At 8 A.M. the next day, Williams resumed his artillery barrage. The Confederates pulled back and Williams began sending his men across Cabin Creek. As his advance was reaching the opposite bank, the Confederates fired their small arms. The Union major in command was wounded and his troops retreated.

Williams had his men return fire and sent new troops to cross the stream, including elements of the Ninth Kansas and the First Kansas Colored. This time they pushed the rebels back four hundred yards to a new position. The Union forces attacked the new line and drove the rebels from the field. Williams had about six hundred men under him; he estimated Confederate strength at sixteen hundred to eighteen hundred. His losses were three killed and forty wounded; the Confederates had around a hundred casualties. During the

Summer Campaign, 1863

battle the white soldiers and officers "allowed no prejudice" of the blacks to get in the way of fighting the rebels. Federal artillery once again played a decisive role, but just as important was the fact that Cooper's fifteen hundred Arkansans couldn't cross a flooded stream to assist Watie's men.

At John Speer's new Lawrence paper, the *Kansas Weekly Tribune,* Blunt was reported as now wanting to drive the rebels "into Texas." Speer added, "We expect to hear from 'somebody hurt' in that region." The next week Speer wrote that Blunt's army was "as gallant a body of men as ever pursued an enemy," and he predicted that they "will not be likely to be surprised or whipped."

On July 5, Blunt decided to march to support Phillips with all the men he could assemble. His relief force included the Second Kansas Battery, the First Kansas Colored, and the Second Colorado Infantry. Blunt left without his supply trains, his men carrying just six days worth of rations. He also left without his staff, except for Col. Thomas Moonlight and Capt. William Tholen. In reporting on the Cabin Creek battle, the *Conservative* echoed the *Tribune's* hopes by saying, "Stirring news may soon be expected from the Arkansas."

Blunt marched from Fort Scott to Fort Blunt in five days, covering some one hundred seventy-five miles. He marched as soon as word arrived of the action at Cabin Creek. He had with him four howitzers, eight field cannons, and between three thousand and four thousand men. En route Blunt decided to attack Cooper while he was moving toward the fort. Writing at the time, Wiley Britton speculated that if Blunt routed the Confederates, Blunt's allies would give him the glory, even though he thought Phillips deserved some of it.

A correspondent from the *Conservative* was full of praise when describing Blunt's arrival at the fort. He reported that Blunt had arrived on a mule, his three (not two) staff members on horses, and all without wagons. Two of the three staff officers had had to draw uniforms upon arrival because they were not expecting to march south. The correspondent told his readers, "no General in the Federal army is more respected, esteemed and beloved by his troops, than General Blunt." The men he had arrived to command were veterans who had served under him before and were willing to go wherever Blunt led. Blunt had reportedly told Phillips not to fire his guns in a salute to him because that would waste ammunition. Blunt also sent word to his soldiers not to let the rebels know he was there; apparently he thought they would run off in fear when they learned that Blunt was on the scene!

The reporter took this chance to editorialize on the war's progress. He wondered why Union generals in the West were often outnumbered and still successful while Eastern generals had many men but failed to win. Why were two regiments sitting in Rolla, Missouri doing nothing, he asked, when the fort "was the only point in General Schofield's Department" under threat? Blunt had very little with which to "whip all creation"; however, the reporter reassured his readers, Blunt was prepared to fight with what he had and would do his best.

When Blunt arrived at Fort Gibson on July 11, Phillips organized a reception in his honor. At the evening reception Phillips praised Blunt for his victories in Arkansas the previous fall. He said that Blunt's presence alone would deter the Confederates from camping too close to the fort.

Blunt then spoke, telling his audience of his swift move to support Phillips. He praised Phillips and his men for their bravery at Cabin Creek. He reported the Union victories at Gettysburg and Vicksburg days earlier. He expressed confidence that with the capture of Vicksburg, the Union forces that had been sent from the department at Fort Gibson would return. With those troops back in the region, a new offensive south could be seriously considered.

The first step in that new offensive came when Blunt decided to drive back Cooper's Confederates in the area. He believed Cooper's full strength was around six thousand soldiers. Though Blunt was apparently sick with a "burning fever," he nonetheless started out after Cooper.

He marched from Fort Gibson on July 15 with around three thousand men, and on that day and the next, he drove back rebel pickets and cavalry. He found Cooper's main body late on July 16 at Honey Springs, some twenty-five miles from the fort. Blunt formed his force into two columns and on the morning of July 17 sent them forward. He kept his men massed so Cooper would be unable to gauge how many men he had. When his force was within a quarter of a mile of the Confederate line, Blunt had his men deploy, and in five minutes they were in line to advance on their opponents.

Cooper, in his report of August 12, claimed that early in the battle he pushed the Union advance back. A rainstorm suddenly stopped the battle, but after the rain ended the Union troops attacked again. One rebel unit mistook orders and left a bridge over Elk Creek undefended. Small parties then started giving way, followed by Cooper's whole army. Further hurting Cooper's chances was that he only had four cannons against Blunt's twelve. What was worse, some Confederate gunpowder got wet during the rainstorm, perhaps because it was an inferior grade of powder.

Not that the Federals, especially the black soldiers, didn't do their part in defeating the Confederates. The First Kansas Colored held the center of the Union advance. They marched to within fifty yards of the rebel line and exchanged fire for twenty minutes, until the rebel line collapsed. The collapse of the Confederate line may have been precipitated by one of the Union Indian regiments, which got between the First and the Twenty-ninth Texas Cavalry. The Indians, of course, pulled back to avoid the crossfire. When the Indian regiment drew back, the Texans assumed all the Federals were retreating and charged. However, the black soldiers held their ground, shot up the Texans badly, and forced the Texans backward. This had the effect of destabilizing Cooper's center, which caused him to disengage and fall back.

In his report after the battle, Blunt said that the Texans had entered the battle with three hundred men and left the field with only sixty. He said that the men of the First had "fought like veterans." A month later he further praised the First as "better soldiers in every respect than any troops I have ever had under my command."

Blunt reported about 80 casualties; he estimated rebel losses at 150 killed, 400 wounded, and about 80 captured. Reportedly, one of the Union wounded was Colonel Williams, the commander of the First. Taken from the rebels were 2 cannons, 500 small arms, 5,000 pounds of flour, and about the same amount combined of salt, meat, and sugar. Also supposedly taken from the rebels were a few hundred handcuffs to be used by the Confederates to lead the black soldiers back into slavery.

After the battle at Honey Springs, the Confederates retreated to

Fort Smith. Although getting sicker every day, Blunt stayed in command and wanted more troops so that he could take the fort. The Confederates were worried about such a move; however, they were also worried that sending troops back into the territory would leave Texas exposed to Blunt. At least one rebel officer was conceding that Blunt's Indian regiments were better armed and had better white officers than theirs.

General Schofield was also concerned about Blunt, but not for the same reason. On July 24 he wrote to Maj. H. Z. Curtis in Fort Scott that he thought Blunt was too far south. General Grant was sending a force up the Arkansas River, and Schofield wanted Blunt to pull back and wait for Grant. On July 30, Blunt wrote to Schofield that, despite being outnumbered three thousand to eight thousand or nine thousand, he was going to attack the Confederates as soon as an ammunition train arrived at Fort Blunt. He said he preferred to attack than to wait to be attacked. He also reported that there were only a few hundred men holding Fort Smith for the rebels.

Schofield did send troops into southwestern Missouri to open communications with Blunt. He refused to send them all the way to Blunt for fear of leaving that part of Missouri defenseless to guerrillas. For this refusal, Schofield was again hammered by the newspapers in Kansas, and on August 14 the *Conservative* wrote, "The pro-slavery policy, which controls at St. Louis, seems determined to sacrifice the Kansas army, to surrender the Indian country, and to open Kansas to the raids of red and white rebels." This tone would carry on throughout the late summer and fall to the point that, on October 24, the *Conservative* would actually encourage giving opium to reluctant generals on the theory that Union general Rosecrans in Tennessee took opium, which had made him eager to fight and pursue rebels.

Though Blunt was quite willing to engage the enemy, his illness during the campaign may have been smallpox or cholera, and it left him so sick at one point that he couldn't ride his horse. He could still communicate, however, and he wrote to Daniel Wilder at the *Conservative*. Parts of that letter appeared in the *Leavenworth Times* via the *State Journal* in an attempt to undermine Blunt. The excerpts centered around Blunt's supposedly telling Wilder that the black soldiers of the First were the best troops he had ever commanded. This attempt at undermining Blunt was confusing because the article is not clear why Blunt's statements are wrong; perhaps the writer of the story objected to Blunt's opinion that the black soldiers were better than the whites he had commanded.

A more clear effort at harming Blunt's reputation came a few sentences later. The author of the article claimed that Blunt used the "personal pronoun 'I'" at least "twice in every line." Blunt's men were credited with having done "a little fighting," though the general was always the victor. It may not have occurred to the article's writer that without leadership soldiers are little better than a mob. He then concluded that upon reading Blunt's missive, he was tempted to suggest that all major generals "drive out the fussy and mealy-mouthed scribblers for the newsprints, and henceforth do their own correspondence."

No doubt the author was being sarcastic, but he probably didn't realize the irony of his comments. Here was one such a "scribbler" lobbing insults at General Blunt—but to what end? Most likely the writer hoped to damage the reputation of that general and the politicians who kept him in command. Thus the author's motives in commenting on the letter are just as suspect as Blunt's were in writing the original letter to Wilder. Such was the devolving political situation in Blunt's home state.

Blunt was well enough to write another personal letter, this one to Maj. H. Z. Curtis. Unlike most of Blunt's personal correspondence, this letter to Curtis has survived to the present. The letter not only reveals Blunt's plans in the first half of August but also gives a glimpse into Blunt's private life and views.

Blunt began his letter by telling Curtis that he had been waiting for mail. Two nights previous, two messengers had arrived in Blunt's camp, but they had only one letter. On the positive side, that letter was from Blunt's wife Nancy. He asked Curtis if he was sending mail separately or with the supply trains. He told Curtis, "If you only knew how *hungry* we poor mortals get for news from America, you would send me mail often."

After telling Curtis of some confused and delayed mail deliveries, he turned to the situation that faced him at "Fort Blunt." He planned to "pitch into" the Confederates as soon as a supply train arrived. He said all his men were eager for action, including the "first nigger." He thought he would have about thirty-five hundred men to put up against nine thousand rebels. He said he had been ordered to fall back, and while he didn't want to take great risks, his men were ready to fight and expected to win.

"I only fear one thing," he wrote. His fear was that "if Holmes & Price should be defeated in central Arkansas and fall back to [the] Red River, Steele, Cooper and Cabell will follow suit before I get ready to give them a lick."

Blunt vowed to pursue the rebels and chase them at least as far as the Canadian River. He would then push down to Fort Smith and "gobble up all the buck-negroes that will make good soldiers." He conceded that this might be "counting the chickens before they are hatched," but his confidence was unshaken. He thought there was plenty of forage to last his army to December, passing along word that locals believed they would have the best harvest in twenty years.

Of course, Blunt could not help but complain about his rivals. In this case he expressed to Curtis his displeasure at the price he had to pay for the corn to feed his army's stock animals. He said that had he contracted the corn at half the price he paid, he "would have been declared a D—D *fraud*" by "*Carney* the *Immaculate.*"

Returning to the possibility of taking Fort Smith, Blunt told Curtis that if he and his staff wanted good "accommodations" he would have to "*put in your requisitions soon with plans and specifications.*" Specifically, he meant, "the number of *female servants* you will require." Blunt then wondered if Carney would allow such "luxuries" if not consulted, "*as I believe the Constitution of Kansas gives him control of such things.*" He said he had to forgo such "luxuries" for the present; "*As Jim Lane would say: 'I have been running strictly on my virtues.'*"

For years there were accusations that Blunt consorted with prostitutes, or "female servants," during the war. For proof most invoked the *State Journal* letter of February 12, 1863. As was stated before, that letter was hardly an accurate view of the situation at the time. But this letter of Blunt's, tucked away in the Moonlight collection at the Kansas State Historical Society, is evidence that cannot be contradicted. Later in life Blunt would pay for his adulterous dalliances, but during his war years, his romps were the subject of jokes and fun.

Blunt continued his letter by telling Curtis that he wanted to write to Moonlight and his staff, but he didn't have time. He asked Curtis to copy his letter, send it to Moonlight, and show it to his staff and to the "B'hoys." It is this copy that has survived and provides the best picture of Blunt the person.

Blunt then told Major Curtis that he had been keeping up with the stories in the newspapers. He passed along word to Curtis that he had read of General Ewing's "gay time" in the District of the Border, and that Ewing had little to do. Interestingly Blunt wrote, "If [Ewing] has no bad luck and continues to win laurels, . . . I think his name will be handed to posterity as a 'Hero' over the rest." This statement is underlined, but whether it was by Blunt at the time of the letter's writing or later by Curtis may never be known.

We can see that despite his feuds Blunt was confident in the wake of his victory at Honey Springs. The Confederates might have had more men, but his army had the momentum. Fort Smith was his ultimate goal, and if that fell, Union control would be extended through half of Arkansas and most of the Indian Territory. All Blunt had to do was march out of the hort and go back on the offensive.

To that end, on August 22 Blunt had marched from Fort Blunt to attack the Confederates who were sixty miles away, along the Canadian River. Blunt's army arrived there two days later only to find that their enemy had retreated. On August 25 he learned of a rebel force at Perryville, about twenty miles south, and he sent three cavalry regiments to attack the Confederates in that area.

The village was an important Confederate supply depot. When the Union troops arrived they captured much and destroyed even more. One of the Confederate commanders there, Brig. Gen. William Steele, reported that he was having problems inducing his Indian regiments to march to his aid or prevent their soldiers from deserting. In the wake of Cabin Creek, Honey Springs, and Perryville, the Confederate hold on the rest of the Indian Territory was slipping away.

On August 31, Blunt discovered twenty-five hundred Confederates several miles from his camp, along the Poteau River. He sent a detachment under Colonel Cloud to attack them. The

Col. W. F. Cloud. Cloud commanded units under Blunt during his 1862 fall campaign, most notably at Cane Hill and Prairie Grove. *Photograph courtesy the Kansas State Historical Society, Topeka, Kansas.*

Col. Thomas Moonlight. Moonligh served as an officer on Blunt's staff anc commanded units under Blunt *Photograph courtesy the Kansas Stat Historical Society, Topeka, Kansas.*

Confederates had formed up on Backbone Mountain, and Cloud attacked on September 1. After a three-hour battle, the rebels were driven off the mountain in an action called either the battle of Backbone Mountain or the Devil's Backbone. Supposedly the rebels retreated when a Texas sergeant misunderstood an order to "lie down," yelled that the general had said "Light out," and started running away.

Three months later, in his report on the campaign, the Confederate general in command wrote that during this battle three infantry regiments and one cavalry battalion fled as soon as it had begun. Afterward his army was plagued with desertions. Even worse for the Confederacy, as a result of the battle Federal forces occupied Fort Smith for the first time since the Civil War started.

Blunt confidently told Schofield on September 11 that "the entire Indian Territory and Western Arkansas" were under his control and that the rebels had been driven to Texas. He asked Schofield to send more supply trains south and requested that if Little Rock was taken, Schofield should also send boats up the Arkansas River with supplies. He even thought it possible to string up a telegraph line to Fort Smith.

Wiley Britton would later write that Blunt's campaign had left the Confederate leadership and their Indian allies "in amazement and deep discouragement." No doubt they were further discouraged on September 10, when Blunt sent word to the people of western Arkansas that Fort Smith was again in Union hands. In this message he made it known that he would protect Union supporters. If the population chose to "disenthral [themselves from] tyranny and oppression" and organize a loyal government, he would support them in their efforts.

As the autumn of 1863 arrived, Blunt's status could not have been higher. In a series of small battles he had cleared the Indian Territory of all but irregular guerilla forces. Fort Smith had been taken, cementing Union domination of northern and western Arkansas. He had proven his doubters wrong time and again. His promotion to major general was now entirely justified.

Back in the spring of 1863, four companies of cavalry had been recruited. The companies were then caught in the dispute between Governor Carney and Senator Lane over the appointments of officers. Ultimately, those companies were formed into the Fourteenth Kansas. By the fall of 1863, elements of the Fourteenth were assigned as General Blunt's personal escort, and at the start of October they were in Fort Scott, waiting for their charge to move south

Blunt's headquarters for his District of the Frontier were to be moved to Fort Smith for a short time. Before he moved to Fort Smith the people of Fort Scott held a party in his honor. Confidence was high that the rebel threat was diminishing, and combined with the victories at Vicksburg and Gettysburg, it is not hard to imagine that partygoers believed the Civil War would soon end. Blunt himself may have felt that way, for around October 1 he announced plans to join a group from Fort Scott that would attend the state fair. Blunt even promised to bring his new brigade band with him to the fair.

Blunt's military band, just before leaving Fort Scott in October 1863. General Blunt, dressed in light-colored clothes, is on the far right. Almost all the members of the band would die days later at the Baxter Springs Massacre. This picture survived thanks to one of the survivors of the massacre and was later put on a card and sold to benefit the Fort Scott Grand Army of the Republic post. *S. A. Douthit photograph, courtesy the Baxter Springs Heritage Center and Museum, Baxter Springs, Kansas.*

But first he had to move his command south. His party left Fort Scott on October 4 with the band and his aides in tow. He planned to visit Fort Gibson first, then continue to Fort Smith. The move required the group to bring the papers and records of the District Headquarters. That same day the wife of Major Curtis left to return to her home in Iowa. Curtis did not return with her; instead he rode with Blunt and the wife of the brigade quartermaster in Blunt's carriage.

The hope was for the column to march fifteen to twenty miles before stopping for the night. Wiley Britton, writing in his daily journal, thought that Blunt would reach Baxter Springs late on October 5. Baxter Springs, the location of a small defensive post, was almost on the southern border of Kansas. Stationed at this post were elements of the Second Kansas Colored Infantry and the Third Wisconsin Cavalry. Although close to Missouri and the Indian Territory, the post was a quiet one and the horrors of war had not yet touched it.

CHAPTER 11

Baxter Springs

There were hints during the previous days that the Union forces at Baxter Springs might be in some danger. Around the third or fourth week of September two civilian mail carriers working along the route from Fort Scott to Fort Gibson were attacked. The leader of the attackers was one of William Quantrill's men, Cy Gordon. He had recognized one of the carriers and spoken to him. From Gordon, the carrier learned that Quantrill's men were short of supplies and that in ten days or so they would need to take some from the nearest Union post. The carrier rode into the small fort at Baxter Springs and told the post commander, Lieutenant Cook of the Second Kansas Colored. Other rumors of rebel and guerrilla activity were already circulating through Kansas in early October. The *Chief* all the way up in White Cloud reported on October 8 that the telegraph wires were hot with reports of marches by rebels or guerillas on either Fort Scott or on Kansas City.

On the morning of October 6, Cook sent forage parties from his company and from two companies of the Third Wisconsin Cavalry, one of which had arrived two days earlier under the command of Lt. James Pond. At noon the post was attacked without warning by rebel guerillas under Quantrill. The Union troops fought back fiercely. Cook was killed, but Pond, who had taken command of the post upon his arrival, managed to avoid Cook's fate. During the fight, Pond manned the fort's lone cannon by himself, firing off three rounds. Within half an hour the battle was over, though ten soldiers had been killed and several more were wounded. The one black soldier killed was shot by his former master, whom he had recognized. Another man was shot by a friend after trying to surrender.

Unaware of the desperate struggle at the post were Gen. James Blunt, his staff, the brigade band, and his escort. Approximately four hundred yards from the post Blunt stopped his column. In front of him were about one hundred men wearing Federal uniforms. At first everyone assumed they were from the fort. But when Blunt noticed confusion among the "Federals," he ordered his escort into line. At that point the raiders opened fire on the column.

Blunt ordered his men to fire back, only to see many of them fleeing in panic. The raiders charged, some three hundred men attacking Blunt's party. Blunt and Major Curtis tried to rally their men but only pulled fifteen men together a mile and a half from where the attack had begun.

Blunt and Curtis helped the quartermaster's wife to mount a horse. All three rode away, the young woman riding for the first time in her life. The trio came to a gully. Blunt and the woman's horse jumped, but Curtis's flinched, having been shot. The horse fell, and shortly thereafter Curtis was shot in the head and died instantly.

The wagon with the musicians had attempted to reach the fort. The driver realized the danger, however, and he turned his team west and fled. Unfortunately, the wagon struck a hole about a mile from where the attack began, lost its front wheel, and knocked the musicians to the ground. Quantrill's men killed as many of them as they could. For some reason, perhaps pure spite, the guerillas then set the wagon on fire.

The small group that Blunt had rallied was able to fight off Quantrill's men. Once the raiders were gone Blunt sent a lieutenant and six men to Fort Scott for additional soldiers. Later Blunt took the survivors to Pond's fort. He arrived with only three other men in his escort still alive.

At first Blunt assumed that Pond's men had been wiped out in the attack, which is supposedly the reason he didn't immediately make for the fort. This explanation is backed by the first report of the attack in the *Conservative*. A man in Leavenworth received a letter from his brother at Fort Scott, which he passed along to the paper. The letter claimed that Blunt's staff, his escort, and Pond's men had been captured.

The first inkling that Pond had of the attack on Blunt's group came from Maj. B. S. Henning, Blunt's provost marshal and member of the Third Wisconsin. During the attack Henning noticed that the raiders were attacking from an angle that suggested they

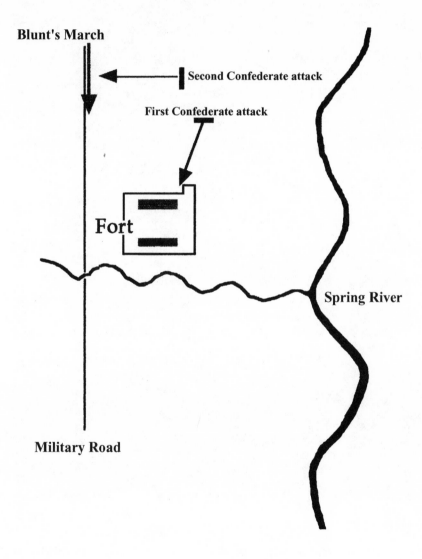

The Baxter Springs Massacre
October 6, 1863

Blunt's March

Second Confederate attack

First Confederate attack

Fort

Spring River

Military Road

Maj. H. Z. Curtis, son of Gen. Samuel Curtis and an officer on Blunt's staff. Major Curtis was among the many Union casualties at the Baxter Springs Massacre. A fort in central Kansas, Fort Zarah, would later be named for him. *From the collection of Dr. Tom and Karen Sweeney, General Sweeny's Museum, Republic, Missouri.*

had missed Pond's camp. On his own Major Henning decided to make a run for Baxter Springs. He slipped past the guerrillas and was even able to liberate a few prisoners who had been taken from Pond's command. When he reached the post, Henning asked Pond to assist Blunt's escort, but Pond had no men available for the task.

At 2 P.M. George Todd, one of Quantrill's guerilla leaders, appeared at Pond's camp with a flag of truce. Todd requested an exchange of prisoners, claiming to have thirteen captives. Pond suspected Todd's motives and refused to parley. Pond was right for later he discovered that the guerrillas had taken no prisoners. Despite the reality, rumors of prisoners persisted for days after the massacre.

Other Union witnesses to the aftermath of the massacre stated that most of the men killed had been shot through the head. Most of the dead had as many as a half-dozen separate bullet wounds. Some of the bodies were observed as being mutilated, and several were thought to have been shot after surrendering. Among the dead was James O'Neal, artist-correspondent for *Leslie's Illustrated Newspaper,* and Maj. H. Z. Curtis, Blunt's assistant adjutant general and the son of Gen. Samuel Curtis.

After the war John Edwards claimed that Curtis was captured alive and unhurt. He said that Quantrill had found an order in Curtis's pocket approving the execution of Quantrill's men if any should be captured. Quantrill supposedly asked Curtis if he would have obeyed that order, and when Curtis replied in the affirmative, he was shot. Edwards also claimed that in O'Neal's possession was a "hypothetical" illustration of Yankees running down Confederates. Though Edwards used this illustration to justify O'Neal's execution, his reason stretches credibility since Confederate soldiers had just killed unarmed musicians in the massacre.

A far darker account of Confederate actions emerged in the *Leavenworth Times* on October 21. An author who seemed to have spoken to survivors wrote to that paper that captured men were shot and killed, even the wounded. He further wrote, "One fiend was seen to dismount and feel the pulse of an inanimate wounded soldier and with cold-blooded, fiendish malignity place his pistol's muzzle against the head of the poor unfortunate and discharge it."

Only about a dozen of the wounded Union men survived, all by feigning death and creeping away in the dark. One man staggered into the fort with five bullet wounds to the face. A sergeant of the Third Wisconsin claimed he was shot by Quantrill himself. The total losses in the two attacks were one hundred and one Federals killed, compared with the loss of only two of Quantrill's men. All of Blunt's papers were taken, and he lost about fifteen hundred dollars in personal property. It also seems that the dead and wounded were stripped and robbed by Quantrill's Confederates.

The next day, reinforcements arrived from Fort Scott. In the immediate aftermath of the massacre, Blunt sent word to Fort Gibson and Fort Smith that Quantrill was on the loose with six hundred men. He ordered that men be sent out to intercept Quantrill before his force could reach the Arkansas River. But Quantrill's men escaped across the river relatively unhindered.

After the battle Quantrill is believed to have said, "By God, Shelby could not whip Blunt; neither could Marmaduke, but I whipped him." His men captured ten supply wagons, two Union flags, and Blunt's sword. Also taken was a flag given to Blunt by some Leavenworth civilians. Quantrill, in his report, said nothing about killing men after they had given up or about killing wounded men. He did claim to have captured Pond's camp, which did not happen at any point during the attack. Although it was not in his official report, Quantrill is supposed to have said that Blunt was killed in this raid.

Other claims, charges, and statements surfaced in the wake of the massacre. All put their own spin on the events, including General Blunt. Blunt wrote that his inadvertent arrival interrupted Quantrill's planned attack on Pond's camp. He believed that this interruption allowed Pond to mount an effective defense. Blunt later stated that he believed that if his escort had stood their ground, he could have driven off Quantrill's men.

Wiley Britton would also write about Baxter Springs. Britton had heard that during the attack on his escort, Blunt had assumed Pond's men had been captured. Britton believed that if Blunt had known the fort was not captured, he would have fought to reach it. He also noted that Pond didn't know that Quantrill's men were attacking Blunt's party, and that if he had known, he might have attacked the raiders in order to relieve Blunt. Britton did not think the affair a blunder on Blunt's part, but an accident. Blunt was still

William C. Quantrill, the most feared of all the region's Confederate guerillas. At Baxter Springs in 1863 his men almost wiped out Blunt's escort. Afterward Quantrill mistakenly claimed he had done what no other Rebel leader had accomplished: killing General Blunt. *Photograph courtesy the Kansas State Historical Society, Topeka, Kansas.*

well-liked by the men, and Britton didn't believe the massacre would diminish the soldiers' support for him.

Fifteen years later W. H. Warner of Girard wrote a narrative of the massacre for a history of the state. He was a doctor and at the time of the attack was serving at Baxter Springs. He was of the opinion that Blunt failed to take the normal precautions, such as sending out advance scouts, that a general should when traveling through open country.

The newspapers of the day also weighed in on the horror at Baxter Springs. On October 9, when the *Kansas City Journal of Commerce* first reported the attack on Blunt, it related that Blunt was captured by Jo Shelby's men. It wasn't until two days later that the paper reported what had actually transpired. While the *Journal* made no editorial comment about the massacre, the *Conservative* used this event as an opportunity to again praise Blunt's bravery and military record.

Opposing that praise was the *Council Grove Press*. In reporting the massacre, the *Press* criticized Blunt for being caught by surprise. It invoked a quote from the Duke of Wellington: "A General surprised is a General disgraced." But in some degree of fairness, the *Press* also called for the hanging of every rebel prisoner in retaliation for the massacre.

The most incendiary reporting on the massacre came from the *Leavenworth Times,* now emerging as the main organ against Senator Lane and General Blunt. Having reported the facts of the engagement on October 9 and 10, the *Times* began to editorialize on October 15. One correspondent, known only as "G," claimed that Blunt's column was attacked by between fifty and one hundred guerillas. "G" also stated that Blunt's escorts were unarmed and that their ammunition was locked in their supply wagons. This seems a suspicious accusation since there is strong evidence that Blunt's men did fire back. Someone may have disputed that account, for on October 22 "G" felt obliged to defend himself. Interestingly, in this defense, references were made to what Blunt had said in the *St. Louis Democrat,* but his words were not reported in the piece; instead readers were told to "see his letter in the Democrat."

Despite the confusing and contradictory writings, Blunt's actions at Baxter Springs on that October day were questionable at best. Certainly he had an obligation to send out advance guards while on the march. The raiding season for Confederate guerrillas wasn't yet over, and in fact they might continue to raid as Blunt traveled south. Therefore, he would have been wise to send out advance guards since he had the responsibility to protect both his men and the unarmed civilians traveling with them. Blunt's lack of caution could have arisen from information he may have received that suggested General Shelby was attempting to move into Missouri. Even though Shelby's men would have been far from the military road, Blunt should have taken precautions to prevent disasters like the one at Baxter Springs. Thus, he bears some responsbility for the catastrophe.

But to place too much blame on Blunt is essentially blaming a victim of the massacre for the massacre. Some of the blame must also fall upon the officers at Baxter Springs. They may have had warnings that a guerrilla force was near or that a raid might be imminent. If they had warnings of an attack, they had a duty to pass along those warnings to their superiors at Fort Scott. Though it might have been difficult for them to sort rumors from actual threats, in the wake of the Lawrence massacre the previous August, they should have taken any stories about guerrilla raids seriously.

The soldiers of Blunt's escort also bear some of the responsibility for the events of October 6. Blunt was probably wrong in saying that if the men had held their ground, they could have defeated Quantrill's raiders. But had they not panicked and tried to flee, they would have stood a better chance of surviving. Though outnumbered, they were soldiers, which the guerillas were not. Guerrillas tend to avoid open battles with regular soldiers. The guerrillas would have pulled back if Blunt's escort had provided a stiff enough resistance. This seems even more likely considering that there were additional soldiers behind the Confederates at Baxter Springs. They would not have allowed themselves to be pinned between two bodies of Union soldiers. Blunt's escort would have suffered casualties, but not on the scale that actually did.

Of course there would have been no massacre at all had not Quantrill and his band initiated the attack. It wasn't for nothing that Quantrill was one of, if not the most, feared guerrilla leader in the region. He was clearly a skilled leader with devoted and ferocious men under his command. He had proved himself at

Lawrence when his men had burned the town and killed over 150 men and boys. A lesser chieftain would not have had the numbers to overwhelm Blunt's escort or the reputation to terrify them.

The blame for the Baxter Springs massacre can be spread around. Many on the Union side made serious errors in judgment. These errors piled together to create the conditions for a disaster. Quantrill and his men were the match that set off the explosion. Ultimately, though, it was General Blunt's responsibility to make certain his trip would be uneventful. He should have made himself aware of the situation before he left. He should have had men escorting him south, and he should have had them ready for any contingency. Therefore any harm to his reputation in the wake of the massacre was due in part to his own failures.

No doubt the massacre was a blow to Blunt's spirits, whether he accepted any blame or not. A message that might have boosted his spirit came from the Cherokee Nation on October 21. On that day the loyal Cherokee authority sent him an official proclamation of thanks for "driving from our borders the enemies of the Cherokee people and the traitors to the Cherokee National Government." The thanks to Blunt was extended all the way back to his victory at Old Fort Wayne. The Cherokees regarded Blunt as "the true peacemaker and benefactor of the land."

Another boost may have come from John Speer in Lawrence. About two weeks after the massacre Speer's *Tribune* reprinted an article from the *Boston Journal* that praised Blunt and General Steele in command against Sterling Price in Arkansas. Blunt had raced through the Indian Territory, cleared "more than 100,000 square miles" of area of rebel forces, and was taking control of the territory while Steele was besting Price and seizing Little Rock.

On the Confederate side, most believed Quantrill's pronouncement that Blunt was dead. But by November Price had learned otherwise when he read in some newspaper that Blunt had been recalled to Fort Leavenworth. While they were still concerned about the feisty general on the loose, Blunt's superiors were becoming exasperated with argumentative commander and his questionable practices.

CHAPTER 12

An Unpleasant Man

On October 24, Senator Lane spoke at the Wilder House in Fort Scott, and following his address, Blunt spoke briefly. Wiley Britton was there, and he observed that Blunt wasn't much of a public speaker. At that time, however, he was unlikely to be in an ideal mood to speak. He was no doubt still touchy about the massacre and the loss of the command of the District of the Frontier only days earlier.

Anything Blunt might have said would likely have done little to enhance or harm the fortunes of his patron Senator Lane. Blunt's victories were small compared with Gettysburg and Vicksburg. Lane himself had survived the Lawrence massacre and joined the pursuit of Quantrill. At this point his association with President Lincoln, and not with General Blunt, would have been the key to Lane's hold on power in Kansas.

In the wake of Baxter Springs, Blunt's fate had been uncertain. Britton wrote that there were discussions among the people he knew concerning whether or not Blunt would keep his command. They wondered if General Schofield might use the massacre as a pretext for removing or exiling Blunt. Of course, the allies of Blunt claimed that he outranked Schofield since Schofield's appointment to the rank of major general had not yet been confirmed. But this would be cold comfort to Blunt if Schofield did indeed force out the Kansan.

Britton, in his *Memoirs of the Rebellion on the Border*, used this situation to complain about the "continual wrangling of politicians, contractors, and sutlers." He disapproved of the charges and countercharges, and observed that such rancor could be thrown at an honest officer as much as a dishonest one. He also believed that the "moneymaking adventurers" should not be taken seriously by those who were trying to crush the rebellion.

Schofield, for one, would have considered himself serious and Blunt the adventurer. Baxter Springs or not, Schofield was determined to rid himself of the difficult general. As early as October 1, Schofield had written to General Halleck that he wanted to relieve Blunt of his command. In the days after Baxter Springs, word spread through the ranks that Blunt would be replaced by Gen. John McNeil, commander of the District of Southwestern Missouri. Schofield did indeed want McNeil to replace Blunt, but he was worried that he had no one to replace McNeil.

When President Lincoln learned of Schofield's thoughts, he asked the general to give him "the particulars of Major-General Blunt's case." Lincoln cautioned Schofield against adding to the difficulties of the Kansas situation before he could deal with another matter. That matter was a group of Kansas radicals enraged by the Lawrence massacre and their belief that Schofield had failed to prevent it.

The "case" to which Lincoln referred stemmed from the previous July when Schofield had reported irregularities in the District of the Frontier under Blunt's command. During the summer Schofield had dispatched three officers to make a special inspection of Blunt's district. Interestingly they also investigated Ewing's District of the Border. Their inspection tour was completed sometime in September, and on October 3 Schofield sent their finding to General Halleck.

Schofield explained his actions in this incident by reporting that he had found other irregularities when he had assumed command of the Department of the Missouri. To stop these irregularities, he had put officers in whom he had confidence into quartermaster and commissary positions. He had further ordered that no contracts could be made with outside firms without the approval of the chief quartermaster.

According to Schofield, the three investigating officers appear to have found instances when Blunt's staff officers were "implicated in frauds upon the Government" or had "failed to protect the Government interests entrusted to them." In his report Schofield never states what exactly Blunt's officers had done. He did admit that similar abuses existed in Ewing's district, but Schofield let him off the hook by stating that Ewing had been in command only a short time and had "labored under peculiar difficulties" that prevented him from obtaining control of his district.

This discrepancy in the treatment of the two men raises questions about why Schofield was calling for Blunt's removal but not Ewing's. If corruption existed in both districts, how was Blunt expected to deal with this problem during the summer while he was on campaign in the Indian Territory? Why wasn't Schofield holding Ewing as accountable as Blunt, especially considering that Ewing had not been as occupied as Blunt was in the summer battles? Was Blunt doing a worse job administering his district than Ewing, or was there another reason for this inequality of treatment?

Blunt, of course, believed the committee had its report written the moment it was assigned. He later accused them of not coming to talk to him in person while he was sick at Fort Smith. He claimed that they only gave a cursory "inspection" but did a great deal of drinking. However, considering that Blunt never directly addressed the committee's accusations with proof of his own, his comments should be taken with at least a few grains of salt.

A second message from Schofield on October 3 contained a few more specifics but was vague about who was being charged. Schofield asked to relieve any and all delinquent officers in his department. These delinquencies included allowing subordinate officers to be absent from their duties with or without reason; drunkenness; lack of discipline; and overall demoralization of the ranks. Schofield wanted this power so that he could punish officers who were so out of line that they were "manifestly unworthy of the consideration of a court-martial."

This request may seem extreme, but it wasn't out of character for Schofield. Days earlier, on September 30, he had asked General Halleck if he could apply one of his general orders on martial law to Kansas newspapers. He sent three clippings, two from the *Leavenworth Conservative* and one from the *White Cloud Kansas Chief.* Neither paper was aiding the rebellion; they were merely criticizing Schofield. The choice of the *Chief* seems especially odd since that paper was no friend of Senator Lane, the man who had been working so hard to get Schofield transferred from the region. Schofield's attempt to shut down the newspapers critical of him strongly hints at a self-centeredness almost as unpleasant as Blunt's.

The papers' criticism of Schofield largely dated from the events of August 21, 1863, when over 300 guerrillas under William

Gen. Thomas Ewing. Ewing was a powerful man in Kansas before the Civil War. He aspired to more power, and to that end he entered the Union army and served under Blunt. However, his victory at Pilot Knob during the Price Campaign did not garner enough publicity for him to capitalize on after the war. *Photograph courtesy the Kansas State Historical Society, Topeka, Kansas.*

Quantrill had attacked Lawrence, virtually burning the town to the ground and killing over 150 men. Schofield had sent many regular soldiers east, leaving Kansas without enough troops to prevent Quantrill's assault. Despite Schofield's support of Ewing's infamous "Order Number 11" to crack down on the guerrillas, cries for his ouster arose and were led by Senator Lane.

Ironically the Baxter Springs massacre also played into the hands of Lane and his fellow radicals. Here was more proof that Schofield was not protecting Kansas as well as he should. Lincoln ignored the radicals' claims, but it seems clear that he was losing confidence in Schofield.

Schofield was finally able to relieve Blunt on October 19, when he sent Gen. J. B. Sanborn to replace McNeil in Springfield. McNeil was to replace Blunt at Fort Smith. Blunt was then to report to Fort Leavenworth for new orders. Perhaps responding to the criticism of his leadership, Schofield increased Ewing's district to embrace all of Kansas.

The *Leavenworth Times* had reported on these reassignments as early as October 3, no doubt adding with glee that Blunt was "under arrest." The next day it claimed that Ewing would take over Blunt's command. It was not until October 21 that the paper correctly reported the development, and then it seemed to express a lack of confidence in Ewing. The *Journal of Commerce* in Kansas City supported the change, but not due to any ill will toward Blunt. Its view was that uniting Kansas with the Missouri border counties would enhance efforts to quash the guerillas.

McNeil's relieving Blunt should have been the end over the dispute between the Kansas general and his superior. But on October 28, Blunt wrote to Schofield from Fort Scott to ask if he could be relieved from that location instead of at Fort Smith, as specified by orders. He also reported that he was leaving Fort Scott with twelve hundred soldiers and three hundred wagons to reinforce Fort Gibson, which he said was again threatened by the Confederates. Blunt promised that when he was "properly relieved" he would indeed go to Fort Leavenworth for new orders.

There can be no reason for Blunt to have written this letter except to further antagonize Schofield. It was his duty, upon receipt of his superior's orders, to immediately proceed to Fort Smith. If he he was unable to stomach that, he could have written to McNeil acknowledging the new district commander, then traveled to Fort Leavenworth. For a man who months earlier had railed against an officer who remained on a burning building instead of obeying Blunt's orders, this letter smacks of hypocrisy and a disregard for the chain of command.

Indeed, in writing a report about his actions during the war, Blunt boasted that he had told McNeil to telegraph Schofield. The message told Schofield that if he wanted Blunt arrested, he should do so himself. It may have included the snide comment that if he did arrest Blunt, Schofield might finally "see a little 'active service.'"

Whether or not that message was actually sent, further conflict between the two generals arose. On November 2, William Weer, still with the Tenth Kansas, sent a message to Schofield about Blunt's departure from Fort Scott. Weer stated that Blunt's wagons were loaded with "contraband of war," which he claimed was to be sold to the rebels. Weer added that he had heard that considerable amounts of "buried treasure" were hidden in Fort Smith and Van Buren. As to why Blunt was defying Schofield, Weer said simply, "Lane has encouraged him."

Thomas Ewing in Kansas City also wrote to Schofield on November 2 about Blunt and the wagon train. Ewing didn't go as far as Weer had about the "character" of what was being transported. He did state his belief that whatever was being carried, Blunt had a financial interest in both the goods and in the contractor transporting them. Ewing also reported that the contractor, one Alexander McDonald of Fort Scott, was going to Fort Smith with an appointment to the position of sutler, though he had not been appointed by the government. Ewing said the appointment was not regular, but that Blunt planned to make it so upon arrival.

That same day, Schofield, no doubt enraged at Blunt, wrote to General McNeil about the matter. He ordered McNeil to stop the wagon the train and search it. If it did indeed carry contraband, Blunt was to be arrested. Should Blunt resist, McNeil was to put Blunt under guard and send him to Fort Leavenworth.

Apparently nothing untoward was found with that wagon train, for there was no further communication relating to it. But then, on November 24, the commander of the Sixth Kansas sent a message to Schofield via Ewing about yet another unsavory train. This one had left Fort Scott with a large load of cotton. Some of the bales of cotton were reported to have been bought at a low price, but most of it had been captured from the rebels. The commander's message ended with the speculation that "some one high in military rank was engaged in the operation." On December 1, McNeil sent word to Schofield that Blunt still had not left for Leavenworth. Instead he was raising a regiment of black troops under authority from the War Department.

An interesting view of Blunt during the last months of 1863 comes from the diary of the post chaplain at Fort Smith, the Rev. Francis Springer. Writing in mid-October, Springer said of Schofield that he had "yet to hear the first man in this army" praise him. He did not know how Blunt felt about Schofield but he suspected it wasn't good. What Springer did know was that the feud between the two generals had put the army at Fort Smith in a "destitute & perilous condition."

Sometime later in 1863, Springer's opinion of Blunt plummeted. He called Blunt a "military poltroon" who was overindulging in food, drink, and women. At one point, Blunt was dragging a young bear around town because he had seen it in an exhibit and bought it. Springer even made note of a rumor that Blunt and his staff were drunk at the time of the Baxter Springs massacre.

Springer also set down an incident that was similar to one reported in an issue of the *Freedom's Champion* much earlier in the year. According to the story, one night Blunt returned to camp from town around midnight. He was met by a guard and challenged. Blunt identified himself, but the guard refused to let him pass without getting the proper countersign. Blunt persisted that he be allowed back inside the camp, and the guard took him into custody. He was taken to the officer of the camp guard before being released. As this and the *Champion* story are similar, it is logical to conclude that the event took place. It had to have been a humbling experience for the victor of Prairie Grove and the former military master of the state of Kansas.

Other views of life at Fort Smith can be seen in letters to the *Conservative* published in December. The first was written by a correspondent. Dated December 1 and published on December 16, the letter made a brief mention of the investigating committee Schofield had sent to the fort. The author alleged that the committee was sent to write an unfavorable report. He said nothing about the other conclusions of the group, but he did say that the committee found that the First Kansas Colored had "soliderlike [*sic*] bearing and were well drilled and disciplined."

If this account is true, then it does throw some questions onto the intentions of that committee. After all, they were supposed to be investigating corruption; why would they need to review the First Kansas Colored? It could be argued that the selection of officers for the regiment might have been irregular, and the committee was looking into irregularities in Blunt's district. But the First was a Kansas regiment, and any problems with its officers should have been dealt with by state authorities, not by General Schofield. On the other hand, the account of the committee's findings on the First Kansas might not be true, but rather more pro-Lane propaganda. Nevertheless it does raise questions about Schofield's motives in dispatching that committee.

The next report from Fort Smith was dated December 7, published December 27, and written from the Thirteenth Kansas. It said that there had been an attempt to celebrate the first anniversary of the victory at Prairie Grove, but a day-long rainstorm wiped out the event. Otherwise, the *Conservative's* readers were told that General Blunt was still waiting for new orders; the soldiers were attending balls and dances; and the officers of the Thirteenth spent their time playing poker, "calling on the fair sex," and talking about who might get the next promotion to brigadier general.

This speculation led to another opinion on the subject of Blunt. "What we want most is men enough to march to the Red river," the author said, "and *Blunt* to lead us." From this it would seem that someone in Fort Smith still had confidence in the combative Kansan.

So, too, did the *Chicago Tribune,* in a piece printed in the *Conservative* two days later. The writer of that editorial expressed satisfaction with rumors of Schofield's impending ouster, saying "We may hope that some justice will be done [to] a gallant soldier whom that Incubus [Schofield] never failed to insult when an opportunity presented." That gallant soldier was Blunt, who the *Tribune* urged be allowed to chase after "Pap Price" and his "crew of raiders."

"Put Blunt at the head of eight or ten thousand troops," claimed the *Tribune,* and "we will speedily hear of a foot race South." The

Tribune blamed Schofield and Missouri conservatives for the Lawrence massacre, and demanded that such a thing not happen again. "Give Blunt a command and we shall soon see the old flag in Northeastern Texas."

The one person who was in Fort Smith and whose opinions we know of by name was Wiley Britton. Britton, still a soldier in the ranks, disagreed with these opinions about a new expedition. He didn't think Blunt would take command of any troops, not because something was wrong with the general, but because Britton believed that the Confederates had no forces nearby that could threaten Blunt into action.

Still, the prospect that Blunt might be turned loose had the Confederates in the region sweating. On November 23, General Steele wrote the adjutant general of the Trans-Mississippi Department of the number of Blunt's regiments and warned, "Should these troops . . . move down the nearest road to Red River, there is no force to resist them." That same day Steele wrote to one of his subordinates that if Blunt was in command at Fort Smith, "We shall in all probability hear from him soon."

No doubt had Blunt known the Confederates' fears, he would have crowed about this to Edwin Stanton in his next letter to the secretary of war, dated December 9. Instead Blunt offered his side of the story concerning the orders that he be relieved at Fort Smith. He claimed he was getting along with McNeil. He also claimed that the ordinary soldiers were unhappy with Schofield and that he was staying at Fort Smith to "inspire [the men] with confidence in my successor."

Blunt told Stanton that the regiment of black soldiers he had been raising was in good enough shape that it was no longer important for him to stay in Fort Smith with it. He asked for a new field assignment or permission to resign if none came. He boldly asserted that he would no longer communicate with Schofield except to charge him with incompetence and cowardice, again riding his "Fall 1862" hobby horse. He launched into a diatribe about Schofield's not having high enough rank to command him because Schofield had a record that couldn't match Blunt's own record. He spent the rest of his letter repeating his accusations about Schofield's actions the previous year.

Three days later Champion Vaughan, former editor of the

Leavenworth Conservative, told Schofield about Blunt's letter to Stanton. Vaughan knew about the letter because the day before Blunt had read it aloud at post headquarters in Fort Smith. After reading it, Blunt supposedly boasted that he had helped stall Schofield's promotion. Vaughan had defended Schofield, he said, and later heard General McNeil express his indignation at Blunt's "vulgar display." Vaughan called upon Schofield to make an example of Blunt and concluded his letter by calling for "war to the knife."

However, the very next day Vaughan sent word to Schofield that Blunt's shrill tone had subsided. How this happened Vaughan doesn't say. Vaughan did say that McNeil thought Blunt was "hand-in-glove" with local army speculators, but he had no proof. Blunt had claimed that he was in Fort Smith to turn over command to McNeil and to attend to "recruiting business." Vaughan told Schofield that neither McNeil nor "any sensible person" believed Blunt. Vaughan concluded his message by saying that Schofield was being spoken of well in Fort Smith, and that "earnest wishes [were] expressed for your final triumph over the 'embattled hosts of darkness,' to all of which do I most heartily cry, 'Amen.'"

While Vaughan might have found Schofield supporters in Fort Smith, in Kansas the general's troubles with Blunt had not enhanced his reputation among Lane and his allies. Worse for Schofield was General Shelby's successful raid into Missouri around the time of the Baxter Springs massacre. In September 1863, Price had sent a brigade under Gen. Joseph O. "Jo" Shelby back into the state. Shelby had been able to take Neosho, but he was defeated near Marshall and withdrew to Arkansas. Then late in December, Stand Watie tried to invade Kansas. They were intercepted by Colonel Phillips at Fort Gibson, but instead of retreating, Watie raided Missouri. With mounting evidence of Schofield's difficulty in suppressing rebels and guerillas, Lincoln had no choice but to dismiss him.

Schofield was sent east, put in command of the Army of the Ohio, and marched with Sherman to Atlanta. Schofield didn't follow Sherman south but remained in the area. He held off a Confederate army at the bloody battle of Franklin, Tennessee, on November 30. After the battle Schofield was ordered to retreat to Nashville. When he felt that his superior, Gen. George Thomas, didn't attack the Confederate positions around that city soon enough, Schofield sent messages behind Thomas's back to Washington. Eventually Thomas did attack and smash the barefoot and hungry rebels. Schofield, it seems, was perfectly willing to circumvent the chain of command, just as Blunt had in 1863.

Schofield would remain unpopular in Kansas into the following year. Well before the political campaign of 1864, Sol Miller at the *White Cloud Chief* had turned against Senator Lane. During the campaign the *Chief*, in its August 11 issue, published an attack on Lane, probably written by Miller. Titled "The Great Kansas Statesman," it accused Lane of associating his enemies with unpopular figures with whom they in fact were not associated. One of these unpopular men, the piece stated, was General Schofield. Lane was accused of "raising a cry" that Governor Carney was working with Schofield, and later that Carney protested against Schofield's removal. Indeed, the only newspaper in Kansas to support Schofield was that of Council Grove, and its support seemed to be for the Schofield of Wilson's Creek fame.

These editorials clearly suggest that it was not simply Lane and Blunt who drove Schofield from the region. Few in Kansas, regardless of their ties to Lane, were happy with the job that Schofield did as department commander. That Schofield didn't know or care how unpopular he had become, even with Lane's rivals and opponents, indicates just how unfit he was for this command. In the end he was unable to stop the guerrillas, make allies in Kansas, or compel Blunt to honesty.

On January 1, 1864, Samuel Curtis returned, this time as commander of the Department of Kansas. This department now embraced Kansas, Nebraska Territory, Colorado Territory, and the Indian Territory. The last territory specifically included "the military post of Fort Smith." Curtis's headquarters were to be at Fort Leavenworth.

John Speer in Lawrence expressed the sentiments of many when he wrote in the *Kansas Tribune* of January 7, "This will be glorious news to Kansas." Schofield had been a "fogy," whereas Curtis "[kept] pace with the progress of the age." Lane's other friendly paper, the *Conservative*, added to the joy by pronouncing that "General Curtis is right . . . and he will soon be here."

William S. Rosecrans was put in charge of the Department of

Gen. Samuel Curtis, Blunt's commanding officer throughout much of the Civil War. His son, Maj. H. Z. Curtis, stationed at Fort Zarah, would serve on Blunt's staff. General Curtis seemed to like Blunt, defending him against the charges of Gen. John Schofield more than once; however, Curtis could not help Blunt during his scandal at Fort Smith in early 1864. *From the collection of Dr. Tom and Karen Sweeney, General Sweeny's Museum, Republic, Missouri.*

the Missouri on January 28, 1864. Alfred Pleasonton, who had commanded the Army of the Potomac's Cavalry Corps, was transferred to the department on March 23. This reshuffling of generals could have created an infusion of energy in the region and led to a new effort to crush the rebellion in the far west. Blunt may have recognized this, for despite his troubles in Fort Smith he was again looking to get back into the field.

On January 9, Blunt was given permission to go to Washington to meet with Senator Lane and members of the Bureau of Indian Affairs. The subjects of this meeting were to be the return of Indian refugees to the territory and the move of Kansas Indians to that region. Blunt used the trip as a chance to meet in person with President Lincoln. Lincoln supposedly assured Blunt that he would give the general cooperation for a new expedition south to Texas, which no doubt was the real reason for Blunt's visit.

On February 23, Blunt was given command of the District of the Frontier, specifically those parts embracing Curtis's Department of Kansas. About a week later, Curtis wrote to Secretary Stanton about the state of affairs in the border region. Curtis reported that the people of Kansas were living in "anxious fear" of new guerrilla raids. He listed losses either in dollar amounts, deaths, or burned homes from raids on Gardner, Olathe, Shawnee, and Springfield. He expressed his hope that despite past "irregularities" Stanton would be sympathetic to the region's plight.

Curtis then brought to Stanton's attention a contradiction in the department lines that had been drawn. He cited an order from General Steele in Little Rock that designated Fort Smith as part of the Department of Arkansas. He also cited a general order from Washington that shifted the Ninth Kansas to that same department. Curtis implied that the first order seemed puzzling because it gave him control of the fort but not the nearby town of Fort Smith. He stated that the second was taking away troops that were guarding the Missouri border. He asked Stanton to give him command of these troops and of Fort Smith so as to restore the refugee Indians and to drive the Confederates into Texas. Curtis was confident that another campaign could secure Arkansas and the Indian Territory, and perhaps bring the war to Texas. Blunt, for his part in this new expedition, later claimed that he had secretly organized three thousand loyal Texans to assist the Union march south.

That same day, February 27, Curtis also wrote to General Halleck, asking for siege guns, field batteries, mountain howitzers, carbines, and revolvers. Curtis wanted this ordinance and small arms to enhance his forts, secure his supply lines, and allow his cavalry units to operate at their best. This request strongly indicates that Curtis wanted to mount another southward strike on the rebels.

Another message on that same day revealed Blunt's staff: Maj. T. J. Weed was to be an aide and head of musters (or the raising of new troops); Maj. B. S. Henning, one of the survivors of Baxter Springs, was to head Blunt's cavalry; Maj. H. H. Heath was given the job of provost marshal; Capt. J. McNutt was Blunt's chief of ordinance; and Maj. M. H. Insley was chief quartermaster.

At midnight on February 28, Halleck told Curtis that while department lines were fixed, they should not be seen as hindrances to cooperation. Curtis replied that same day that this message didn't address the problem of Fort Smith. This was a troubling problem because there was both a town of Fort Smith and an actual fort. According to all these orders, General Steele had jurisdiction over the town, while Curtis controlled a two-hundred-square-foot "stone enclosure" just outside the town. Curtis pointed out the oddity of him controlling the enclosure while soldiers within fifty miles of it belonged to another department. If this was so, Curtis expressed his preference for the words "Fort Smith" being struck from his department's description. He then repeated the list of raids on Kansas and concluded with a call for an offensive against Texas.

Perhaps because of the communication from Halleck, Curtis issued a new general order that day spelling out the districts under his command. Blunt's District of the Frontier was to cover all of Curtis's department south of the state of Kansas. Curtis advised his district commanders to cooperate with commanders of adjacent districts whenever possible.

Someone in the Fort Smith area apparently did not understand that message for on March 9, Blunt wrote to Curtis to say that Gen. John M. Thayer, commanding the Department of Arkansas' District of the Frontier, wasn't getting along with him. He asked for the district boundaries to be changed. Blunt also said that the soldiers and lower-ranked officers nearby wanted him to take

command, boasting that "they will cheerfully comply with whatever I may ask of them in defiance" of their superiors.

On March 15, Thayer sent out two messages on this situation. In
one addressed to Charles Dana, assistant secretary of war, he said
that Blunt had told Curtis that he (Thayer) had agreed with Blunt
to refer the question of jurisdiction to the War Department.
Thayer said he had not agreed and added, "There is no question
at issue between us." The other message was to his superior, Gen.
Frederick Steele, in Little Rock, and among other things it stated
the same belief that he had told Dana about jurisdiction.

That same day Curtis wrote to Halleck about the situation. He
reported that Blunt was attempting to assume command of troops
in the area, which were were obeying the department lines and
reporting to Thayer. Curtis did point out to Halleck that only his
orders could move those troops back under Blunt's command. On
March 28, Halleck told Curtis that the problem was being referred
to Stanton and newly promoted Lt. Gen. Ulysses Grant. Grant
would investigate the matter and decide what was to be done.

The cause of this problem might be found in a letter written to
the Confederate commander of the Indian Territory. On April 12,
one T. S. Scott wrote to a Gen. Samuel Maxey that he had learned
that Blunt and Colonel Cloud were maneuvering to supersede
Thayer so that they could begin another expedition. Said Scott,
"Blunt and Cloud are at Fort Smith; they will gather the means;
they have the dash—won't they make the attempt? I think so." This
perspective changed just over a week later, because on April 21, J.
B. Magruder speculated to H. E. McCulloch that Confederate victories in Louisiana might stop Blunt from advancing toward Texas.

But the real reason for Blunt's actions is suggested by a letter
written by Col. W. R. Judson, who was left in command of the
Department of Arkansas while General Steele was in the field. The
letter, written on April 7 and received by General Halleck early on
April 15, stated that Blunt had taken over the quartermaster's
office in Fort Smith. The officer Blunt had in charge of transportation and supplies was a "strong sympathizer" of the contracting
firm McDowell and Company. Judson claimed that the army was
being run for the benefit of this firm. He said that when he had
made an application to Blunt for transportation, he was refused
and insulted.

Halleck promptly forwarded Judson's telegram to General Grant. He recommended that Blunt, who he said seemed "to be a very quarrelsome man," be relieved. He pointed out to Grant that there continued to be serious accusations against Blunt. The telegram got results; two days later Secretary Stanton ordered that both the Indian Territory and Fort Smith be transferred to the Department of Arkansas. Stanton also ordered Blunt to report to Curtis in Fort Leavenworth for new orders.

On that same day, April 17, Curtis told Blunt that he thought it unlikely that any new troops would be forthcoming for any new expedition south. As the message from Stanton apparently had not yet arrived, Curtis also said that he had no resolution to the Fort Smith matter. Importantly, Curtis told Blunt not to interfere with "a single man" in any other department until this matter was cleared up.

Again Blunt disregarded this advice, for on April 18, Judson was writing to Gen. Nathan Kimball in Little Rock that the influence of the McDowell firm was growing stronger. Blunt's quartermaster was refusing to do anything without Blunt's order, "not even to the issuing of a pair of pants." Blunt had also managed to gain help from someone in Little Rock so that he could place another of his men in charge of a wagon train bringing supplies. Judson warned that if action wasn't taken, he would have to submit to Blunt's authority or allow his men to starve.

Kimball immediately wrote back that he would give orders to try to stop Blunt. He told Judson to seize any transportation in his district. He also ordered Judson to send his letter and Kimball's reply to General Halleck, and promised that he would not let Blunt interfere with Judson's command. General Steele wrote similar orders to Judson on April 18, and told Judson to inform Blunt that if he had a supply request, he could send it through the proper channels. He gave Judson permission to arrest any officer that interfered with Steele's order. Not too long after these orders were issued, Blunt was forced to resign from his command.

Blunt would later blame Halleck for the whole mess, despite the fact that he was the one causing problems. Blunt expressed the belief that Halleck hated Kansas and that he was a "special object" of Halleck's "malice." Of course Blunt never acknowledged any responsibility, nor did he admit to engaging in speculation.

Evidence contrary to Blunt's claim of innocence comes from the pen of Sol Miller in White Cloud. In a piece simply titled "On It" in the September 8, 1864, issue of the *Chief,* Miller claimed that these two words could be phrased as part of a question. If a man was "on it," he was in favor of "robbing and swindling the Government." Blunt was accused of being "on it" for having amassed a fortune of half a million dollars through his schemes. Two months later the *Oskaloosa Independent* published a similar exposé of fraud. While not naming Blunt in its story, there were strong implications in the piece that Blunt had something to do with the corruption in military supplying.

That second story also contains reasons as to why this misconduct took place. The region was far from the view of the Lincoln administration, and the information they did receive came from Senator Lane. From all accounts, Lane was at the center of the "swindle." What's more, the one senior officer who tried to correct the problem was the incompetent and unpopular General Schofield. The situation was never thoroughly dealt with, and in the end only Blunt paid a price by being ousted from command of the district.

However, Blunt's actions and responses may have hurt the reputation of his chief political patron. The attacks on corruption were part of an overall campaign against Senator Lane. His term was soon to expire, and the state legislature elected that fall would vote to fill that seat. Lane was in a heated contest with Governor Carney not only for the Senate seat but also for political control of the state Republican Party and Kansas politics. Blunt's recklessness in Fort Smith would have done nothing to help Lane and everything to hurt his chances. It is therefore probable that Lane either played some part in Blunt's removal or looked the other way instead of fighting for "his" general.

For a time in 1864, Blunt was a general without an army to lead or a campaign to wage. His name even dropped out of most newspapers. The *Tribune* mentioned his April resignation a month after it had occurred. The *Conservative* did run a piece from St. Louis that again called for Blunt to take the field, but it offered no opinion of its own on Blunt's future. When he was finally given a command a few months later, it was of a few hundred soldiers and carried the inglorious responsibility of chasing hard-to-find nomadic warriors across western Kansas.

In the meantime, the dustup at Fort Smith played a small part in the larger political war between Carney and Lane. Claims and counterclaims flew back and forth as the state's newspapers took sides. The charges of corruption against Blunt that surfaced in 1864 appeared largely in anti-Lane papers. Blunt himself was not up for any political office. His priority should have been lobbying to restore his reputation and obtain a field command. But he apparently refused to stay away from the ballot fight, and joined in a big way on July 31, 1864.

On that day the *Conservative* printed a very long letter from Blunt in which he severely denounced Carney. In response to Carney's allegations of war profiteering, favoritism, and corruption, Blunt claimed that because he had never sought high office, his judgment was far superior to the governor's. He accused Carney of bragging about his integrity while hiding any crimes he might have committed and decrying others. Blunt insisted this was something he had never done. In relation to bragging, Blunt's assertion is true, but considering the alternative that he suggests, this characteristic is hardly a virtue.

Blunt also wrote that when Carney had been nominated, he heard expressions of surprise from Republicans serving with him. The surprise was due to the fact that Carney was only a successful merchant, not an active Republican. Blunt then followed this statement onto a slippery slope by concluding that Lane's friends had voted for Carney "under protest." A disinterested observer might note that such a statement hardly made Lane look good since in 1862, Carney was Lane's candidate. On the other hand, Carney had become Lane's rival, so it might not be any fault of Lane's that he had failed to see that Carney had ambitions of his own.

Blunt's ire then turned from the political to the personal. He charged that Carney had broken promises he had made to Blunt when Carney became governor. At their first meeting in January 1863, Blunt had asked for Carney's help in changing the commissary and quartermaster officers at Fort Leavenworth. Carney had agreed to write letters supporting Blunt's position. He had also agreed to Blunt's suggestion that Carney promote officers to Kansas regiments in a "regular" way. The general went into great detail as to how the governor had broken both promises. Blunt insisted that when he took command in April 1862, the Kansas troops had been demoralized. "What I have accomplished," he said, "be it little or much, is a matter of history." But had he gained the cooperation of "State authorities," he claimed that he might have done much more.

Blunt repeated the charge he had made before that various superiors had singled him out as the "special object of copperhead malice and hatred." He pointed again to Schofield as unwilling to protect Kansas from rebel incursions. He alleged that Carney had opposed the efforts to remove Schofield and instead colluded with the governor of Missouri to retain him. To support this allegation, he printed a letter from one of Lincoln's secretaries to a Kansas official, M. W. Delahay. The letter did suggest that Carney lobbied the Lincoln administration against Schofield's removal. But it was written months after the fact, and the author conceded that he couldn't remember the specifics of the conversations in question. It may well be this accusation of Blunt's that later caused Sol Miller to charge that Lane was trying to tie Carney to Schofield.

Blunt continued his letter by shifting his attention to the case of the Fourteenth Kansas and the commissions of its officers. Blunt insisted that he didn't know why he was given authority to recruit the regiment and that he had not sought it. Having been given the orders to do so, he claimed he raised it properly; commissions were only given to those who deserved them and only upon recommendation of a serving officer. But while Blunt was in the Indian Territory, Carney had "interfered" with the Fourteenth and left it demoralized.

Finally Blunt attacked Carney for trying to assemble two regiments of "One Hundred Days men," most likely meaning two "home guard" regiments. Carney had asked Lincoln that he be allowed to raise these regiments, and he had made his request public. In response Blunt, through his letter, also made public the president's refusal to grant Carney permission. Lincoln had called Carney's request "obviously" political, which it no doubt was. But in disclosing the letter, Blunt again did no favor to Lane for later in the letter Lincoln told Carney that "there is not a more foolish or demoralizing way of conducting a political rivalry, than in these fierce and bitter struggles for patronage."

Blunt concluded his message by calling for harmony between the area's civil and military authorities. He again charged Carney with "duplicity and perfidy" in his dealing with him. He boldly predicted that Carney was "pass[ing] to that oblivion to which he is fast hastening." He finished in typical Blunt style: "Even now I feel like asking pardon of your readers for spending so much ammunition on a *dead carcass,* and if ever I should have occasion to claim their indulgence again, I hope it will be in treating a *live subject.*"

Of course Blunt's missive didn't go without some reply, which came from the *State Journal* on August 4. The *Journal's* opinion was about as sarcastic as Blunt's comment, and unfortunately about as relevant. The editorial responded to Blunt's conclusion by saying, "The 'dead carcass' is all that he can possibly find time to attend to." It then accused Blunt, without substantiation, of trying to discourage enlistments in the Second Kansas in 1861, when he had not received a lieutenant's commission. The editorial concluded by implying that President Lincoln was no friend of Kansas and had in his letter insulted Carney.

The only other recorded instance of Blunt taking the political stage in 1864 was on August 10, when he spoke at a pro-Lane rally in Junction City. Blunt followed Lane to the platform after a long and colorful speech by the senator. Blunt spoke briefly to express his support for Lincoln. The reporter for the *Conservative,* writing about the meeting later, said that Blunt's letter had "blunted the ardor" of Carney's supporters.

The reporter had concluded his piece with information on Indian deprivations in the area. Part of the reason that Blunt was able to speak at the meeting was that he had been transferred to Fort Riley and assigned to deal with the plains tribes and their raids on white settlements and wagon trains. During his remarks at the rally, Blunt, alluding to his new post on the plains, assured his audience that he was determined to protect them. His assignment was for an intractable problem, but Blunt was trying to make the most of his exile.

The situation on the western plains had started to deteriorate early in 1864. Throughout that spring and summer, reports of unrest and attacks by the "hostiles" came in to Curtis's headquarters. One such report, dated July 15, said that the Cheyenne, Arapaho, and Commanche were unhappy that buffalo hunters were killing the beasts for hides and tallow in violation of treaties between these tribes and the federal government. This was one source of the tribes' anger, and they retaliated by raiding settlements and mail routes between the Republican and Smoky Hill Rivers.

Not everyone took these reports seriously, as exemplified by a letter Halleck wrote to Grant on August 17. The subject of the letter was the stories of Indian uprisings throughout the West. Halleck expressed his view that reports of trouble were caused by Indian agents and speculators. He did concede that it would be bad publicity to withdraw troops to the East while mail routes were under attack, forts were threatened, and settlers were killed.

More serious were Indian raids on wagon trains along the Santa Fe Trail and other western trails. These trails were vital arteries connecting the Far West and the Pacific Coast with the East, and they were used by both civilians and the military. In fact the attacks on mail carriers and wagon trains on the Santa Fe Trail became so bad that the transit stations between forts were abandoned. The final straw came on July 17 when Kiowa warriors raided Fort Larned and stole over 170 army animals.

General Curtis immediately took the field with four hundred men and two cannons to prevent the tribes from shutting down the Santa Fe Trail. He marched out of Fort Riley to the trail, then followed it to a spot along Walnut Creek just north of the "Great Bend" of the Arkansas River. There he established Fort Zarah, named for the son he lost at Baxter Springs. He took his column thirty miles farther southwest to Fort Larned, split his command into three detachments, and attempted to draw the Indians into battle. Curtis's men failed to find them, and deciding that the threat had eased, he returned to Fort Leavenworth.

After this expedition, General Blunt was given his new assignment. On July 25 he was put in charge of the new District of the Upper Arkansas. The district took in western Kansas and eastern Colorado south of the Solomon River, with Blunt's headquarters at Fort Riley. His staff consisted of three officers and his command contained a few hundred soldiers.

Even this exile did not diminish Blunt's thirst for administrative power. On August 10 he wrote to Curtis that settlers in north-central Kansas were asking for protection. And in addition to the plains tribes, Blunt had to put down unrest among the

Pottawatomies who were living close to Fort Riley. To deal with the general Indian situation, Blunt requested that his district be enlarged north to the Kansas-Nebraska border. One wonders what Curtis must have thought when he read Blunt's request.

Curtis's earlier campaign had not lessened the fear travelers had of Indian attacks. The attacks had resumed as before, compelling Blunt to act. Late in September, Blunt assembled a force at Fort Larned and set out after the raiding tribes. His force found a camp of Cheyennes, Arapahos, and Kiowas about seventy-five miles west of the fort on September 25. He attacked the camp, and when the Indians scattered, he pursued them for a few days. Blunt reported that his men had killed nine and had wounded many more at the cost of two soldiers killed and seven wounded.

By this time winter was not far away, and most believed that the raids would soon end. Meanwhile, on the other side of the state, a new raid was brewing. This raid would have dramatic consequences for both the military and the political situations in Kansas. It would also present Blunt with a chance to redeem himself before the Civil War came to an end.

CHAPTER 13

Opportunities Won and Lost

The Union troops in Arkansas had not been idle during the plains uprising. A combined Federal effort to drive Confederate troops completely out of the state had begun in the spring of 1864. The plan was for Gen. Nathaniel Banks to drive north from New Orleans while General Steele was to drive south from Fort Smith and Little Rock. The two armies were to converge on Shreveport, Louisiana, crushing the rebel forces between them. Steele's effort south succeeded though Banks's drive north failed; therefore Steele had to pull back. But as he did so, he defeated Sterling Price at Jenkin's Ferry on April 30.

Price still had designs on retaking Missouri for the Confederacy, despite the fact that the South was in trouble. Grant had Lee pinned around Petersburg, and Sherman was driving toward Atlanta. Nevertheless Price decided to mount one final invasion of his home state. Over the summer of 1864, he raised an army of between twelve thousand and fifteen thousand men to wage his campaign.

On August 4, Price was given orders to make St. Louis his objective. The hope was that if he took that city, he would have enough supplies to sustain his army. Such a victory might also prove a strong rallying point for the Confederacy. Price was advised not to allow his men to commit any "wanton acts of destruction" and to prevent them from taking revenge on anyone. He was told that if he had to retreat from Missouri, he should do so via Kansas and the Indian Territory. Price was to use that retreat as an opportunity to raid those areas of anything of military value.

Price himself hoped that this campaign would take some of the pressure off the rebel armies in the East. He counted on a general rising of the population of Missouri. He believed that he could capture enough supplies not only to maintain his army but also to hold any territory he conquered.

Price had not been able to act in complete secrecy, however. As early as July 22, Senator Lane had warned General Rosecrans that Price was assembling an army. But it was not until September 6 that General Steele in Little Rock detected that Price was preparing to move. Successful demonstrations by Confederate forces had been able to cloak Price's movements. Finally on September 17, Curtis, returning from his campaign on the plains, sent word to Rosecrans, Halleck, and Governor Carney that Price had crossed the Arkansas River.

In the meantime Stand Watie had been on the move again in Indian Territory. In June he captured a steamer along the Arkansas River loaded with Union supplies, and as a result he was promoted to brigadier general; he would be the only tribal chief to achieve the rank of general in the Civil War. On September 19 he followed up his June attack by capturing at Cabin Creek a Union wagon train worth over one million dollars. This was the biggest victory Confederates ever had in the territory, and Confederate hopes soared as Price marched north. Price claimed to have twelve thousand men in his army, two-thirds of whom were armed, and fourteen cannons as his forces entered Missouri.

The first problem for Price's campaign arose on September 26 at Pilot Knob. Gen. Thomas Ewing, who had been put in charge of a district in eastern Missouri, took approximately one thousand men to Pilot Knob, a village at the end of a railroad line out of St. Louis. He correctly guessed that Pilot Knob would be an early target of Price's army. He quartered his men in a nearby fort where they would have the advantages of four siege guns, eight howitzers, and six field cannon. On September 26, Ewing's men were attacked by two divisions of Price's army, and inflicted some fifteen hundred casualties on the rebels at little cost to themselves. The next day troops from the Tenth Kansas delayed further advance by Price at Harrison. These actions bought time for General Rosecrans to assemble his forces in Missouri and for Kansas authorities to prepare for Price's possible invasion.

In his report to Governor Carney on September 17, Curtis suggested that he might need the militia in southern Kansas called up in order to deal with Price. Perhaps to further the matter, Curtis said the same thing to Gen. George Sykes, who was commanding that part of Kansas. On September 20, as he reported the Cabin

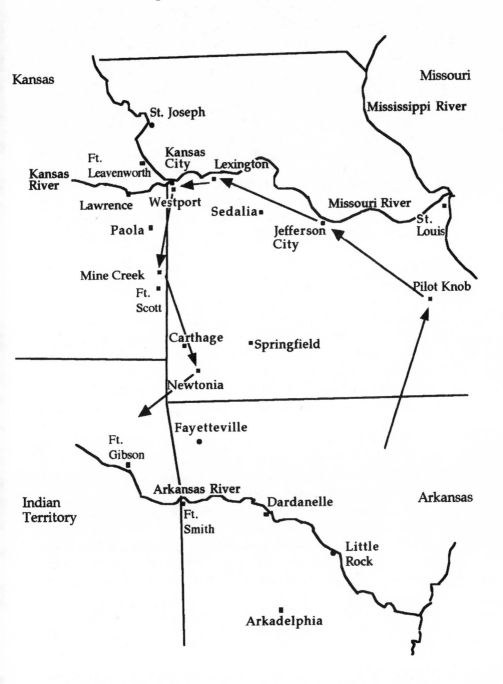

Movement of Price's Army, September & October 1864

Kansas

Missouri

Mississippi River

St. Joseph

Kansas City

Ft. Leavenworth

Lexington

Kansas River

Lawrence

Westport

Sedalia

Missouri River

St. Louis

Paola

Jefferson City

Mine Creek

Ft. Scott

Pilot Knob

Carthage

Springfield

Newtonia

Fayetteville

Ft. Gibson

Arkansas River

Dardanelle

Arkansas

Indian Territory

Ft. Smith

Little Rock

Arkadelphia

Creek attack to Carney, Curtis again suggested that the governor prepare the militia. Curtis knew he did not have enough "regular" troops in the field to cope with the oncoming threat, and he would have to rely on the Kansas State Militia to assist. But this reliance presented a new problem, as he stated in his official report on the campaign:

> The whole country was engaged in the great National and State political campaign, the very crisis of which seemed to culminate with Price's progress through Missouri. Motives, measures, and men were all distrusted. The Senators, Governor, and people, commanding, composing, and controlling this militia reserve were all fiercely engaged in this political strife. No time for using the militia could be more unfavorable. The ballot-box, not the bayonet, was the weapon sought by the militia, and it required the greatest exertions to draw attention of officers and men from the political to the military necessities of the hour.

Part of the problem stemmed from the rivalry between Carney and Senator Lane. Carney suspected that Curtis's requests were being made under Lane's influence, especially since Lane had been issuing warnings about Price for some time. Carney assumed that Lane was trying to save his flagging campaign to be reelected senator by dragging out the old Confederate hobgoblin, Sterling Price.

Lane's reelection bid was in trouble because by the fall of 1864 the scandals and allegations of corruption were finally catching up to him. Furthermore several Leavenworth politicians were unhappy with the ticket's nominee to the House and were withholding their support from Lane. Lastly but most importantly, Carney was mounting a strong challenge to Lane's Senate seat. Carney, concerned about the militia's absence and the resulting loss of votes during the upcoming election, was only interested in allowing the militia to staff posts in Kansas if Curtis took his troops south, which would prove that Price was a threat. So on the same day that Curtis was telling Rosecrans that Price might have twenty-six thousand men under him, Carney and his allies were certain that Price would not come toward Kansas.

On September 22, Curtis wrote to General Blunt to inform him of Price's moves and of other developments on the plains. At the time, Curtis believed that Carney was calling out the militia. He advised Blunt to deploy some of his forces to protect the Santa Fe Trail and to bring the rest to Council Grove to await orders. Blunt, of course, could not immediately comply because he was in the field chasing Indians.

On September 24, Curtis and Rosecrans speculated to each other about news that Price was near Cane Hill and moving north. Within days of that conversation, word arrived of the action at Pilot Knob, and on October 2 Rosecrans informed Curtis that Price was seventy-five miles west of St. Louis. Rosecrans reported that he was concentrating two forces to resist Price, one at St. Louis and the other at Jefferson City.

The day before Rosecrans' message, the *Conservative* alerted its readers, and perhaps the whole state, that Price was on the move. On October 5, Curtis formally requested that Governor Carney call up the Kansas militia, telling Carney that Price was fifteen miles south of Jefferson City and that Union forces were approaching Price from the direction of St. Louis. Curtis wanted the militia to gather at Olathe and serve for thirty days. Carney stalled for some time before finally complying with Curtis's request, and orders were given for the militia to gather at four points with militia headquarters at Olathe.

The next day Curtis spoke briefly at a political meeting in Leavenworth in which he only encouraged the audience to support the president and his party. He said even less to General Blunt on October 9: "You will proceed at once to Olathe and report to me for orders." Blunt no longer had to chase Indians; he was again doing what he did best, fighting the Confederate army.

Around noon on October 10, Rosecrans informed Curtis that Price was now heading for Leavenworth. He added that telegraph communication might be interrupted. That evening Curtis promised Rosecrans that he would "give Price a warm welcome if he comes this way." Sometime during that day Curtis reported what Rosecrans had told him to Governor Carney and all his commanders.

That same day Blunt entered Olathe from the west. Curtis had already decided that General Sykes' health wouldn't hold up under the strain of a military campaign and that a younger man should replace him. For his part, Sykes didn't like Blunt being sent into the field at Olathe, and he requested that he be relieved. He was, and Blunt took over his command on October 11.

The pro-Lane press expressed confidence in Blunt's return. So did the people of Paola, who turned out at his hotel and asked him to speak. Blunt reportedly told the crowd that he did think the danger from Price was enough to justify the call-up of the militia. He said he wanted to "meet Price at the threshold and hurl him back." Finally he expressed his hope that the militia would not halt at the state line if they had to take offensive action against Price.

At first the anti-Lane press downplayed the danger to Kansas posed by Price's movements. On September 24 the leading anti-Lane newspaper, the *Leavenworth Times*, printed a letter from one "Armigo" at Fort Smith in which it communicated that the only rebel activity was small guerilla raids. Three days later it reported on the Confederate march but said that Jo Shelby was in charge of a "large cavalry force." The following day, September 28, the *Times* finally reported the complete story of Price's invasion, but its editors may have still believed that it was Missouri and not Kansas that was in the greatest danger.

Indeed on October 6 the *Times*, under the headline "Price's Invasion—Public Peril and Public Duty," expressed the view that Price was more a problem for Missouri than for Kansas. The author of this piece accurately mentioned the Confederate moves against the main Missouri railroads and the effort to retake the state for the South, but seemed to believe that Missouri was the only goal of Price's army. At worst, he wrote, Price's cavalry might "make a raid westward into Kansas." The writer didn't think the rebels were strong enough to take Fort Leavenworth, but he thought calling the militia into service was "proper to strengthen the public confidence and security." For the time being, partisan politics would be put aside so as to meet the Confederate threat.

In the days after the militia call-up, Blunt and Curtis kept in contact as to how well the militia was assembling, what weapons they needed, and what Price might be doing. As he had expressed in his Paola remarks, Blunt wanted to go on the offensive against Price to prevent the Confederates from reaching Kansas. Curtis was thinking along those same lines but told Blunt to focus on assembling the militia first.

During the second week of October, Blunt was also put in command of the First Division of Curtis's army, which consisted of the volunteer cavalry regiments and the militia units from southern

Kansas. The Second Division, under militia Maj. General George W. Dietzler, was composed of the bulk of the state militia. In all, Curtis's army numbered about fifteen thousand men.

Halleck ordered that Curtis concentrate his forces at Fort Scott, thinking that Price would be forced southward around Lexington. Blunt believed that Price might get farther west than Lexington. He argued that a concentration at Olathe and Paola could resist Price if he approached Kansas but could also strike Price's flank if he did turn south. Curtis agreed with Blunt's views, and he had the Union forces gather at those two towns. To discern Price's true intentions toward Kansas, Blunt sent scouts east from Paola. Blunt also put up fortifications around Olathe in case the Federals had to fight a defensive battle.

Militia commander Dietzler and his aides, including the former governor, Charles Robinson, and Marcus Parrott, were all anti-Lane and anti-Blunt men. So when Price didn't immediately appear while Curtis and Blunt made their preparations, they began speculating that the call-up was a Lane stunt. Their view was supported by the *Freedom's Champion* in Atchison, which on October 13 said, "We are inclined to think that the danger [to] Kansas from this invasion has been exaggerated."

The tone in the *Leavenworth Times* also changed along these lines. On October 16 it reported positively on the militia preparations to resist Price. Interestingly, though, the *Times'* correspondent gave his readers the impression that it was Curtis, Dietzler, and Carney who were working together. General Blunt was not mentioned even once.

Then two days later the *Times* pronounced the militia deployment as "Lane's Last Fraud." Its correspondent claimed that Lane and Blunt were abandoning the Kansas town of Wyandotte to chase after "ten guerillas" at Hickman's Mill. Another report called the campaign a "humbug" because small groups of rebel raiders supposedly were menacing the area, while Price's main army was nowhere in sight.

On October 13, the day the *Champion* expressed its doubts, Curtis received reports that some of Price's men were north of the Missouri River attacking the Hannibal and Saint Joseph Railroad while Stand Watie was marching on Humbolt. Curtis decided both were rumors intended to draw the militia away from the Kansas

City area. He made his skepticism of these reports clear to his officers in order to increase their confidence.

But the skepticism in the Kansas ranks grew to the point that on
October 15 Brig. Gen. William H. Fishback tried to send three
militia regiments from Olathe back to Paola. Fishback tried to
claim that the move was to protect southern Kansas, but no doubt
it was a first step in sending the men home. Furthermore Fishback
told Blunt's acting adjutant general that he was under Dietzler's
orders and not Blunt's. One militia regiment, the Sixth, under the
command of James D. Snoddy, did start marching south. On
October 16 Blunt personally stopped the Sixth and arrested
Snoddy and Fishback; supposedly the men cheered Blunt when he
returned them to camp. Fishback apologized for his error, was
released from custody, and served honorably during the campaign. Snoddy, about whom one officer said that "[d]ifficulties are
bred around him where ever he goes," was kept at Paola for at least
a month.

When, on December 24, Blunt wrote his official report on the
campaign, he seems to have forgiven both men. He wrote that he
had discovered that the two officers were merely "instruments" of
Governor Carney and the militia leadership. The men had been
chosen to "carry out their mischievous and disgraceful designs."

While these events were unfolding, Senators Lane and Samuel
Pomeroy arrived to act as Curtis's aides. Curtis allowed them to
speak to the wavering militia and others so as to stamp out the
rumors that were harming his army. But the problems in obtaining
accurate information about Price's wherabouts continued to create trouble among the Kansas militia.

This led Lane's opponents both in Kansas and in the militia to
wonder, "Where is Price?" Most believed that Rosecrans would
catch up to Price well before the rebels appeared in front of
Kansas City. The *Journal* of Lawrence on October 20 confidently
stated that if Price was not at Lexington, he must have escaped.
The *Times*, meanwhile, began to demand that the militia be sent
home, and on October 19 it presented an editorial claiming not
only that Kansas was in no danger from the rebels, but also that the
call-up was disrupting the local economy. The burden of defeating
Price ought to be shifted to Rosecrans' army, it said, and the
Kansas militia should no longer "be required to ferret out" rebel

bushwhackers. In a separate item on that day, the *Times* claimed that Blunt had arrested Fishback and Snoddy "because they refused to pass over their commands to Jim Lane, for a raid into Missouri and Arkansas."

The pro-Lane press tried to counter this rhetoric, but they appear to have been in the minority. As early as October 8, the *Conservative* was warning of Price's advance. Presaging the rising tide of disbelief, it had urged. "The people must arouse. . . . This is no *scare*. You must stop the enemy or suffer your homes to be devastated."

However, Dieztler was so unconcerned that on October 15 he allowed a regimental band to come to his headquarters in Shawnee and play a concert. After the concert Dietzler spoke to the crowd, followed by the anti-Lane candidate for governor. The affair ended with "happy exchange[s] of sentiments appropriate to the occasion."

Certainly the *Times* was by far the closest among the the state's newspapers to the Carney faction. The *Conservative* alleged that one of the *Times'* editors was on "Carney's staff." For its part, the *Times* continued to trumpet the governor's line that Price presented no danger to Kansas; that the militia should be disbanded and sent home; that martial law should be lifted; and that Lane and his candidates should be defeated at the polls.

The skeptical chorus reached its peak on the night of October 17 when a mass meeting was held in Shawnee. Led by Lane's militia opponents, the meeting was held close to Carney and Dietzler's headquarters. Speakers loudly denounced Lane's "stunt," and a crowd hanged the senator in effigy. Blunt did not escape their ire; the crowd took a mule from a local man, painted "Blunt" on its side, and paraded it around their meeting site.

The editor of the *Times,* who was supposedly on Carney's staff, pronounced a few days later that Price was south of the Arkansas River. The *Conservative*, when reporting this "news," denounced it and blamed Carney, Dietzler, and their allies for preventing the Kansas militia from taking action against Price's army. "The effort of these men to create disaffection with the militia is most certainly criminal," the *Conservative* asserted flatly. Later the *Conservative* printed a telegram from Fort Scott that essentially told the *Times* to stop lying about the situation.

Decades later Samuel Crawford blamed Curtis for the militia

imbroglio. He believed that Curtis should have arrested the militia leaders who were harming the morale of their men. He felt that if Curtis had done so, he could have been free to move his army east into Missouri. Price would have been trapped there, Crawford claimed, and Kansas would never have been in any danger.

But Kansas was in danger. On October 22, two days after the *Times* had asked "How Much Longer!", it was urging "To Arms! To Arms! Victory or Death!"

Another newspaper that had also asked "Where is Price?" during these mid-October days was Kansas City's *Daily Journal of Commerce*. Though asking that question, it also said that "unless he travels very soon" he wouldn't get away. It expressed confidence that some Union force would "gobble up" Price's army. Its editor wrote that Curtis was ready for a fight and that "Kansas could well afford to have turned out *en masse* to secure such a result."

Previously, on October 12 scouts had informed Curtis that Price was definitely marching west from Jefferson City toward Lexington. When Curtis informed Blunt, Blunt began moving his advance units into Missouri. On October 14, Blunt took two brigades toward Lexington while the third camped on the west bank of the Big Blue River. One of Blunt's aides on the march was Sen. James Lane, his old patron.

Curtis then took the field to personally command his army. He seemed to be concerned about his troops, especially the militia, getting into an open battle with the rebels, and he was hoping that Rosecrans would be able to defeat Price before the rebels reached Lexington. Curtis's plan was that, if Rosecrans should triumph over Price, his forces could get into Price's flank and pursue him out of the region.

There continued to be confusion over Price's movements as the days progressed. Blunt passed along rumors gathered by his scouts that Price was marching toward Fort Scott on October 15. The picture became clearer the next day when word came that Sedalia had fallen.

After the battle at Pilot Knob, Price's campaign had not gone as he had expected. The people of Missouri did not rise up to celebrate his men as liberators. Rosecrans had put a strong force behind him, preventing the rebels from taking Jefferson City.

Since some of his men were unarmed, Price had no choice but to keep moving in the hope of finding some place to make a stand and defeat the Union army. He believed that such a victory might win Missourians to his side. He thus had continued to march west after his defeat at the state capital.

Early on the morning of October 17, Blunt heard from a spy who had gotten into Price's camp. The unnamed spy reported that Price had twenty thousand men. Price's men believed that they would follow the Missouri River to Lexington, and from there they would advance to Kansas City. At this point the rebels expected to turn south toward the Indian Territory and Arkansas. Blunt related this information to Curtis, and Curtis passed it to Dietzler and his other officers.

On the day Blunt heard from his spy, three hundred Union cavalrymen from the Second Colorado dashed into Lexington and seized the town. The following afternoon Blunt arrived on the scene with two thousand men and several howitzers. After the intense battle that ensued, Price would estimate Blunt's force at between three thousand and four thousand men.

The action began on October 19 when Blunt sent out a reconnaissance in force from Lexington to determine the number of men Price commanded and to slow down his westward advance. Blunt wanted to hold the line at the Little Blue River, but Curtis could not get the militia to deploy any farther east than the Big Blue. Blunt wanted to extend his lines south to Lone Jack, link up with Rosecrans' men coming from the east, and combine to launch a massive assault on Price. Curtis apparently decided not to take Blunt's advice, concluding that there wasn't enough time to carry out such an effort and that the Kansas militia would not march too far into Missouri.

Once the reconnaissance was completed, Blunt staged a contested retreat from Lexington back to the Union position along the Little Blue. The last to pull back was the Eleventh Kansas under Col. Thomas Moonlight, who withdrew after dark. Blunt wanted to make a full-blown stand at the Little Blue. Instead Curtis ordered Blunt to leave Moonlight with a few hundred men at a bridge over the Little Blue to slow the Confederate advance. Blunt left Moonlight on October 20, ordering him to burn the bridge if the rebels attacked and to resist until Blunt said otherwise.

This delay would turn into the battle of the Little Blue. The Confederates attacked Moonlight's men at 7 A.M. on October 21, and his men fought for two hours, slowly withdrawing about two miles. Within two hours, another Union regiment arrived to support Moonlight. At 10 A.M. Blunt came on to the field to personally manage the Union resistance, "regardless of shot and shell," reported one Maj. Chapman Charlot. Curtis also arrived at the field to direct the action. Lane later described Curtis as "the bravest of the brave" for doing this.

During the battle Blunt brought in more fresh troops and continued to stall Price, despite Blunt's being outnumbered. As in the old days, the Union artillery used canister shot to devastating effect. As Blunt's force pulled back, the Eleventh Kansas Cavalry held off Price until Blunt safely withdrew his forces to Independence. One of the guerrilla leaders, George Todd, was killed during this battle. The crucial bridge over the river was indeed destroyed by Moonlight's men.

The Union officers believed that Blunt's men had been heavily outnumbered at this battle. When his men had finally retreated to Independence, they were able to withdraw without losing any artillery. Blunt later complimented his men on their calm and orderly retreat in the face of superior numbers. Some two thousand men had held up Price for over a day.

At first the Confederates thought they had beaten Blunt and captured all his artillery. A Confederate deserter later reported that the rebel officers under Shelby argued over who had been leading the Union troops at Lexington. Some claimed that it could not have been Blunt because he supposedly held no command. In reference to that assumption, Shelby said in a famous remark, "It was either Blunt or the devil."

With the battle of the Little Blue, the dissension among the Kansas militia suddenly quieted. At least one paper was still trying to claim that Price was south of the Arkansas River. But Curtis told Blunt that his stand against the Confederate general was smashing these sorts of rumors, which were harming his chances of mounting a successful defense. That same day Curtis heard that Gen. Alfred Pleasonton, leading Rosecrans' advance from St. Louis, was closing on Price's rear. Curtis sent word to Pleasonton that he had formed a strong defensive line along the Big Blue River. He asked

Pleasonton to attack so that Price's army might be trapped between them.

A few days later, the *Kansas City Journal of Commerce,* still printing with the Confederates almost at their door, praised virtually every field officer at the battle of the Little Blue. But as it was exulting in the Union stand, it was reporting that Union pickets near the Big Blue position were being driven back and that skirmishing had begun. These skirmishes would lead to the next battle in the campaign, the battle of the Big Blue River.

The same day that fighting raged at the Little Blue, Dietzler's division came up to the Big Blue River and formed a line with Blunt's men. Price attacked this line the following day, October 22. He had sent General Shelby to ride along the Federal line and scout. Shelby found no weak spots, but he did find the end of the

An illustration drawn by Union veteran Samuel J. Reader. It shows the Battle of Big Blue, one of the engagements at which Blunt was present during the Price Campaign. It does not appear to show any particular moment of the battle, during which the Union line was flanked by Price's Confederates. In the course of the campaign, the artist was briefly captured, but he managed to gain freedom and return to his friends in Kansas. *Photograph courtesy the Kansas State Historical Society, Topeka, Kansas.*

line near Byram's Ford. Price then crossed the river and attacked the Federal line from the north.

Throughout the morning Blunt, Curtis, and their aides kept watch over their position along the Big Blue. At 11 A.M. reports arrived of rebel attacks on Byram's Ford and Hinkle's Ford. In response Blunt sent reinforcements to hold the line, which held until 3 P.M., when it was flanked near Byram's Ford. Union forces withdrew and made it to lines around Kansas City by 6 P.M. An hour later word came that Pleasonton was attacking Price's rear. Pleasonton, having come up the Missouri River from the east, drove Price's forces in confusion through Independence. Once again Price's advance on Kansas was slowed by stubborn Union resistance.

After the battle, Pleasanton and Curtis began making plans to join their forces. Before this could happen, though, there seems to have been some debate among Curtis's senior officers about their future course of action.

The trouble seemed to have begun on the afternoon of October 22. At a council of war, Curtis proposed taking his men back across the Kansas River to Leavenworth. Everyone else at the council, including Blunt and Senator Lane, wanted to stand and fight Price's army. This may have alarmed other senior commanders for later that night some of them approached Blunt about arresting Curtis and putting Blunt in command. Blunt asked if the army would support him, and he was told yes. He then approached Curtis, who was arguing with Lane.

"General Curtis," Blunt asked firmly, "what do you propose to do?"

Curtis hesitated a moment, then replied, "General Blunt, I will leave the whole matter to you. If you say fight, then fight it is."

Blunt said fight and asked to concentrate his forces near Westport. Curtis apparently agreed, and the concerned officers seem to have returned to their commands. It is a question to this day whether or not this incident actually occurred. It is recorded in Samuel Crawford's autobiography; James G. Blunt, never mentioned it.

From his writings after the war, it is clear that Blunt was unhappy with some of Curtis's actions during October 1864. He seemed skeptical of Curtis's fortified line along the Big Blue. At the Little Blue he claimed that Curtis interfered with his order of battle, and after Westport, Curtis did not seem to want to pursue Price as closely as Blunt did. But Blunt never used the harsh language that he had in describing the earlier actions of Schofield, Robinson, Carney, and Halleck.

Furthermore, it's important to recall that Curtis's son served under Blunt for at least a year. Young Major Curtis died at Baxter Springs, while Blunt survived. Though Blunt might not have had the same feelings toward General Curtis that he did for Senator Lane, it seems reasonable to conclude that he did not dislike Curtis.

The fact that Blunt doesn't mention this incident does not in itself suggest that it never took place. If it did happen, Blunt might have omitted Curtis's hesitation in the face of battle in deference to a superior he liked and got along with. It could also be that the conversation never happened and that Crawford's memory (or his ego) was playing tricks on him. Crawford was harshly critical of Curtis's actions during the Price campaign, and this might also be a reason for him to invent or enhance the encounter. But in the end the incident, even if it occurred as reported, would have had little effect on the next day's battle.

A similar but far more crucial incident may have occurred on the rebel side. Shelby called on Price to launch an attack on Curtis and to then take up a position along the Big Blue to hold off Pleasonton. The other Confederate generals advised Price that a retreat south was a better option. Price decided to listen to Shelby, and he kept his men on the field south of Wesport, Missouri.

On the surface this seems to have been a questionable decision. Blunt's force facing Price was in Westport, while the rest of Curtis's army was in Kansas City. Pleasonton was approaching the Confederate rear with three brigades, while a fourth was also advancing. The stage was thus set for the battle of Westport.

At 5 A.M. on October 23, Blunt's men moved forward to attack the Confederate line. General Curtis had found a local seventy-five-year-old man to guide him through Brush Creek to a spot where some of his men could attack the rebel position. Curtis ordered Blunt to attack, then told Dietzler to advance as soon as he heard Blunt's men open fire.

Blunt's movement placed him between two rebel forces. He pressed the rebels hard during the opening hours of the battle but gained no ground. He called for reinforcements from the state militia, but because it would take time for them to dismount and join him, Blunt ordered his men to pull back to Brush Creek. Blunt may also have been under orders from Curtis to withdraw. But when Shelby's men drove forward, Blunt ordered a counterattack. Shelby's men broke and ran, and the tide of battle started to turn.

One of Blunt's staff officers later reported that the general was "every where at the front," giving orders and encouraging his men. He was exposed to bullets and shell fire but remained cool and confident. Blunt's bravery is best seen when, during the battle, he and his staff came upon a Union howitzer stationed in front of a farmhouse along the road bordering the state line. A small group of rebels was advancing on the gun from the east, and the gun crew had no infantry support. Blunt formed his staff, which drew pistols and fired off a few shots before Blunt's escort regiment, the Fourteenth Kansas, arrived and drove the rebels back.

As before, the Union commanders used their artillery to great effect. As Curtis's men moved down the creek, Curtis found that more Union units were pressing the rebels back. Deciding that the time was right, Curtis ordered a cavalry charge, telling Blunt to support the charge with an advance of his own.

At the other end of the battlefield, Pleasonton moved his brigades into action. They soon drove the Confederates away from their positions along the Big Blue. At about 1 P.M. Pleasonton's men appeared near the Westport battlefield. Now facing two Union armies, the Confederates retreated from in front of Curtis's line. To hold off a rout, the rebel cavalry counterattacked; however, an artillery barrage from Pleasonton's forces pushed them back, bringing on a general withdrawal by Price's entire army. The rebels ran for at least ten miles before stopping for the day.

At Indian Creek, about ten miles south of Westport, Pleasonton's and Curtis's staffs met, including Blunt, Lane, and Governor Carney. The combined Federal army continued five more miles, pushing Price farther south. The Union command finally stopped at Little Santa Fe and camped for the night.

If the *Journal* in Kansas City had been exultant after the Little Blue, it was positively giddy at Price's defeat at Westport. It described Price's men as an "inferior" race and the war as one of "Christian civilization against barbarism." It called the rebel soldiers "miserable, degraded, hungry wretches" on an "errand of plunder and devastation." The editor praised the Kansas soldiers who, under "the good Providence of God," had driven back the rebel "invaders."

As Price's army withdrew from the Kansas City area, the threat to northern Kansas diminished. Martial law in that part of the state was revoked, and militia units from the region were allowed to go home. But Price was still a threat to Kansas and had to be dealt with. To chase Price out of the region, Blunt was given one division, Pleasanton another, and Moonlight a brigade.

The pursuers found Price along Mine Creek in southern Linn County, Kansas. On October 25, Union units, some of which were under Samuel Crawford, attacked the rebels along the creek. During the battle Crawford sent word to Blunt recommending that Blunt, who had been in the rear of the Union advance south from the Kansas City area, bypass any troops in front of him and come to the front. Crawford hoped that one good attack would crush Price's army once and for all.

Blunt, however, was piqued over having been in the rear when the army crossed the Marais de Cygne River. Blunt was still angry when Crawford's man approached him with the request. Blunt refused to move, using language that Crawford later termed "terse and vigorous." In his autobiography Crawford called Blunt's conduct mutinous. Considering that he wrote that description almost fifty years later, it is likely Crawford never forgave Blunt for his actions on this day. Interestingly, in Curtis's report, he names members of his staff who were at Mine Creek. He also mentions that at least one officer of Blunt's staff was there, but Curtis does not mention Blunt himself.

But even if there was trouble in the Union ranks, the battle of Mine Creek was another resounding defeat for Price. In addition to losing eight hundred men and nine artillery pieces, three brigadier generals were captured. Worse still, also taken was one of Price's chief generals, John S. Marmaduke. After the battle Price's men continued fleeing south.

Blunt had had no part in the engagement, and when Blunt did finally begin moving, he ignored the rebel retreat and instead marched to Fort Scott. He was followed to the town and fort by Pleasonton's men. Crawford went to Curtis to ask that both Blunt and Pleasonton be ordered to attack the fleeing rebels. Curtis gave the order, but both officers said their men were too tired.

Following the battle, a dispute broke out between Curtis and Pleasonton over where rebel prisoners would be sent. This dispute may have also been caused by problems between Curtis and Pleasonton's superior, General Rosecrans. When Rosecrans had arrived at Little Santa Fe after the Westport battle, he actually criticized Curtis's actions and plans to pursue Price, and he accused Senator Lane of running "the machine." Once he had finished his outburt, Rosecrans marched back to St. Louis, leaving behind a strained relationship with Curtis.

The hard-luck General Price could take no advantage from these disputes. His army was again beaten as he tried to cross the Osage River in Missouri. He failed to seriously threaten Fort Scott or to acquire Union supplies. His men tried obstructing the path of the pursuing Federals, but in doing so they were also leaving behind important war supplies.

Price's men also had taken some prisoners on the march, but after hearing reports of maltreatment, Curtis arranged a release of the Kansas prisoners on October 27. Curtis may have believed that Price was contemplating surrender due to the supposed condition of Price's army. When Union forces reached Granby, Missouri, they learned that Price was at Newtonia. Contrary to what Curtis thought, the locals told the Union officers that Price was still defiant.

Blunt had three brigades under him as he carried out his part of the chase for Price. As his men approached Newtonia, Blunt decided to allow Moonlight to rest and feed his horses, while he would continue on with two brigades. When Curtis learned of this, he ordered Sanborn to rush to Blunt's assistance.

For his part, Price made camp at Newtonia, thinking he was no longer being chased by the Federals. In reality Blunt marched south all day and night. His men came upon Price on October 28. Blunt would later call this battle of Newtonia, the "warmest contested field we have had in the campaign."

Blunt only had three regiments with him, the Second Colorado and the Fifteenth and Sixteenth Kansas. But even though he had only one thousand men, Blunt decided to attack. He was confident that his small division could hold their own, and that when reinforcements arrived, there would be a rout. When they arrived, they saw steam rising from the local flour mill. This mill appeared to be the last spot that a flour mill was still operating in the area and, consequently, the last place that grain could be obtained by any army. The importance of the grain made taking Newtonia and driving Price south all the more vital.

The Confederates were camped about two to three miles south and west of town. When the battle opened, the rebels formed up west of town in a cornfield in front of the McClain farm. Blunt drew his pistol and rode to the skirmish line, personally directing the moves of his units. Artillery again had a vital impact for the Union side, and Blunt's bravery seemed to instill confidence in his soldiers.

Blunt was attacking men under General Shelby, who was holding the rear guard of Price's column. Blunt estimated his opponent's strength at two thousand, while Shelby believed Blunt's to be over five thousand.

As the day wore on, no Union reinforcements arrived. In danger of having his line flanked, Blunt ordered a withdrawal of three hundred yards. Confederate officers tried to force their men into charging. Only one succeeded in moving his regiment, and he was driven back by a countercharge. At this point Shelby may have asked Price to send reinforcements in order to drive Blunt back farther. Unfortunately for both, Price sent no one to Shelby's aid

Just as the Union ammunition was running out, Sanborn arrived. A day earlier, on October 27, Brig. Gen. John Sanborn, commanding one of Pleasonton's brigades, had taken his command south from Fort Scott in the hope of catching part of Price's army. Throughout the next thirty-six hours his men marched over one hundred miles. Sanborn reached Newtonia at 4 P.M. on October 28 to find Blunt pulling back and his line about to be encircled.

Sanborn's horses were too tired to make a cavalry charge so he dismounted his men. Blunt persuaded him to launch an attack just north of town. Then, as Sanborn's brigade charged, Curtis arrived. Sanborn's assault drove the rebels from the area at sunset, and according to Sanborn, the rebels were driven back three miles before the pursuit was ended.

The next day Rosecrans ordered all pursuit of Price to stop and all Union forces to return to their headquarters. However, as early as October 15, Halleck had given orders to Rosecrans that once

Price was driven from Missouri, he was "to pursue him as far as his troops can follow." Halleck repeated these orders directly to Rosecrans on October 27. Curtis, Blunt, and the other Union commanders did want to continue the chase. They were understandably upset about Rosecrans' order but helpless to do anything but obey. They were eventually able to get orders to resume the pursuit, but by this time Price had too much of a lead to be caught.

Curtis did try to catch Price but the Confederates were able to cross the Arkansas River unhindered. On November 6, 1864, Curtis's advance reached the river, a battery fired a round southward, and the campaign came to an end.

When Rosecrans wrote an order, dated December 8, 1864, praising his troops, he mentioned the actions of Pleasanton and Sanborn but completely omitted Curtis and Blunt. His message ignored the holding actions at Lexington and the Little Blue. It attributed the defeat of the rebels at Westport to Pleasanton and at Newtonia to Sanborn. By contrast Sanborn gave credit for the latter to Blunt for making a stand.

At one skirmish during the Union pursuit under Col. Frederick Benteen, an odd artifact was retrieved and given to Blunt. In 1863, possibly in very early October, a flag had been presented to Blunt at Leavenworth. When Blunt's escort was massacred at Baxter Springs, this flag was captured by Quantrill's men. Benteen's men found the flag in pieces in a traveling bag. The flag was sewn back together with only a small part of an inscription on it missing.

In spite of the recapture of Blunt's flag and the many Confederate losses and humiliations, Sterling Price tried to claim some victory from his campaign. His claims would never hide the harsh reality, however. The army that he brought back to Arkansas was five thousand men, less than half to two-thirds of the force with which he had entered Missouri. He lost several engagements, never retook Missouri, and left the Confederacy in the West in a precariously weak position.

It is interesting to note that Price had odd estimates of Union strength during the campaign. He later said that he had hesitated taking Jefferson City because he thought the Federals had fifteen thousand troops in the city, which was an erroneous assumption. He also believed that Blunt had from three thousand to four thousand men at Lexington; that there were between six thousand and eight thousand men under Blunt and Curtis at Big Blue; that three thousand Federals attacked him at Mine Creek; and that some three thousand men under Blunt attacked his army at Newtonia.

This inflation might make sense if Price was trying to explain defeat, but Price refused to do even that. In his report he claimed that his army had marched over fourteen hundred miles, had taken three thousand prisoners and eighteen cannons, and had destroyed ten million dollars in property in Missouri. He also related that his men were welcomed everywhere. Price failed to mention that he did not take St. Louis or Jefferson City, the main goals of his campaign. He also omitted that he was defeated at Pilot Knob, Westport, Mine Creek, and Newtonia, and that his claims of public support were an outright lie.

It is true that the guerrillas who had been raiding and killing Union supporters in Kansas and Missouri did flock to Price's army. But many of those who joined Price were killed or wounded during the march. George Todd, described as the cruelest of the men who rode with Quantrill, was killed at the battle of the Big Blue River. "Bloody Bill" Anderson, another of Quantrill's bushwhacker allies, was killed in northern Missouri by local militia while under Price's orders to destroy a railroad. It isn't far off to say that Price did more to end the guerilla war in the region than a slew of Union generals, including Blunt. Perhaps because of all these factors, the Confederate politician Price had hoped to inaugurate as governor of Missouri denounced the general's mismanagement of the campaign and accused him of being physically and mentally incapable.

The Union commanders, including General Blunt, were also well aware of Price's failures. Blunt sent a report of the battle of Newtonia to Senator Lane, which Lane then had published in Kansas newspapers. In that report Blunt said that a spy in the rebel camp (thought to be James Butler "Wild Bill" Hickok) had told him that Price had planned to take Kansas City. Furthermore Price had told his recruits from Missouri that Kansas could not raise enough troops to hinder his march.

The true beneficiary of Price's actions was obviously not the Confederacy, but Sen. James H. Lane and his allies. Price did indeed invade, just as Lane had been claiming. Governor Carney had blundered in not calling out the militia soon enough, and the anti-Lane faction had come close to destroying the militia's ability to fight, for they had demoralized the soldiers by questioning their necessity in the campaign against Price. Lane's supporters, on the other hand, could claim that Lane's "friends," Generals Curtis and Blunt, had saved Kansas. What's more, Lane's nominee for governor was Col. Samuel Crawford, the "victor" at Mine Creek.

This view of events was summed up by J. T. Hunt, who had taken over the *Emporia News* from Jacob Stotler. After the election, Hunt told his readers of the October 17 meeting at Shawnee, during which Carney's supporters had mocked Lane and his desire to call up the militia. Hunt then wrote that while this "drunken and disgraceful farce" was transpiring, Lane was looking for the enemy. When the Confederates were found, Lane remained with Curtis's army until Price was forced from the state.

"Who is the patriot and soldier?" Hunt asked his readers. "The men who hung Lane in effigy, or the man who marched to the front and [did] his duty as a soldier?"

The *Conservative* editors and correspondents were more gleeful, but no less on target. On October 27, under the heading "Lost," it offered a "liberal reward" for a copy of a proclamation Carney supposedly wrote. In the proclamation Carney decried the battles as "humbugs" and "Jim Lane Frauds." "The said document can be of no use to any but the author," the *Conservative* said, but since it was evidence of Carney's "bravery, loyalty, and disinterestedness" it was no doubt worth the price to obtain it.

The *Conservative's* rival, the *Times*, tried to put the best face on things. It tried to claim on October 27 that if there was any dissension in the Kansas militia, it was because Lane had taken "supreme command" and that Blunt had put cannons behind the men to force them into Missouri. The next day the *Times* repeated the old, and ultimately discredited, charge that Lane had conspired to call up the militia in order to prevent them from voting in the November election.

Perhaps the most infamous attempt by the *Times* to harm Lane came when it printed a quote from General Pleasanton. Supposedly the general had said, "If the people of Kansas think they are at all indebted to me, tell them to beat Jim Lane." The *Daily Monitor* of Fort Scott responded by asking Pleasanton about the remark. He denied that he had said anything of the sort;

instead he had sent a note to Lane expressing his gratitude to the senator for his work during the Price invasion.

It was therefore no surprise that when Kansans went to the polls on November 6, they gave Lane unquestioned control of their state. Crawford was elected governor by a landslide, Lane's allies took other offices, and the new state legislature was all but certain to return him to the Senate.

Blunt, too, was able to gain from Price's failed crusade. His bravery had reclaimed the reputation that he had lost in Fort Smith the previous spring. The image of "Blunt the Contractor's Friend" was replaced with that of "Blunt the Battlefield Hero." James G. Blunt was a winner again as the Civil War began to wind down.

Blunt's first duty as a newly acceptable figure was to deal with disturbing reports about the actions of one of the units in his command. As the Kansas regiments returned home from chasing Price, Blunt began to receive complaints from Missouri and Arkansas citizens about the Fifteenth Kansas. That regiment was part of the brigade commanded by Charles Jennison, the man who had wanted for himself the promotion to brigadier general conferred on Blunt back in 1862. Reports surfaced in November that the Fifteenth had engaged in pillaging and house burning on both their march south and their return to Kansas. Officers in Jennison's brigade who didn't approve of this jayhawking sent official protests to Blunt. By this point in the war such actions were no longer tolerated. Jayhawking had not stopped guerrilla activity, and by now many people in the region were impoverished by years of war and had little to be stolen.

On December 8, 1864, Blunt wrote to Gen. J. M. Thayer, commander of the part of Arkansas overrun by the Fifteenth. He asked Thayer to obtain information about the conduct of the Fifteenth in the form of affidavits from loyal citizens so as to be sure that the complaints were true and not rebel propaganda. Blunt also told Thayer that he would investigate Jennison and his men. While Thayer was unable to get sworn statements, Blunt was able to obtain his own evidence in the matter.

Two days earlier, Blunt had reduced the subdistrict that Jennison commanded. Jennison responded by sending Blunt a letter, which insulted both Blunt and Senator Lane. Blunt promptly relieved Jennison of the command of his regiment and demanded that Jennison report to him at Paola under arrest. Blunt also sent a letter of rebuke to Jennison. The letter seems to lack the force of Blunt's temper, possibly because Blunt knew Jennison still had pull in state politics. Blunt may have considered that his letter might be published, and it could be unfortunate for him if his remarks were too inflammatory. Lastly, it may well be that Blunt had learned that his temper had gotten him into trouble and could do so again if he didn't keep it under control.

Jennison did turn himself in. His confinement in Paola was very loose, allowing him to go on hunting trips and family visits. But when Jennison asked to be completely released from arrest on December 23, Blunt refused. Jennison then sent letters to anti-Lane newspapers denouncing his arrest as a political ploy by Lane. Jennison also claimed that he was being held because he would not take part in the "public stealing" carried on by unnamed government officials in Paola. Blunt was undaunted by Jennison's rants and a court-martial was convened on January 30, 1865, to try Jennison on charges of disobedience, insubordination, and conduct unbecoming an officer. Jennison was found not guilty of the first two but convicted of the third and sentenced to a formal reprimand.

Those charges were for Jennison's disobedience of one of Blunt's orders. The question of Jennison's plundering during the Price campaign was still unresolved, and Blunt continued the investigation. Jennison was court-martialed a second time in May, this time on the specific charges related to the looting carried out by the Fifteenth Kansas. After a three-week-long trial, Jennison was convicted on three of the charges filed and dishonorably discharged from the army.

In the meantime Blunt had also resumed command of the Indian Territory. Not everyone in the territory welcomed him back. Over the winter, a group of Cherokees told General Grant that they wanted to stay under Maj. Gen. J. J. Reynolds' authority and didn't want Blunt to resume command. Their reason for their dislike of the general was that they blamed Blunt for thefts of cattle and corn while he was previously in control of the territory.

These thefts were partly caused by pro-Union refugees from Arkansas and pro-Union Indians living close to the major posts in the region. These populations were sometimes driven to the posts by both Union and Confederate outlaws who had taken their property. Some of these refugees might have engaged in theft in order to feed themselves.

Wiley Britton believed that Blunt cooperated with Kansas legislators in an attempt to break up the outlaw gangs. He did not believe that Blunt sanctioned them, profited from them, or had anything else to do with the outlaws. Britton thought that Blunt was hampered because powerful politicians in Kansas were involved in this "trade." Since Blunt owed his commission to some of these politicians, Britton reasoned later, Blunt had decided that he couldn't afford to anger them by cracking down as hard as he would have liked.

When spring came, Blunt found himself under the command of John Pope in what was now the "Military Division of the Missouri." On April 22 he sent Blunt to Reynolds in Little Rock with orders to raise a cavalry force of five thousand men. The object of Blunt's campaign was Texas and the Confederate force remaining there under Kirby Smith.

Texas had long been the wintering ground for the bushwhackers who plagued Kansas and Missouri. It was the location to which the dispirited remnants of Price's 1864 army had retreated. In the minds of the Union military and political leadership, Texas was the feared final stronghold of the Confederacy. To end the war, Texas would have to be taken, and Blunt was to be given the task of leading the invasion.

On May 2, Reynolds sent Blunt to Fort Gibson, where he was to take command of the new Fifteenth Kansas Cavalry; the Fourteenth Kansas; the Sixth Kansas, which had recently consolidated with the Ninth Kansas; and the Second Kansas, which was to be consolidated with the Fifth and Seventh Kansas. Blunt was also to reorganize the Indian regiments, and had bought horses from Canada to turn that regiment into cavalry. He was also to receive artillery support and an engineer regiment to assist in his campaign.

But by May 15, only one regiment, the Fourteenth, had reported to Blunt, and no horses had arrived. Blunt could only report that he had plenty of forage on hand. The Arkansas River had gone down, though, and Blunt was unsure when the next supply boat might arrive. Two days earlier messages of concern had passed among the Confederates south of Fort Gibson. They had already heard that Blunt was assembling a cavalry force to march into Texas. Douglas Cooper said his information put Blunt's force at fifteen thousand, but he thought the number was exaggerated. No matter the numbers, the Confederates seemed to think Blunt was ready to move.

In fact the horses for Blunt's expedition still had not arrived by May 27, and Blunt only had two regiments on hand, consisting of a total of twelve hundred men. Blunt reported to Pope that two regiments weren't moving because generals in neighboring districts were not allowing them to march without their permission.

That same day Blunt got word from George Cutler, government agent to the Creek tribe, that unknown Kansans were driving Creek cattle out of their land and into Kansas. On June 2 Blunt ordered that the cattle be seized and only returned to a lawful Indian agent. He also ordered that anyone holding the stolen cattle be arrested and held.

By now the war in the East was long over. Blunt received a message on June 1 from Little Rock speculating that rebel soldiers observed moving northward were heading home. The next day Kirby Smith signed the terms of capitulation on board a U.S. warship in the harbor of Galveston, Texas. Although not every rebel commander had given up, the Civil War was now over throughout the country.

Smith's surrender meant that there was no longer a need for a Texas campaign. On June 3, Blunt was relieved of command of the pending expedition. He stayed in Fort Gibson until June 18, when he headed to Leavenworth to be mustered out. He resigned from the army shortly thereafter, and on July 29, 1865, his resignation was formally accepted.

James G. Blunt was a civilian again. He had just turned thirty-nine. He had a new life ahead of him and, with some of his reputation regained, a good chance of advancing the social ladder of post-Civil War Kansas.

CHAPTER 14

Fade Away

After the war Blunt moved to Leavenworth. At times he returned to his practice of medicine, but apparently he also engaged in various business deals. Indeed, mere months after the fighting stopped, Blunt was asked to use some of the connections he had made during the war. In September or early October 1865, Blunt returned to the Indian Territory. He traveled to Tahlequah to attend the annual Cherokee Council to lobby them about a railroad.

Joining him was Kansas City businessman Kersey Coates. Coates was one of the leaders of a new railroad company, the Kansas & Neosho Valley. The immediate goal of the K&NV was to build a line along the eastern border of Kansas from Kansas City to the territory, though they held a larger goal of pushing the line to the Gulf of Mexico. Coates and his group were determined to make Kansas City the railroad hub of the postwar West. They were beginning to engage railroads to the east in the idea of crossing the Missouri River into Kansas at that city instead of at Leavenworth or at Atchison. They had also taken an interest in the Union Pacific, Eastern Division, which was building west and had already reached Topeka.

The K&NV men most likely had employed Blunt for his knowledge of the territory and the Cherokee. They wanted to gain an exclusive land grant from the tribe that would allow them to build the K&NV south through the territory to Texas. In this Blunt and Coates did not succeed, but Blunt seems to have made an impression on the group. Later when Coates traveled to Washington to get Federal help for the K&NV, he took Blunt with him to help lobby the government.

Blunt, for his part, seemed to take little more interest in the K&NV project. He had no role in the company when James Joy, the powerful head of the Chicago, Burlington & Quincy railroad, became involved. He took no part when the road, renamed the Missouri River, Fort Scott & Gulf, tried to be the first to the reach the territory, nor in the MRFS&G's fight with settlers in the Cherokee Neutral Lands in southeast Kansas. But he did present the company with a bill two years later for services rendered, and he was paid fourteen thousand dollars for his assistance.

In October 1865, Col. Thomas J. Anderson, the adjutant general for Kansas, requested James Blunt to write a report of his actions during the Civil War. At first Blunt decided against writing such a report. He believed that there was enough information already published in newspapers and elsewhere so that he didn't need to bother with the task. But after a later personal meeting with Anderson, Blunt changed his mind.

This report, dated April 3, 1866, and apparently written in Washington, was never published as an official military report because the manuscript was lost. It was rediscovered in 1898 in the capitol building in Topeka and given to the Kansas State Historical Society two years later, but it was not published in its entirety until 1932. The manuscript of this report runs to 116 pages, with the 117th page in fragments. The whole document probably never included more than 120 pages. When printed in the *Kansas Historical Quarterly,* it took up almost 65 digest-sized pages.

This report has come down to the present as "General Blunt's Account." It is a narrative of his actions and experiences during the war. But it is also filled with verbal assaults on his rivals, mainly Halleck, Schofield, Carney, and Robinson. It not only provides Blunt's point of view on his battles and feuds, but also gives insight into the character of the man who wrote it.

One of the first impressions it provides any reader is that Blunt was willing to use the nastiest language possible in attacking his opponents. He repeats many of the charges against Schofield that he made in the incendiary letters he wrote to Lincoln and Stanton in 1863. He questions the loyalty of General Halleck and the competence of General Fremont, and he accuses both Governors Robinson and Carney of undermining his authority.

These attacks lead to an obvious question: why should Blunt include those attacks in what is supposed to be an official document?

One answer comes from combining a reading of Blunt's report with the incident of the burning warehouse in Van Buren. Taken together and with other Blunt writings in the official records of the Union army, they suggest a man who could not control his anger. James Blunt never seems to have learned to hold his tongue or command his rage. When something happened that he didn't like, he exploded, either failing to consider or outright ignoring any consequences. If Blunt couldn't vent, as at Mine Creek, he simply sulked.

Another answer is that Blunt seems to have been too self-centered to care about what he said of others. Blunt was supremely confident in his abilities and his record. But no matter the talent or success of a person, a vicious insult reflects poorly on that individual's character. Lost in his accomplishments, Blunt failed to notice that impugning the character of others only made him appear petty and egotistical.

Returning to the questions about his involvement in corruption, Blunt seems to have believed that his string of victories put him above reproach from anyone else. This is likely the reason why he never took Schofield's investigation seriously. Even after the war, as he wrote his report, he continued to disregard these serious allegations as simply motivated by jealousy or lack of loyalty to the cause.

Related to this matter of loyalty is another possible explanation for Blunt's tone. Blunt's rise was largely due to the influence of Senator Lane. And like Lane, Blunt seems to have shared in the "spoils" of lucrative army contracts. Blunt's return from the plains may have been partly engineered by Lane, and his part in fending off Price in turn aided Lane's ascendancy. Clearly James Blunt was still a "Lane man" when the Civil War ended.

At the time Blunt wrote his report, Lane's political fortunes had rather abruptly reversed. Lane's one political patron had been President Lincoln, who was assassinated days after Lee surrendered to Grant at Appomattox. Although Lane talked like a radical, in action he was more a moderate like Lincoln. Thus, with Lincoln's death, the Radical Republicans in the House and Senate gained control of the party.

To maintain his grip on patronage in Kansas, Lane cast his lot with the new president Andrew Johnson. But Johnson was no radical, and soon he and the Radical Republicans came into conflict over how harsh the policy of Reconstruction should be toward the South. Lane chose Johnson's moderate Reconstruction despite the president's weakness and the sentiments of Lane's constituents back in Kansas. Within a year of his reelection to the Senate, Lane lost most, if not all, of his influence over Washington and Kansas, and within two months he would be dead of a self-inflicted gun-shot wound.

Therefore it's logical to conclude that Lane's sudden downfall may also account for the tone Blunt takes in writing his report. Blunt's main targets for his bombasts, Robinson, Carney, and Schofield, were all men with whom Lane and Blunt had conflicts. When Blunt writes of first taking command of the Department of Kansas, he claims that this "was the signal" for an attack on him and on those "with whom I had held intimate personal or political relations." And practically the only Kansas politician about whom Blunt has absolutely nothing negative to say is Senator Lane.

Perhaps Blunt, seeing his old patron and friend losing power, and possibly his will to live, was motivated by loyalty to Lane in letting loose his verbal grenades. Unable to control his anger at the situation, worried that Lane was about to be erased from history, and wanting to set the record "straight" in his own self-centered way, James Blunt composed a public document filled with broadsides at their mutual enemies in order to defend the man to whom he owed almost everything.

Blunt returned to the public stage in Topeka on July 4, 1866. Despite the fact that Senator Lane had shot himself three days earlier, Blunt's appearance was a festive occasion. The war had been over for a year, the nation was healing, and Blunt was to present battle flags to Governor Crawford and the state of Kansas. Even the news from Lane was hopeful; he appeared to be recovering from his wound.

To mark the presentation of the battle flags, Blunt gave a twenty-minute speech. Blunt began his remarks with a typical patriotic invocation of the American Revolution and the meaning of the "stars and stripes." From there he threw out a bit of chest-thumping about the meaning of the American flag during the recent rebellion and how it had withstood the assault of "traitorous hands." He reminded his audience that the small state of Kansas had provided more men per capita for the Union war effort than any other state. He concluded by formally presenting the flags to the state government so that veterans, orphans of fallen soldiers, and other citizens could see the banner under which the Kansas boys had fought.

The one remarkable thing about Blunt's speech is how unremarkable it actually was. It contained much of the familiar Blunt bombast, this time in the service of Fourth of July patriotism. Except for the touches on treason, it had none of the usual Blunt broadside attacks. It is a bland speech, the sort that anyone calling upon the spirit of the Fourth might make.

It could be that with the war over and his narrative written, Blunt felt no need to carry on his struggles. Blunt may have also felt the celebratory mood of the occasion was an inappropriate time to refight old battles. And perhaps the shadow of Lane's attempted suicide put Blunt in a somber mood. With such a dark event surrounding the occasion, Blunt wasn't motivated to give a speech that called attention to himself.

This would not be the last time that Blunt and Lane would be tied together. Lane's death on July 11 left a vacancy in the U.S. Senate. Governor Crawford would have to appoint a successor.

Crawford's choice was complicated due to the evolution of national and state postwar politics. Andrew Johnson had followed Lincoln to the presidency after Lincoln's assassination, and he soon came into conflict with Radical Republicans in Congress. By the time of Lane's death, Johnson and the radicals were at odds. To maintain a hold on the important federal patronage, Lane had bucked the radicals and remained a Johnson supporter. But Crawford found he would need support from radicals in Kansas if he were to be reelected governor.

In June, Crawford tried to make it known that he was joining the radical faction. He was still a Lane man, and the radicals therefore distrusted his stance. Lane's death was both an opportunity and a dilemma. Crawford had the opportunity to appoint someone the radicals liked, thus ensuring his renomination at the state convention two months later. His dilemma was in the large number of candidates for the Senate seat. It would be hard for Crawford to choose one without angering some powerful interest or individual.

There were at least four possible candidates for Lane's Senate seat. First was John Speer, still an influential newspaperman and probably the person closest to Lane. Next was the Rev. H. D. Fisher, a clergyman and a politician with backing from religious interests. Also in the running was former governor Thomas Carney, backed by Leavenworth businessmen. In addition Crawford's former superior, James G. Blunt, had joined the race.

After Lane's funeral, Crawford toured southern Kansas, accompanied by Blunt. As a result most assumed Blunt had the inside track on the appointment. There would have been strong arguments in Blunt's favor. He was still popular with veterans and with Lane's friends. He also had become a national figure during the war, something that the other three candidates were not. And for his part Blunt still liked Crawford; this would be important if the two were to get along for the four years left in Lane's term of office.

It isn't clear whether there was any faction opposed to Blunt, but that does not mean his appointment would not have had serious disadvantages. Despite his stature, Blunt still might have carried the baggage of the corruption allegations launched late in the war. Blunt was not a politician, and Crawford may have wondered if his popularity would have translated into votes. There was no doubt that Carney and Blunt didn't get along, so Blunt's appointment would have prevented Crawford from gaining support from Carney's backers.

But perhaps Crawford's biggest obstacle to appointing Blunt was his knowledge of the personality of his former commander. Crawford probably knew better than almost anyone the severity of Blunt's temper and his use of indecorous language when angered. In the Senate such a man could get both himself and his state in trouble. What was worse for Blunt, Crawford seems to have carried around his bitterness about Blunt's actions at Mine Creek after the war ended. While Blunt may have liked Crawford, the governor might not have liked the former general. It may not have been factional politics but personal feelings that kept Blunt from taking Lane's place in the Senate.

After briefly considering the possibility of not making an appointment, on July 19 Crawford chose a dark horse, Edmund G. Ross. Ross had served in the army and was once Speer's partner at the *Tribune*. Although completely unexpected, the Ross appointment

Samuel Crawford, an officer who commanded units under Blunt in the general's 1862 fall campaign from Old Fort Wayne to Van Buren. Crawford would also serve alongside Blunt during the Price Campaign of 1864. That service led to Crawford's election as Kansas governor. *Photograph courtesy the Kansas State Historical Society, Topeka, Kansas.*

had advantages over the other three candidates. Fisher had no strength with veterans; Speer was tied through Lane to President Johnson; and Kansas's other senator, Samuel Pomeroy, distrusted Carney. Edmund Ross had come out against Johnson, was not seen as a threat by Pomeroy, and had worked with Speer.

Immediately accusations appeared in the Kansas press that Crawford had chosen Ross more or less at random. However, other newspapers hailed the appointment, and soon everyone was on board Crawford's bandwagon. Crawford was easily renominated and won the election in a landslide. When the state legislature convened early in 1867, it formally voted for Ross to complete Lane's term.

Ross generally supported the Radical Republican agenda. But in May 1868, on the eleventh article of impeachment against President Johnson, Ross cast a "not guilty" vote. Vilified at the time, historians now consider Ross's vote a seminal act of bravery. Johnson was not impeached, and Ross became famous.

It's unlikely that Blunt would have voted as Ross had, considering his hatred of southerners, Democrats, and moderates. But it is even more unlikely that he ever would have been given the chance to cast that vote. There were too many reasons for Governor Crawford not to appoint him to fill Lane's seat. This would mark the end of the political career of James G. Blunt, which had started in Anderson County back in 1858 and taken Blunt to the Wyandotte convention.

Some time after moving to Leavenworth, Blunt gained admission to the Kansas bar as a lawyer. In 1869 he moved to Washington and began acting as a solicitor of claims before the federal government. He would also returned to Maine with his family for summer visits in the years following the war.

Before leaving the state, Blunt briefly reentered politics in the fall of 1867. Two referendums were on the ballot that year: one would give women the right to vote and the other would give that right to black men. Several prominent men lent their support to the latter and actively opposed the former. From September 17 to September 20, Blunt joined four other men in a speaking tour of northeastern Kansas in favor of "manhood suffrage."

Earlier on September 5, Blunt had attended a meeting in Lawrence that passed resolutions against "female suffrage." This is interesting mainly because at the 1859 Wyandotte convention Blunt had said that if women "shall ask to be put upon an equality with men," he would not object. How is it that Blunt's opinion had changed in eight years? An answer comes when some of the names of the men at that Lawrence meeting are recalled. Present were Chief Justice Samuel Kingman; Attorney General George Hoyt; future governor John Martin; Blunt's old militia nemeses George Dietzler and James Snoddy; George Martin, editor of the Junction City newspaper; Jacob Stotler, formerly of the Emporia paper; former convention colleague Ben Simpson; and future senator Preston Plumb, the former publisher of the *Buck and Ball.* Blunt may not have wanted to interfere with the desires of so many leading men.

It may also be possible that Blunt feared that the issue of women's suffrage might negatively impact the fight for black men's suffrage. This view was expressed in the *Leavenworth Conservative.* "Negro suffrage" was the cause Blunt believed in, and it was the reason he went on the short speaking tour in September. In Topeka he told his audience of the heroism of the black soldiers under his command. An account after the meeting reported that Blunt's remarks on the subject were "loudly applauded." Despite this support, however, both measures were defeated.

Unfortunately, after his entry into politics Blunt became mired in two scandals that further harmed his reputation as well as history's view of him. The first occurred in October 1867 when Blunt joined two other men in an effort to buy a portion of the "Black Bob" Reservation. The reservation had been granted to the Shawnee tribe in 1825, and by the end of the war it consisted of some thirty thousand acres in Johnson County. The tribe had split into two factions, and it was to the "Black Bob" group that Blunt and his allies applied.

They persuaded the group to sell their patent claims to the land on the reservation to the three whites. Blunt and his friends in turn sold those patents to land speculators. Government agents were aware of the situation by December but were unable to resolve the mess due to a new dispute between settlers and other land speculators.

It is unknown how Blunt fared in this scheme, but in the second scandal, which came about after he moved to Washington, he ended up in court facing fines and jail time. In the spring of 1873,

Blunt and the head of the finance division of the Bureau of Indian Affairs went to trial. They were charged with fraud in connection with payments made to the North Carolina branch of the Cherokee tribe.

The Kansas newspapers apparently didn't report this indictment. Indeed the only known commentary on the matter was made in the *St. Louis Dispatch* and reprinted in an Anderson County newspaper. The *Dispatch* claimed that other former officers had committed worse offenses than Blunt, but because they were West Point graduates, they had escaped such consequences. Wrote its correspondent, "To be a volunteer officer even now is to be declared guilty without a trial."

The resolution of the case is as confusing as its cause. That same newspaper in Anderson County reported in December 1874 that the case, obviously a civil matter, was decided against Blunt and in favor of the plaintiff. The damages in the case came to over fifty-four hundred dollars. However, Daniel Wilder's *Annals of Kansas* reported that on April 15, 1875, the case against Blunt was discharged. Although the charges against Blunt and the results of the case are confusing, his fraudulent behavior toward the Carolina Cherokee fits with his pattern of corruption during the war. Unfortunately for James Blunt this event would not be his last negative appearance in the press; life would soon deal him one final humiliation.

Three years later Blunt began to act in a way that attracted concern. The symptoms of this odd activity came on quite suddenly. In the fall of 1877 Blunt wrote to the secretary of the Kansas State Historical Society from his home in Washington. Kansas was beginning to memorialize John Brown, and this prompted Blunt to send a letter detailing his own encounters with the famed abolitionist. The letter he wrote is long, twelve legal-sized pages, and it is occasionally too detailed in certain descriptions—but there is a narrative thread, the handwriting is legible, and there are few cross-outs or other signs of erratic writing.

But just a year later, when Blunt returned to Leavenworth, he seemed to conduct himself in an odd manner. Then, on February 5, 1879, a warrant was issued for Blunt's arrest for larceny in Washington. Apparently Blunt had endorsed a check issued by the

U.S. Treasury that was made out to someone else. The unusual aspect of the episode was that Blunt made no effort to avoid having this "fraud" discovered.

When Blunt appeared in court, several friends of his, including perhaps some U.S. senators, stated that Blunt's mental state was deteriorating. Blunt was promptly committed to a local asylum, and his doctor issued a certificate of insanity. Later news accounts referred to Blunt's condition as a "softening of the brain."

This may seem like a vague diagnosis, but in the late 1870s illness in general was not well understood and even less was understood about mental illness. The medical profession was working to understand the causes and symptoms of various diseases. The rate of progress was starting to accelerate, but the level of medical research was still low compared with the medical science of the twenty-first century.

This lack of understanding is especially evident when considering the cause of General Blunt's rapid mental deterioration. According to *The Penguin Dictionary of Psychology,* the term "softening of the brain" was used to describe the physical damage to brain tissue and the central nervous system caused by syphilis. The symptoms included paralysis and a progressive loss of mental capacity. STDs were common during the Civil War and were largely spread through prostitution. From Blunt's own references to "female servants" as well as his reputation for dalliances with women, it seems clear that he was consorting with prostitutes during the war. Blunt's sudden onset of mental illness, which proved fatal, would most likely have been caused by the final stage of syphilis.

But the cause of these symptoms was not known at the time Blunt was committed. Research into sexually transmitted diseases such as syphilis was in its infancy, and public perceptions of these diseases bordered on hysteria. If sex was rarely discussed in public during this Victorian time, then STDs were not mentioned at all, even in the private conversations between doctors and patients. Blunt, therefore, had the misfortune to become sick at a time when mental illnesses were not well known, when STDs were a taboo subject, and when both were only understood in terms of innuendoes and stereotypes.

Blunt's illness was an enemy he could not defeat. He lived in confinement for only two years before he died on or about July 27,

1881, at the mental hospital where he had been living. He was survived by his wife, a son, and a daughter. The daughter seems to
have been married to a son of Rufus Gilpatrick, the man who had
brought Blunt to Kansas some twenty-five years earlier. His body
was brought to Leavenworth, where Blunt had spent much of his
controversial Civil War career, and he was buried in the Mount
Muncie Cemetery.

CHAPTER 15

Tarnished Glory

The military record of Maj. Gen. James G. Blunt is largely one of successful battles and campaigns. Unlike the other successful generals of the Civil War, Blunt had not attended West Point, and he was not a professional soldier before the war. How is it that this Kansas abolitionist was able to earn such a strong record?

One of the few articles that dwelled on Blunt's character came from the *St. Louis Republican* and was republished in the *Conservative* on July 3, 1863, while Blunt was at the height of his success. From this article we might get a handle on how he was able to accomplish so much.

The article described him as having "bravery that borders upon reckless daring." That Blunt was aggressive cannot be doubted. At Old Fort Wayne he charged the enemy despite being outnumbered. He raced to support Herron at Prairie Grove, and after the first day he was eager to continue the battle. His 1863 campaign after Honey Springs was a series of fast strikes that put much of the Indian Territory in Union hands. And finally, at Newtonia in 1864 he again pitched into his opponent although he commanded inferior numbers. Aggression is an important quality for a successful general. It reflects a willingness to seize opportunities and take risks to achieve goals.

It's also worth noting Blunt's personal bravery on the battlefield. The Civil War was one of the last in which the deeds of commanders could encourage their men, and Blunt's courage may have aided in his achievements by inspiring his men to ever braver actions on the field. Blunt was certainly fearless, and that fearlessness may have rubbed off on his men, to the advantage of Blunt's war record.

The benefits of bravery are related to another quality that leads to victory, determination. Blunt certainly seems to have had a hunger for victory. What's more, along with many of his men, he was a radical abolitionist. This meant they were fighting for a cause, always important in war and especially so in a civil war. By contrast, their Confederate opponents often seemed less than certain of their cause or were simply conscripted to fight. It does not seem to be an accident that many of Blunt's wins were marked by the flight of his enemies.

The *Conservative* article attributed other advantages to Blunt, among them "a big head, full of active brains; [and] judgment that is intuitively correct." These characteristics apply to another aspect of his success, his overall competence. Blunt seemed to have common sense in dealing with military matters. At Prairie Grove he didn't panic when he found rebels in his rear; instead he moved and attacked. At Honey Springs he massed men to cloak their numbers. At Westport he found a gap in the rebel line and attacked there. In general, Blunt seems to have made enemy forces his goal instead of enemy-controlled posts or towns. Blunt did complain about lack of support, but he always made do with the resources available.

One of those resources was artillery, and this too was key to Blunt's achievements. In several battles it was Union cannons that broke rebel charges, opened gaps, or sent rebels fleeing. Perhaps the most dramatic example of this was at Old Fort Wayne, where the capture of a rebel battery sent the Confederates into a retreat despite their having superior numbers on the field. Blunt himself may or may not have been skillful at using artillery; there isn't enough evidence to make any conclusions. But he was certainly blessed with quality cannons and competent artillery crews and officers.

Theodore Gardner of the First Kansas Battery made a casual remark in an article for the Kansas State Historical Society that sheds light on this matter. In writing about Cane Hill, Gardner said that at that battle the First "did nothing in particular except to demonstrate the advantages derived from preparedness."

This suggests that Blunt's artillerymen had enough ammunition and time to practice before going into battle. Gun crews need time and munitions to learn how to fire their guns properly and quickly, how to find the range of a target, and how to move their guns around a battlefield. If Blunt's men had the opportunity to learn and enhance their skills, this would certainly account for their devastating effect in battle after battle. A competent and practiced soldier will almost always beat an incompetent and unpracticed one. The competence of Blunt's artillerymen may have been the key to his record of victories.

Blunt's military record and overall competence may stem from his high school education. If indeed he was educated at a military academy, he would have learned at the very least the basics of strategy and tactics. He may also have been taught drill, marching order, and cavalry and artillery skills. These would not have been helpful in battle against West Point graduates, especially imaginative officers like Robert E. Lee. But Blunt wasn't facing men like Lee; he faced men who were political appointees like himself. Unlike them, though, Blunt apparently had military training beyond that of the ordinary soldier of the day. Logically, a general armed with the basics of military education should do better than one without that training.

The clearest evidence of this advantage comes from the battle of Honey Springs. In his report Blunt noted that he marched his men to the field in columns to disguise their numbers. When they arrived, Blunt was able to move his men from columns into battle line within minutes. A general with common sense could see how column formations could hide his strength. But it would take some military training to know how to efficiently change from marching column to battle line and to relate that method to subordinates in order to carry out the maneuver.

So with such a good record on the field and so many skills to his advantage, what was it that prevented General Blunt from being more successful? Why wasn't he able to achieve more? Why wasn't he given the chance to move to a more important theater of the war?

The most obvious answers come from Blunt's character flaws, which were legion. He was clearly self-centered, had a bad temper, and was somewhat hypocritical. In Fort Smith he was said to have been overeating, drinking, and indulging in the pursuit of "loose women." In Blunt's time these were viewed as serious moral lapses that did not befit a major general. Word of them would have kept him from advancing his career, gaining more acceptance, or moving to a more high-profile post. But there was one flaw in particular that kept him from rising farther or being selected for a more prestigious command.

Put simply, Blunt couldn't see points of view other than his own or those close to his own. This prevented him from understanding rival generals and politicians, the reasons they might be opposed to his policies, and the ways he could address that opposition. Indeed, time and again Blunt answered his critics not with arguments in his favor but with harsh insults.

His inability to understand the perspective of others also prevented Blunt from taking criticism from those he didn't respect and led directly to his downfall in the spring of 1864. If he had taken into account Schofield's justified concerns about corruption and acted to stop it, he could have survived the ordeal with his reputation intact. Instead he merely lobbed incendiary letters and thumbed his nose at Schofield. While Schofield was soon replaced, others who disliked Blunt remained active in both the political and military scenes. They didn't forget Blunt's actions, and when he tried to "take" Fort Smith, they became a chorus that President Lincoln could not ignore. Blunt had put Lincoln in the position of having to discipline him, and that's exactly what Lincoln did when he removed Blunt from the Indian Territory and sent him into exile on the Kansas plains.

This flaw in the way he dealt with others also made it hard for people to like him. A general without friends doesn't have particularly good prospects. Those who wrote about Blunt after the war expressed admiration for his deeds but never expressed positive feelings for the man. Samuel Crawford doesn't seem to have liked Blunt personally, certainly not by the end of the war. Richard Hinton, who actually served with Blunt in 1864, gave many descriptions of Blunt's bravery. However he said little about the man personally, and he didn't present a biography of him in his book, which he did for General Curtis and Senator Lane.

And speaking of Blunt's chief patron, it's interesting to note that the two principal biographers of Lane mentioned Blunt sparingly in their books. One of these biographers was John Speer, the newspaper editor who knew both Lane and Blunt personally. Blunt's character flaws make one wonder if Speer's omission was intentional. Although he defended the general during the war, once it was over and Blunt was deceased, perhaps Speer felt that his obligation to Blunt was concluded.

Any discussion of personal feelings about the general inevitably leads to the feud between Blunt and John Schofield. Recounting their incendiary correspondence is not necessary. What is worth noting is that some of what officials in Washington knew of the feud came from Schofield. Blunt never really presented explanations for his actions; instead he offered only insults about his critics. Taking this reaction into account, it comes as no surprise that Blunt was never given the chance to play a more prominent role in the Civil War.

Not that he bears the complete blame for his relatively inconspicuous role in history. A look at the writings of Wiley Britton suggests that Blunt may have been held back by his chief rival, Schofield. Britton was one of the first to write about the trans-Mississippi theater. He spent the war as an ordinary soldier in one of the Kansas regiments and saw action under Blunt in 1862 and 1863. Britton published his 1863 memoirs, and early in the twentieth century, he wrote books about the western theater of the war. This body of work makes Britton's views worth taking into consideration.

Britton's view of the Blunt-Schofield feud is interesting because he was not a partisan in the political arena and did not have a commission tied to any high-ranking officer. For example, when Lane tried to assemble an invasion of western Missouri in the wake of the Lawrence massacre, Schofield intervened to prevent the invasion. Britton later wrote that though radicals might not like what Schofield did, his actions were "approved [of] by sober minded people everywhere in the State."

When discussing Schofield's relief of Blunt's command, Britton wrote that newspapers at the time, as well as members of the general public, thought that Blunt was removed because "he had been winning too many laurels." Britton did not disagree with this view, as he did with Lane's planned invasion of Missouri in September 1863. He reported that the soldiers liked Blunt because he was with them in battle, and he never made excuses or needed prodding by superiors. Britton also doesn't seem certain that Schofield was indeed ill in late 1862. He does state that there were officers who criticized Schofield for not being with the Army of the Frontier at that time.

What is even more intriguing is Britton's observation that while Blunt was being lauded for his victories in Arkansas and the Indian Territory, Schofield was being bitterly denounced for "incompetency

Wiley Britton, Union veteran and author. Britton served in units under Blunt's command in 1862 and 1863. His positive view of General Blunt probably reflected the prevailing sentiments of the men in the ranks, who only cared about taking orders from a winning commander. *Photograph courtesy the Kansas State Historical Society, Topeka, Kansas.*

and imbecility." Furthermore, while Britton stated that as an administrator Schofield was one of the best, he added that at that time Schofield had no battlefield victories to his credit.

It's interesting to note that when Schofield finally got around to writing his autobiography, he had very little to say about his feud with Blunt. Reading through the official wartime correspondence, it is clear how Schofield felt toward his rival. Therefore, it seems odd that long after the war Schofield didn't express himself in regard to this matter. It's possible that with the passage of time Schofield thought his rivalry with Blunt was a petty affair not worth including in his autobiography. It may be just as likely, though, that Schofield may have realized that he was wrong about as much as he was right when it came to Blunt.

In a strange sort of way Blunt and Schofield almost deserved each other as rivals. Blunt was successful on the battlefield but unscrupulous as an administrator, while Schofield was usually upright but had no accomplishments and appeared to be jealous of Blunt's. If Blunt had more integrity, he would have easily out-shined Schofield and probably never would have been bothered by him or his comments. On the other hand, if Schofield had a good record of victories, he either could have used that record to intimidate Blunt into compliance or could have fired Blunt without suffering any consequences from Blunt's political allies.

The feud had little effect on the outcome of the war, but it may have kept Blunt from contributing to a more decisive victory. In early 1864, General Curtis was lobbying for an expedition to Texas under Blunt's command. While other Union campaigns in the region may have hindered its initial approval, Blunt's own behavior may have contributed to the final rejection of the expedition. Washington may not have been interested in the project because of the possibility of having to deal with such a troublesome general at such an important time.

It seems likely that had Blunt been given the opportunity, he would have made significant inroads into Texas. He might have even taken the state out of the war. That could have had an interesting effect on the Confederate leadership in the spring of 1865. Would Jefferson Davis and his cabinet have tried to flee if Texas could not have offered the rebels sanctuary? Might the fall of Texas ended the war differently, for better or for worse?

In the end this is just idle but intriguing speculation. Far more factual are the many instances of Blunt's moral flaws. These flaws do raise an important question: why did Blunt persist in behavior that he knew or should have known was wrong?

Blunt's egotism and arrogance might have contributed to his persistence in those behaviors. As was stated earlier, Blunt had trouble taking criticism from those he disagreed with or didn't like. He may have decided consciously or otherwise to spite his critics by going his own way. He may have also decided that because he was fighting to end slavery, anything he did was right and just. Instead of "my country right or wrong," Blunt believed "my cause right or wrong."

Another explanation might be that Blunt was not quite the leader he thought he was. One aspect of leadership is the willingness to do what you think best despite what others might caution. A true leader does not follow the crowd; rather he makes his own way. While Blunt may have had the military ability to achieve victory after victory, he may not have had the will to reject influence on his personal decisions. Without a doubt Blunt went along with corruption rampant in the region. It seems clear that despite being older and married, he went along with his younger staff in consorting with "female servants." Most of all, Blunt went along with most of Senator Lane's schemes, no matter how problematic or questionable they were.

Although James G. Blunt had some of the qualities important to be a successful general, he didn't have enough to be a truly great general, much less to be a good person. At various times in his military career Blunt's flaws overshadowed his accomplishments. He won many battles but won few friends or admirers. Without these allies to defend him, Blunt was unable to establish a legacy that would survive after he died. In the end, if James G. Blunt's important triumphs were forgotten, ignored, or downplayed, the blame only falls upon him. In that way the story of Maj. Gen. James Gilpatrick Blunt is indeed one of tarnished glory.

Bibliography

BOOKS

Compendium of National Biography. *A Biographical History of Darke County, Ohio.* Chicago: Lewis Publishing Company, 1900.

Banaski, Michael E. *Embattled Arkansas, The Prairie Grove Campaign of 1862.* Wilmington, N.C.: Broadfoot Publishing Company, 1996.

Britton, Wiley. *The Civil War on the Border, Volume I and Volume II.* 1899. Reprint, Topeka: Kansas Heritage Press, 1990.

——. *Memoirs of the Rebellion on the Border, 1863.* 1882. Reprint, Lincoln: University of Nebraska Press, Bison Books,1993.

——. *The Union Indian Brigade in the Civil War.* Reprint, Topeka: Kansas Heritage Press, 1994.

Castel, Albert. *Civil War Kansas—Reaping the Whirlwind.* Lawrence: University Press of Kansas, 1997. Originally published as *A Frontier State at War* (Ithaca: Cornell University Press, 1958).

Connelley, William E. *A Standard History of Kansas and Kansans.* Chicago: Lewis Publishing Company, 1918.

Crawford, Samuel J. *Kansas in the Sixties.* 1911. Reprint, Topeka: Kansas Heritage Press, 1994.

Cutler, William G. *A History of the State of Kansas.* A. T. Andreas, 1883.

Davis, Kenneth S. *Kansas, A History.* New York: W. W. Norton & Company, 1984.

Edwards, John N. *Shelby and His Men: or, The War in the West.* Waverly, MS: Gen. Joseph Shelby Memorial Fund, 1993.

Furry, William *The Preacher's Tale, The Civil War Journal of Rev. Francis Springer, Chaplain, U.S. Army of the Frontier.* Fayetteville: University of Arkansas Press, 2001.

Gause, Isaac *Four Years with Five Armies.* New York and Washington: The Neale Publishing Company, 1908.

Glaab, Charles N. *Kansas City and the Railroads.* State Historical

Society of Wisconsin, 1962; Lawrence: University Press of Kansas, 1993.

Goodrich, Thomas. *Black Flag—Guerilla Warfare on the Western Border, 1861-1865*. Bloomington: Indiana University Press, 1999.

Hinton, Richard J. *Rebel Invasion of Missouri and Kansas and the Campaign of the Army of the Border Against General Sterling Price in October and November 1864*. 1865. Reprint, Topeka: Kansas Heritage Press, 1994.

Johnson, Robert Underwood & Clarence Clough Buel, ed. *Battles & Leaders of the Civil War*. New York, 1888.

Josephy, Alvin M. Jr. *The Civil War in the American West*. New York: Alfred A. Knopf Publishing, 1991.

Kansas Constitutional Convention: A Reprint of the Proceedings and Debates of the Convention Which Framed the Constitution of Kansas at Wyandotte in July, 1859. Topeka: Kansas State Printing Plant by the authority of the state legislature, 1920.

Lickteig, Dorothy, comp. *Anderson County Early Gleanings, Volume 1, 1867-1900*. N.p., 1993.

Lickteig, Dorothy and Dorothy M. Sommer, ed. *Greeley's Golden Years—Greeley, Kansas, 125 Year History*. N.p., 1982.

Marsh, William R. "The Military Career of James G. Blunt: An Appraisal." Master's thesis, Kansas State Teachers College, 1953.

McPherson, James M. *Battle Cry of Freedom—The Civil War Era*. New York: Oxford University Press, 1988.

Miner, H. Craig. "The Border Tier Line: A History of the Missouri River, Fort Scott & Gulf Railroad, 1865-1870." Master's thesis, Wichita State University, 1967.

Monaghan, Jay. *Civil War on the Western Border, 1854-1865*. New York: Bonanza Books, 1955.

Moore, Frank, ed. *The Rebellion Record, A Diary of American Events*. Vol. 7. 1864. Reprint, New York: Arno Press, 1977.

Oliva, Leo E. *Fort Larned—Guardian of the Santa Fe Trail*. Kansas State Historical Society, 1997.

Potter, Joseph W., ed. *The Bangor Historical Magazine*. Maine Genealogical Society Special Publication, no. 14. Camden, ME: Picton Press, n.d.

Prentis, Noble L. *Kansas Miscellanies*. Topeka: Kansas Publishing House, 1889.

Schofield, John M. *Forty-Six Years in the Army*. 1897. Reprint, Norman: University of Oklahoma Press, 1998.

Starr, Stephen Z. *Jennison's Jayhawkers*. Baton Rouge: Louisiana State University Press, 1993.

Steele, Phillip W. and Steve Cottrell. *Civil War in the Ozarks*. Gretna, LA: Pelican Publishing Company, 2000.

Tenney, Luman Harris. *War Diary of Luman Harris Tenney, 1861-1865*. Cleveland: Evangelical Publishing House by Frances Andrews Tenney for private circulation, 1914.

The War of the Rebellion: A Compilation of the Official Records of the Union and Confederate Armies. Washington, D. C., 1881-1901.

Thompson, Kenneth E. Jr. *Civil War Maine Hall of Fame—Political, Judicial, and Military Leaders 1861-1865*. Portland, ME: The Thompson Group, n.d.

Welch, G. Murlin. *Border Warfare in Southeastern Kansas, 1856-1859*. Linn County Publishers, 1977.

Wilder, Daniel Webster. *The Annals of Kansas, 1541-1885*. Topeka: Kansas Publishing House, 1886.

Winterbotham, John C. *Lamoine and its Attractions as a Place of Summer Sojourning*. Lamoine and Mount Desert Land Company, 1887.

PERIODICALS

Blunt, James G. "General Blunt's Account of His Civil War Experiences." *Kansas Historical Quarterly* 1, no. 3 (1932).

Cornish, Dudley Taylor. "Kansas Negro Regiments in the Civil War." *Kansas Historical Quarterly* 20, no. 6 (1953).

Cory, Charles E. "The Sixth Kansas Cavalry and Its Commander." *Kansas Historical Collections* 11 (1910).

Denison, W. W. "Battle of Prairie Grove." *Kansas Historical Collections* 16 (1925).

Farlow, Joyce and Louise Barry, ed. "Vincent B. Osborne's Civil War Experiences." Part 2. *Kansas Historical Quarterly* 20, no. 3 (1952).

Gardner, Theodore. "The First Kansas Battery." *Kansas Historical Collections* 14 (1918).

Greene, Albert R. "Campaigning in the Army of the Frontier." *Kansas Historical Collections* 14 (1918).

Kitts, John Howard. "The Civil War Diary of John Howard Kitts." *Kansas Historical Collections* 14 (1918).

Napier, Rita G. "Rethinking the Past, Reimagining the Future."
Kansas History 24, no. 3 (2001).

Plummer, Mark A. "Governor Crawford's Appointment of
Edmund G. Ross to the United States Senate." *Kansas Historical
Quarterly* 28, no. 2 (1962).

NEWSPAPERS

Atchison Freedom's Champion, July 19, November 15, December 20
and 27, 1862; January 3 and 31, March 7, April 11, May 16, 20,
and 23, June 13, 1863; August 18, October 13, 20, and 27, 1864.

"Both Armies Low on Ammunition on Night of December 7th."
Prairie Grove Enterprise, August 18, 1960.

Buck and Ball (Eleventh Regiment, Kansas Volunteers), December
6 (15), 1862.

Council Grove Press, October 12 and 19, 1863.

Ellsworth (Maine) American, August 8, 1917; November 14, 1974.

Emporia News, September 28, 1861; April 19, May 10, July 26, 1862;
January 1, 8, and 10, February 21, June 20, October 31, 1863;
November 12, 1864.

Fort Scott Bulletin, May 10, 17, and 31, 1862; October 11, 1862.

Fort Scott Daily Monitor, October 28 and 31, November 4, 1864.

Kansas City Daily (Western) Journal of Commerce, January 4, February
17, May 16, June 12, July 23, October 7, 9, 11, and 21, 1863;
October 18, 22, and 24, 1864.

Kansas Daily Tribune (Lawrence), October 15, 1864; October 20,
1864; October 22, 1864; November 2, 1864; September 6, 1867;
July 28, 1881.

Kansas State Journal (Lawrence), September 26, 1861; April 17,
June 5, July 3, and 10, December 4, 1862; January 29, February
13, 1863; August 4, October 20, 1864.

Kansas Weekly Tribune (Lawrence), February 19, May 21, June 4,
July 9 and 16, October 17, 1863; January 7, May 12, 1864.

Lawrence Republican, September 26, 1861; April 17, 1862.

Leavenworth Daily Conservative: July 31, September 21, 24, and 26,
1861; April 12, May 6, June 12, 15, 17, 19, and 20, July 10, 15,
and 20, August 6, and 26, September 24, October 9 and 29,
November 2 and 13, December 2, 3, 4, 10, 11, 13, 14, 16, 17, 28,

and 31, 1862; January 13 and 15, February 14, March 22, May 6 and 7, 1863; June 12, 13 and June 14, July 3, 9, 22, 25, and 26, August 14, September 24, October 9, 10, 11, and 24, December 16, 27, and 29, 1863; January 5, May 15, July 31, August 16 and 18, 1864; October 1, 7, 8, 9, 16, 20, 21, 22, 26, and 27, 1864; July 6, 1866; September 5 and 6, 1867.

Leavenworth Daily Times, September 14, 21, and 26, 1861; April 12, May 6 and 7, June 17, July 12, 13, 18, 26, and 29, August 5, October 7, November 11, December 2, 14, 18, 20, and 21, 1862; July 2, 3, 11, and 25, August 16, October 3, 4, 9, 10, 15, 21, and 22, 1863; April 19, July 29 and 30, September 24, 27, and 28, October 6, 16, 18, 19, 20, 22, 27, and 28, 1864; July 8, 1866; February 12, 1879; July 28, 1881.

Leavenworth Weekly Conservative, August 8 and 15, 1861; June 19, 1862.

Mechem, Kirk. "Kansas' First Major General." *Wichita Eagle* (Sunday Magazine), September 16, 1934.

O'Connell, Wayne A. "'General Jim' Blunt Helped Shape Early History Of Southeast Kansas." *Baxter Springs Citizen,* August 20, 1951.

Oskaloosa Independent, April 25, 1863; November 20, 1864.

Taylor, Harold O. "Missed Baxter Springs Massacre—Thirteen-Year Old Cavalryman Left Units Two Days Before on 300-Mile Dispatch-Taking Ride." *Pittsburg Headlight-Sun,* October 6, 1968.

Topeka Capitol, July 30, 1881.

Topeka Commonwealth, February 13, 1879; July 29, 1881.

Topeka Weekly Leader, September 12 and 26, 1867.

White Cloud Kansas Chief, October 17, 1861; May 8, December 4 and 11, 1862; January 1 and 8, 1863; August 11 and 18, September 8, 1864.

PAPERS

1850 Census Record, Harrison Township, Darke County, Ohio. Ohio Historical Society.

Blunt, James G. Letter to the secretary of the Kansas State Historical Society, October 12, 1877. John Brown Collection. Kansas State Historical Society.

Carney, Thomas. Letter to Abraham Lincoln, June 25, 1863. Thomas Carney Papers. Kansas State Historical Society.

——. Letters to McDowell, June 15, 16, and 26, 1863. James L. McDowell Papers. Kansas State Historical Society.

——. Letter to Edwin Stanton, November 16, 1863. T. C. Stevens Papers. Kansas State Historical Society.

Gilpatrick, Mrs. J. H. "Reminiscences of Mrs. J. H. Gilpatrick and her mother, Mrs. James G. Blunt, Leavenworth, November 1905." Miscellaneous Gilpatrick Papers. Kansas State Historical Society.

Thomas Moonlight Papers. Correspondence, 1863. Kansas State Historical Society.

Index